Adobe®
Photoshop®
Elements 8
Digital
Classroom

WILEY

Wiley Publishing, Inc.

Adobe® Photoshop® Elements 8 Digital Classroom

Published by
Wiley Publishing, Inc.
10475 Crosspoint Boulevard
Indianapolis, IN 46256

Copyright © 2009 by Wiley Publishing, Inc., Indianapolis, Indiana
Published by Wiley Publishing, Inc., Indianapolis, Indiana
Published simultaneously in Canada
ISBN: 978-0-4705-6692-3
Manufactured in the United States of America
10 9 8 7 6 5 4 3 2 1

For general information on our other products and services or to obtain technical support, please contact our Customer Care Department within the U.S. at (800) 762-2974, outside the U.S. at (317) 572-3993 or fax (317) 572-4002.

Please report any errors by sending a message to errata@agitraining.com

Library of Congress Control Number: 2009937270

About the Authors

The AGI Training Team is comprised of Adobe Certified Experts and Adobe Certified Instructors from American Graphics Institute (AGI). The AGI Training Team has authored many of Adobe's official training guides, and works with many of the world's most prominent companies helping them to use creative software to communicate more effectively and creatively. They work with marketing, creative and communications teams around the world, and teach regularly scheduled classes at AGI's locations, and are available for private and customized training seminars and speaking engagements. More information at agitraining.com

Acknowledgments

Thanks to our many friends at Adobe Systems, Inc. who made this book possible and assisted with questions and feedback during the writing process. To the many clients of American Graphics Institute who have helped us better understand how they use Photoshop Elements and provided us with many of the tips and suggestions found in this book. A special thanks to the instructional team at AGI for their input and assistance in the review process and for making this book such a team effort.

Credits

Writing
Chad Chelius

Series Editor
Christopher Smith

Executive Editor
Jody Lefevere

Technical Editors
Greg Heald, Eric Rowse, Jerron Smith

Editor
Marylouise Wiack

Editorial Director
Robyn Siesky

Editorial Manager
Cricket Krengel

Business Manager
Amy Knies

Senior Marketing Manager
Sandy Smith

Vice President and Executive Group Publisher
Richard Swadley

Vice President and Executive Publisher
Barry Pruett

Senior Project Coordinator
Lynsey Stanford

Graphics and Production Specialist
Lauren Mickol

Media Development Project Supervisors
Christopher Leavey

Proofreading
Jay Donahue

Indexing
Broccoli Information Management

Stock Photography
iStockPhoto.com

Contents

Starting Up

About the Photoshop Elements 8
Digital Classroom XXI

Prerequisites. XXI

System requirements. XXII

Starting Adobe Photoshop Elements 8. XXII

Loading lesson files XXIII

Managing catalogs XXIII

Creating a new catalog XXIV

Switching Catalogs. XXIV

Reconnecting to missing files XXV

Reconnect missing files window XXV

Working with the video tutorials XXVI

Setting up for viewing the video tutorials. XXVI

Viewing the video tutorials XXVII

Additional resources XXVIII

Lesson 1: Importing your Photos into Adobe Photoshop Elements

Starting up 1

How Photoshop Elements works 2

The welcome screen. 3

Getting photos into the Organizer
using the Photo Downloader. 4

Getting photos from a camera or card reader 4

The Photo Downloader 6

Get photos from a scanner. 8

Get photos and videos by searching 9

Setting a Watch Folder. 10

Adding files and folders to the Organizer 11

Getting a still image from a video frame 13

Workspaces. 16

Organizer basics 16

How to get help. 19

Photoshop help. 19

Support Center 20

The Inspiration Browser. 20

Self study. 21

Review 21

Lesson 2: Organizing Your Photos

Starting up 23

Understanding the Organizer workspace 24

Photo Browser 25

Options Bar. 25

Timeline. 26

Properties 26

Albums. 27

Keyword Tags 27

Analyzing photos in the Organizer 28

Rotating photos. 28

Hiding photos 29

Reviewing photos. 35

Compare photos side by side 35

Stacks 37

Organizing using albums 37

Creating a new album 37

Creating album categories. 40

Creating a Smart Album 41

Tagging your photos 43

Adding ratings 43

Adding keywords and categories. 44

People Recognition 47

Finding your photos. 51

Find photos by star rating. 51

Find photos by keyword 51

Find photos using the keyword Tag Cloud 52

Self study. 53

Review 53

Lesson 3: Fixing Common Photographic Problems

Starting up 55
Welcome screen 56
Understanding the Editor workspace 57
The Project Bin 58
The Panel Bin 58
Editing modes: Full, Quick, and Guided 58
Using Quick Fix. 58
Using Auto Smart Fix 60
Auto Levels 61
Auto Contrast 62
Correcting color automatically 63
Comparing images in Full Edit View 65
Using the Navigator 65
The Guided Edit mode. 67
Fixing an underexposed or dark image 68
Fixing an overexposed or light image. 69
Using Full Edit mode 71
Removing a color cast 72
Correcting skin tone. 73
Photomerge Exposure. 75
The Toolbox. 77
Using tools 78
Red Eye Removal tool 78
Whitening teeth 80
Enhancing blue skies 82
Sharpening 86
Cropping images. 89
Rotating images 90
Resizing images. 91
Recompose 93
Self study. 95
Review 95

Lesson 4: Adjusting Exposure

Starting up 97
Welcome screen 98
Understanding exposure 98
Exposure adjustments with blending modes 99
Improving underexposed images 99
Improving faded or overexposed images 102
Making adjustments manually 104
Adjusting brightness and contrast manually 105
Adjusting shadows and highlights manually 106
Making tonal adjustments using Levels 108
Histogram 108
Making tonal adjustments using Curves 111
Comparing images in Full Edit view 112
Using adjustment layers 112
Correcting selected parts of an image 115
Hue/Saturation adjustments 115
Working with selections 117
Using the Quick Selection tool 118
Saving selections. 118
Moving selections to a new layer 119
Self study. 123
Review 124

Lesson 5: Adjusting Color

Starting up 125
Welcome screen 126
Understanding color 126
HSB color 127
About image modes. 129
Bitmap mode 129
Grayscale mode 129
Indexed Color mode 129
Switching image modes 130
Comparing methods of adjusting color 130
Understanding Edit Guided 130

Understanding Edit Quick 130
Understanding Edit Full 131
Adjusting tonal range in Full Edit 131
Making a duplicate of a file 131
Restoring shadow and highlight detail 132
Correcting color in Full Edit 132
Correcting color casts using Color Variations 133
Removing a color cast using Levels 134
Adjusting color curves in an image 135
Adjusting color saturation and hue 136
Adjusting saturation in specific areas 137
Making selections 138
The importance of selections 138
About the selection tools 139
Using the Selection Brush tool 140
Add to or subtract from a selection 142
Smoothing selection edges with anti-aliasing and feathering 142
Blur the edges of a selection by feathering 143
Saving selections 145
Modifying a new selection with a saved selection 145
Inverting a selection 146
Converting to Black and White 147
Adding color to areas of an image 148
Saving and exporting images 148
About saving images and file formats 148
Self study 151
Review 151

Lesson 6: Sharing Your Photos

Starting up 153
Welcome screen 154
Sharing photos 154
Creating an online album 155
Sharing options for online albums 159
Stop sharing an online album 160

Sharing photos by e-mail 161

Attaching a photo to an e-mail 161

Sending a photo using Photo Mail 164

Setting up Adobe E-mail Service 166

Using the Quick Share panel 168

Sharing photos using online services 168

Ordering prints 168

Ordering a printed photo book 170

Printing photos 173

Printing photos in the Organizer 173

Adding photos using the Print
Photos dialog box 177

Printing a contact sheet 178

Printing a picture package 180

Setting page and printer options 182

Specifying measurement units for printing 183

Backing up and synchronizing files 183

Backing up and synchronizing
files to *Photoshop.com* 183

About synchronized albums on *Photoshop.com* 184

Starting backup or synchronization 184

Stopping and restarting backup
or synchronization 186

Exporting photos 186

Self study 188

Review 188

Lesson 7: Working with Type

Starting up 189

Welcome screen 190

Placing text on a layer 191

Formatting a text layer 192

Editing a text layer 193

Making cartoon bubbles 195

Adding text over the cartoon bubble 198

Adding effects to type 200

Adding text to multiple images 202
Warping type 204
Adding a layer style to type 205
Creating an animation with text. 206
Adding a stroke 208
Getting the layers ready for animating. 209
Time to animate 210
Self study. 211
Review 211

Lesson 8: Photo Retouching: Secrets of the Pros

Starting up 213
Working with what you have. 214
Using the histogram. 215
Working over the image 216
Improving your image. 218
Brushing on corrections 221
Self study. 227
Review 228

Lesson 9: The Art of Illusion: Photo Composites

Starting up 229
Welcome screen 230
What is a photo composite?. 230
Understanding layers. 231
Working with layers 232
Creating a new blank file 232
Creating a type layer 233
Combining images 234
About the Layers panel 235
Editing layers 236
Converting the Background layer
into a regular layer 236
Selecting a layer 237
Showing or hiding a layer. 237
Changing the stacking order of layers 238

Locking or unlocking a layer 239
Deleting a layer 239
Using opacity and blending modes 239
About opacity and blending options in layers 239
Specifying the opacity of a layer 240
Specifying a blending mode for a layer 240
Using the Magic Extractor 241
Flattening an image 245
Completing the composite 246
Working with clipping groups 247
About layer clipping groups 247
Creating a clipping group 247
Using Layer styles 248
Working with layer styles 249
Hiding or showing all layer
styles in an image 250
Change the scale of a layer style 250
Copying style settings between layers 251
Removing a layer style 251
Self study 251
Review 252

Lesson 10: Making Photoshop Elements Creations

Starting up 253
Creating a panorama 254
Creating a slide show 255
Adding text to your slide show 260
Adding graphics 263
Applying transitions 264
Panning and zooming 265
Reordering slides 267
Setting the slide order 267
Drag and drop on the storyboard 267
Quick Reorder menu 267
Working with audio 267
Adding audio 268

Adding narration. 268
Choosing an output option 269
Save as a file 269
Burn to disk. 270
Send to TV 270
Creating a photo calendar 270
Self study. 277
Review 277

Lesson 11: Photoshop Elements for Digital Photographers

Starting up 279
Working with Camera Raw files 280
Understanding the Camera Raw dialog box 281
Using the Camera Raw dialog box 283
Saving a DNG file. 290
Vignetting a photo 292
The basics of filters 295
Sharpening an image with Unsharp Mask. 295
Using Undo History for comparisons. 299
Using the Blur filter to create depth of field 300
Self study. 303
Review 303

Lesson 12: Photoshop Elements for Artists

Starting up 305
Creating a new document from scratch 306
Using brushes to add style to your work 307
Creating texture with brushes and gradients 307
The Impressionist brush 312
Using shapes creatively. 314
Working with patterns. 316
Creating patterns 316
Applying patterns. 317
Scrapbooking made easier. 318
Creating a texture 318
Creating a text effect 324

Adding text to the background. 331

Add images and create a border. 334

Self study. 337

Review 338

Lesson 13: Creating Web and Video Graphics

Starting up 339

The differences between print and the screen. 340

Resolution and color for the Web and video. 340

Preparing images for the Web. 341

Web image formats 342

Saving files for the Web. 343

Preparing images for video 349

Safe margins. 350

Saving files for video 351

Self study. 353

Review 353

Lesson 14: Using Adobe Bridge

Starting up 355

What is Adobe Bridge? 356

Navigating through Bridge 356

Using folders in Adobe Bridge. 358

Making a Favorite 360

Creating and locating metadata. 361

Using keywords 363

Opening a file from Adobe Bridge 365

Searching for files using Adobe Bridge. 365

Searching by name or keyword 366

Using the Filter panel. 367

Collections. 367

Stacks 368

Automation tools in Adobe Bridge 369

Automated tools for Photoshop Elements:
Web Photo Gallery 369

Saving or uploading your Web Gallery 372

Automated tools for Photoshop Elements:

PDF contact sheet. 373

Changing the view 374

Integration with Photoshop Elements 376

Self study. 376

Review 376

Appendices

Appendix A - tools 377

Appendix B - Keyboard Shortcuts 383

Appendix C - Understanding Digital Files 389

Understanding Resolution 389

Understanding Color Modes & Bit Depth. 389

Understanding File Formats. 390

Starting up

About the Photoshop Elements 8 Digital Classroom

Adobe® Photoshop® Elements lets you edit and organize your digital images. While it is a powerful product that includes some of the same capabilities found in the professional Photoshop products, the Elements version makes image editing simple and accessible. Photoshop Elements is more than editing, and organizing—it empowers story telling with images and video, the ability to personalize and create galleries, calendars, and other projects with your images, both in print and on the Web.

Adobe Photoshop Elements is available for the Mac and Windows operating systems. The Windows version includes the Organizer workspace where you can sort and organize your images. The Mac OS version does not include the organizer, instead Adobe included the Adobe Bridge software that ships with their Adobe Creative Suite software to assist you with organizing your images. For many years Adobe neglected the Mac OS with Photoshop Elements being several versions more advanced on the Windows platform. The features for editing are now the same, but they are not for organization. Because of this, the Mac OS organization features are different from what is described in parts of this book. Because of these differences, we have included a section just for Mac OS users at the end of this book on how to use the Adobe Bridge. Because of the differences between the Windows and Mac OS versions of Photoshop Elements, parts of Lesson 1 and Lesson 2 will not apply to Mac OS users.

Adobe Photoshop Elements Digital Classroom is like having your own personal instructor guiding you through each lesson while you work at your own speed. This book includes 14 self-paced lessons that let you discover essential skills and explore the new features and capabilities of Photoshop Elements. Each lesson includes step-by-step instructions, lesson files, and video tutorials, all of which are available on the included DVD. This book has been developed by the same team of Adobe Certified Instructors and Photoshop experts who have created many of the official training titles for Adobe Systems and other books in the *Digital Classroom* book series.

Prerequisites

Before you start the lessons in *Adobe Photoshop Elements Digital Classroom,* you should have a working knowledge of your computer and its operating system. You should know how to use the directory system of your computer so that you can navigate through folders. You need to understand how to locate, save, and open files. You should also know how to use your mouse to access menus and commands.

Before starting the lessons files in *Adobe Photoshop Elements Digital Classroom*, make sure that you have installed Adobe Photoshop Elements. The software is sold separately, and not included with this book. You may use the 30-day trial version of Adobe Photoshop Elements available at the *adobe.com* web site, subject to the terms of its license agreement.

System requirements

Before starting the lessons in *Adobe Photoshop Elements Digital Classroom*, make sure that your computer is equipped for running Adobe Photoshop Elements 8, which you must purchase separately. The minimum system requirements for your computer to effectively use the software are listed below.

Windows OS

- Microsoft® Windows® XP with Service Pack 2 or 3, Windows Vista®, or Windows 7
- 1.6GHz or faster processor
- 1GB of RAM
- 2GB of available hard-disk space
- Color monitor with 16-bit color video card
- 1024x576 monitor resolution at 96dpi or less
- Microsoft DirectX 9 compatible display driver
- DVD-ROM drive
- Web features require Microsoft Internet Explorer 6 through 8 or Mozilla Firefox 1.5 through 3.x

Mac OS

- Mac OS X v10.4.11 through 10.5.8 or Mac OS X v10.6
- Multi-core Intel® processor
- Certified for 32-bit version of Windows
- 512MB of RAM (1GB recommended)
- 2GB of available hard-disk space (additional free space required during installation)
- 64MB of video RAM
- 1,024x768 display resolution
- Microsoft DirectX 9 compatible display driver
- DVD-ROM drive
- QuickTime 7 software required for multimedia features
- Internet connection required for Internet-based services

Starting Adobe Photoshop Elements 8

As with most software, Adobe Photoshop Elements is launched by locating the application in your Programs folder. If necessary, follow these steps to start the Adobe Photoshop Elements 8 application:

Windows

1   Choose Start > Programs > Adobe Photoshop Elements 8.

2   Use the Welcome Screen to determine if you will organize or edit your images.

Mac OS

1   Open the Applications folder, and then open the Adobe Photoshop Elements 8 folder.

2   Double-click the Adobe Photoshop Elements 8 application icon.

Menus and commands are identified throughout the book by using the greater-than symbol (>). For example, the command to print a document would be identified as File > Print.

Loading lesson files

The *Photoshop Elements Digital Classroom* DVD includes files that accompany the exercises for each of the lessons. You will need to copy the entire lessons folder from the supplied DVD to your hard drive.

For each lesson in the book, the files are referenced by the file name of each file. The exact location of each file on your computer is not used, as you may have placed the files in a unique location on your hard drive. We suggest placing the lesson files in your Documents folder or on your desktop.

Copying the lesson files to your hard drive:

1   Insert the *Photoshop Elements Digital Classroom* DVD supplied with this book.

2   On your computer, navigate to the DVD and locate the folder named Lessons.

3   Drag the Lessons folder to your hard drive.

Managing catalogs

In the Windows version of Photoshop Elements, the catalog organizes and displays the images and videos you use with Photoshop Elements. The Mac OS version of Photoshop Elements does not utilize the concept of the catalog but is just as effective. If you are a MacOS user, see Lesson 14, "Using Adobe Bridge," to learn how to organize your photos without the catalog. When you start Photoshop Elements and identify photos on your computer, or import them from your digital camera, a catalog is automatically created for you. The files themselves are not imported directly into the catalog, rather they remain on your hard drive in their original location, and the Photoshop Elements catalog keeps track of their location along with related information about the files, such as when the image was taken, and the kind of camera used.

Photoshop Elements uses only one catalog at a time. Because you will be working with many sample images in this book, you may wish to organize the exercise files in their own catalog, separate from your personal images. This is not required, but is an option if you prefer to keep the exercise files separate from your personal images. If you create a separate catalog for the images used in the book, you will need to switch back to your personal catalog after you have completed the exercises in this book, or any time you wish to work with your personal images.

Creating a new catalog

If you wish to store the exercise files for this book separately from your own images, you may create a new catalog. You can open only one catalog at a time, so you will need to follow the instructions in Switching Catalogs in the next section when you want to access your personal images. This step is not required, but allows you to store the sample images separately from those used in the book. To create a new catalog:

1   With the Photoshop Elements Organizer open, choose File > Catalog.

2   Choose Custom Location, then press Browse. Navigate to the location where you have stored your lesson files that you copied from the DVD, such as your Desktop or your Documents folder and press OK. This will be the location where your catalog will be stored.

    If you wish to store your catalog for the book exercises in the location of the other catalogs, choose the Catalogs Accessible By All Users option instead of choosing Custom Location.

3   Press New and type **Digital Classroom** in the Enter A Name For The New Catalog dialog box, then press OK. A new catalog is created and stored in the location you have specified.

If you backup and synchronize photos using Photoshop.com, *be certain to disable the backup and synchronization before creating the new catalog because the backup and synchronization features only work with files in a single catalog. This only applies if you are creating a new catalog to use with this book, and only if you use* Photoshop.com *to backup your images automatically. To disable the backup and synchronization, follow these steps:*

1   In the Organizer, choose Edit > Preferences > Backup/Synchronization. The Backup/ Synchronization Preferences window appears.

2   In the Backup/Synchronization Preferences window, disable Backup/Synchronization.

3   After you switch back to your personal catalog, return to the Backup/Synchronization preferences and enable Backup/Synchronization so that your personal images are backed-up using Photoshop.com.

Switching Catalogs

If you create a separate catalog for use with this book, you will want to switch back to the catalog containing your personal images after you complete the exercises. To switch back to your personal catalog, follow these steps.

1   In the Organizer, choose File > Catalog. The Catalog Manager dialog box appears.

2   Select the catalog you wish to open from the list of catalogs in the Catalog Manager window, then press Open.

    If you wish to access the files from this book, you will need to repeat this process to return to the Digital Classroom catalog.

You can choose which catalog is used at the time you start the Organizer. Press and hold the Shift key while starting the Organizer. You can do this from the Editor mode by pressing and holding Shift, then clicking the Organizer button while continuing to hold the Shift key. A window appears in which you can choose the catalog to use.

Reconnecting to missing files

Once you start working with Photoshop Elements, you should use the program to organize, rename, and delete your image files. If you move your files using your operating system, Photoshop Elements will likely lose track of them, and a missing file icon appears in the Photo Browser. These steps are provided in case you accidentally move your images outside of Photoshop Elements, or receive a warning regarding missing files. You can return to the section if this occurs, but you do not need to perform these steps unless your image files are missing.

If you have moved an individual file using your operating system, and Photoshop Elements can't locate it, you can use the Photo Browser to identify the new location of the file using these steps.

1   Working in the Photo Browser, click to select a missing file and choose File > Reconnect > Missing File.

2   If you have multiple files that are missing, choose File > Reconnect > All Missing Files without selecting the images that are missing. Photoshop Elements will search for all missing files and reconnect them automatically.

Reconnect missing files window

If Photoshop Elements notices files are missing, the reconnect Missing Files window may appear. Use these steps to reconnect the files.

1   In the Reconnect Missing Files dialog box, select one or more missing files from the Files Missing From Catalog list, located on the left side of the dialog box. To select more than one file, Ctrl+click the files you wish to reconnect.

2   On the right side of the dialog box, under the Locate The Missing Files section, click the Browse tab to see the last known folder location for the file. If you know the new location of the files, navigate to the new location, then select a folder or hard drive and press Find. Photoshop Elements will search the location you specify for the selected files. Press Reconnect after the files are located.

Working with the video tutorials

Your *Photoshop Elements Digital Classroom* DVD comes with video tutorials developed by the authors to help you understand the concepts explored in each lesson. Each tutorial is approximately five minutes long and demonstrates and explains the concepts and features covered in the lesson.

The videos are designed to supplement your understanding of the material in the chapter. We have selected exercises and examples that we feel will be most useful to you. You may want to view the entire video for each lesson before you begin that lesson. Additionally, at certain points in a lesson, you will encounter the DVD icon. The icon, with appropriate lesson number, indicates that an overview of the exercise being described can be found in the accompanying video.

DVD video icon.

Setting up for viewing the video tutorials

The DVD included with this book includes video tutorials for each lesson. Although you can view the lessons on your computer directly from the DVD, we recommend copying the folder labeled *Videos* from the *Photoshop Elements Digital Classroom* DVD to your hard drive.

Copying the video tutorials to your hard drive:

1   Insert the *Photoshop Elements Digital Classroom* DVD supplied with this book.

2   On your computer, navigate to the DVD and locate the folder named Videos.

3   Drag the entire Videos folder to a location onto your hard drive. It is important to copy the entire folder, and not just the player.

Viewing the video tutorials

The videos on the *Photoshop Elements Digital Classroom* DVD are saved in the Flash projector format. A Flash projector file wraps the Digital Classroom video player and the Adobe Flash Player in an executable file (.exe for Windows or .app for Mac OS). However, the extension may not always be visible. Projector files allow the Flash content to be deployed on your system without the need for a browser or without the installation of any other player.

Playing the video tutorials:

1   On your computer, navigate to the Videos folder you copied to your hard drive from the DVD.

2   Open the Videos folder and double-click the PSEvideos_PC (Windows) or PSEvideos_ Mac (Mac OS) to view the video tutorial. If you have difficulty viewing the files after copying them to your hard drive, you may view them directly from the DVD.

3   Press the Play button to view the videos.

The Digital Classroom video player has a simple user interface that allows you to control the viewing experience, including stopping, pausing, playing, and restarting the video. You can also rewind or fast-forward, and adjust the playback volume.

A. *Go to beginning.* *B*. *Play/Pause.* *C*. *Fast-forward/rewind.* *D*. *Stop.* *E*. *Volume Off/On.* *F*. *Volume control.*

Playback volume is also affected by the settings in your operating system. Be certain to adjust the sound volume for your computer, in addition to the sound controls in the Player window.

Additional resources

The Digital Classroom series goes beyond the training books. You can continue your learning online, with training videos, at seminars and conferences, and in-person training events.

DigitalClassroomBooks.com

The *DigitalClassroomBooks.com* site includes updates, notes, and makes it easy for you to contact the authors. You can also learn more about the other books in the series, including many books on popular creative software.

Learn from the authors

The authors of the Digital Classroom seminar series frequently conduct in-person seminars and speak at conferences, including the annual CRE8 Conference. Learn more about regularly scheduled classes at *agitraining.com* and their annual conference at *CRE8summit.com*. The authors also provide private classes for groups and organizations, including speaking engagements. Contact the authors at *DigitalClassroomBooks.com*.

Resources for educators

Contact your Wiley publishing education representative to access resources for educators, including instructors' guides for incorporating this Digital Classroom book into your curriculum. Get more information at *Wiley.com*.

Follow the authors on Twitter

Follow the Digital Classroom authors on Twitter at *Twitter.com/agitraining*.

What you'll learn in this lesson:

- Adding files to the Organizer
- Understanding workspaces
- Using the Photo Downloader
- Creating an album

Importing your Photos into Adobe Photoshop Elements

Adobe Photoshop Elements is an easy-to-use solution for organizing and editing your digital photos. You will be up-and-running, creating beautiful photographs before you know it. To start, you'll need to import images from your camera or computer.

Starting up

You will work with several files from the Lessons folder in this lesson. Make sure that you have copied the Lessons folder from the supplied DVD onto your hard drive. In order to access these files in the Organizer, you need to import them, which you will do in this lesson.

Before you start, note that the Photoshop Elements Editor remembers the last panel layout that you used. Before starting, make sure your tools and panels are consistent with the examples presented in these lessons by resetting the panels, by choosing Window > Reset Panels within the Editor.

If you aren't ready to start working with your own images, you can jump ahead to "Adding Files and Folders to the Organizer" on page 11 to start working with files from the DVD that came with this book.

See Lesson 1 in action!

Use the accompanying video to gain a better understanding of how to use some of the features shown in this lesson. The video tutorial for this lesson can be found on the included DVD.

How Photoshop Elements works

The fact that you're reading this book indicates that you probably already own or are considering purchasing a digital camera. It's probably also accurate to say that you've been taking pictures and truly enjoying the flexibility that digital photography has to offer. The ability to shoot as many images as you like—or at least as many as will fit onto your camera's memory card—is one advantage that digital photography has over traditional film cameras. Another advantage is that you can choose which images to keep and which ones to delete from your camera's memory card, instead of sifting through the photos that you had developed at your local photo store, picking out the good ones, and throwing the bad ones away. With digital photography, you only pay for the good photos!

So you've figured out how to shoot pictures with your digital camera but you've found that the clunky interface on your camera requires a lot of time to sift through the images in order to delete the poor photos that you don't want. In addition, your photos may be accumulating on your camera's memory card, requiring you to constantly remove images to make room for new ones. These are only a few of the problems that people are faced with in this new world of digital photography, and this is where Adobe Photoshop Elements fills a void.

Photoshop Elements provides you with the ability to import, organize, adjust, and output your images in limitless ways. Photoshop Elements makes organizing and editing photos a snap, by giving you the tools needed to accomplish everyday tasks without the complexity of the full version of Photoshop. With Photoshop Elements, you can utilize keywords, tags, ratings, and other features to identify your images so that you can search for and find them easily in the future. You'll never lose an image again. Let's get started!

The welcome screen

When you launch Photoshop Elements, the Welcome screen opens automatically. The welcome screen is a gateway to the workspaces that are available within Photoshop Elements. Workspaces are different environments built into Photoshop Elements that allow you to perform different tasks. You'll get a closer look at workspaces later in this book.

When you launch Photoshop Elements, the welcome screen appears. The welcome screen is the launch pad from which you will navigate to different areas of Photoshop Elements. There are two main categories available in the welcome screen:

Organize (▦): This is like a digital filing cabinet. You can rename your files, add keywords, add ratings, and categorize your photos. Lessons 1 and 2 cover the Organizer.

Edit (✎): This is where you can make adjustments to your photos. Fix exposure, color, and contrast, remove redeye, and much more. Lessons 3, 4, and 5 are focused on editing.

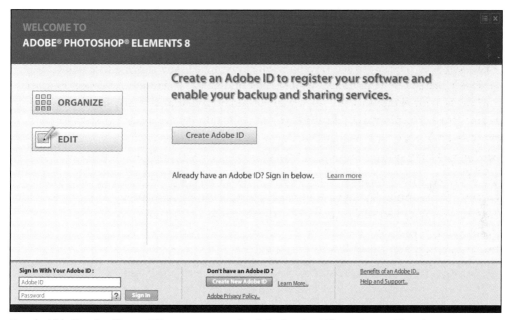

From the Adobe Photoshop Elements Welcome screen, you can launch the Organizer, Editor, or sign on to Photoshop.com to share your images.

Getting photos into the Organizer using the Photo Downloader

The Photoshop Elements Organizer is your creative hub. It can be used to organize your entire photo library, as well as perform a few quick editing tasks. It is not a simple file browser like your operating system uses; it is more of a photo management system, allowing you to organize, tag, and manipulate content. Before you can use it to the fullest, you must first import your images into the Organizer.

Getting photos from a camera or card reader

Photos that you shoot with your digital camera are not usually stored on the camera, but on a removeable memory card plugged into your camera. To get the photos from your camera onto your computer, you must have a physical connection from your camera to your computer. This connection is usually in the form of a USB cable supplied with your camera. With many computers, it is also possible to remove the memory card from the camera and insert it into a card reader. This method generally offers faster importing of your photos, but either method ultimately yields the same results. For details on how to connect your camera to your computer, consult the instructions that you use with your camera. Photos are copied onto your computer using the Adobe Photoshop Elements 8.0 Photo Downloader. The Photo Downloader allows you to choose the location on your computer where you would like the files copied during import.

Import photos automatically

When you plug your camera or card reader into your computer, Windows prompts you with a dialog box asking what you want to do. Depending on the applications that you have installed, your dialog box will look slightly different than the one shown in the figure below. If you choose *Organize and Edit using Adobe Photoshop Elements Organizer 8.0*, the Adobe Photoshop Elements 8.0 Photo Downloader displays on your screen.

The AutoPlay dialog box appears when you connect a camera or card
reader on a Windows computer. This dialog doesn't appear on Mac OS.

Import photos manually

Depending on your configuration, Windows may not display a dialog box asking you which application to use to access the photos on your camera's memory card, and you may have to launch the Photo Downloader manually. To do so, press the Organize button (⊞) from the welcome screen, then follow the steps below to import the photos.

1   Select File > Get Photos and Videos > From Camera or Card Reader.

2   From the drop-down menu in the Source area, choose the digital camera or card reader.

Once you have selected a device, all photos on it are loaded into the viewer.

3   In the Import Settings section, press the Browse button to choose the folder you would like to copy your photos to. If you are using a single folder to hold all your images, you can create a subfolder based on a variety of options in the Create Subfolder(s) drop-down menu.

4   If you would like to automatically rename the photos as they are being copied to your computer, choose a renaming method from the Rename Files section.

5   Set the Delete Options to control what happens to the original photos on the camera or card reader after they are copied to your computer.

6   Press Get Photos to copy your photos. Press Cancel if you are not connected to a camera or card reader.

The Photo Downloader

During import from a camera or card reader, Photoshop Elements uses the Adobe Photoshop Elements Photo Downloader. The Photo Downloader aids you when importing files into Photoshop Elements. This dialog box has two different modes: Standard and Advanced.

Standard mode

In Standard mode, the Photo Downloader provides you with some basic options. The Source section allows you to define a specific device (camera or card reader) from which to import files.

Standard mode in the Photo Downloader offers a quick and easy way to import your photos.

The Import Settings section allows you to determine what occurs during import as you're importing images.

Location: The location on your hard drive from which you would like the files to be imported.

Create Subfolder(s): Organizes the photos into subfolders based on a variety of date formats, including shot date and import date.

Rename Files: Renames the files during import so that they correspond to the date the photos were taken, today's date (current date), or a custom name.

Delete Options: Determines what to do with the original photos on the camera or card reader once the files have been imported onto your hard drive. You have the following choices: Do Not Delete Originals, Verify and Delete Originals, or Delete Originals immediately after copying them.

Advanced mode

In advanced mode, thumbnail previews of all the images on the camera or card reader are displayed and you can choose which photos you would like to download to your hard drive. Additional options are also available.

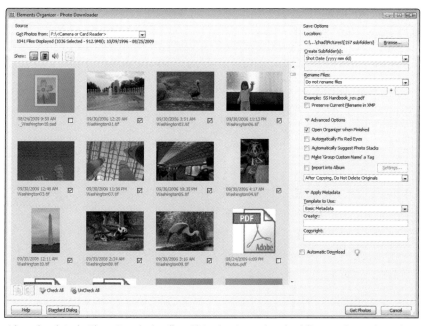

Advanced mode in the Photos Downloader offers additional options, such as the ability to apply metadata to images during import.

Open Organizer when Finished: Opens the Elements Organizer workspace after importing the photos.

Automatically Fix Red Eyes: Analyzes your photos on import and automatically fixes red eye in any image.

Automatically Suggest Photo Stacks: Suggests that multiple photos that appear similar be grouped together in a stack.

Make 'Group Custom Name' a Tag: Applies the custom name tag of the specified group to the selected photos. Use this option only if you have assigned custom groups.

Import into Album: Allows you to import the photos into an existing album, or allows you to create one during import.

Advanced mode lets you apply metadata to your photos during import. Metadata is information about the photos that you are importing, such as the photographers name, the date the image was taken, copyright status, and more. Metadata is discussed in greater detail in Lesson 2, "Organizing Your Photos." Below are options you can choose when applying Metadata.

Template to Use: Allows you to use a pre-configured metadata template to automatically apply common metadata to your images.

Creator: Type the name of the person who took the photograph.

Copyright: Type copyright information related to each image.

Click the *Automatically Download* checkbox to automatically launch the Adobe Photo Downloader and import the photos on the card using the default preferences.

Get photos from a scanner

Photoshop Elements can be used to operate many scanners, allowing you to scan your traditional photos and prints, and open them directly in the program.

1   If the Photo Downloader dialog box is open, you will need to press Cancel before you can perform this step. Choose File > Get Photos and Videos > From Scanner.

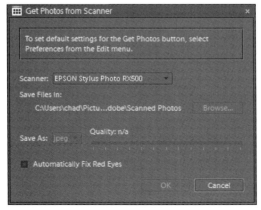

The Get Photos from Scanner dialog box.

2   Choose your scanner from the drop-down menu.

3   Press the Browse button to choose the folder in which you would like to save your scans.

4   From the Save As drop-down menu, select the format in which you would like to save your image. See Appendix C for an explanation of file format options.

5   Press OK to begin scanning, or press Cancel if you are not connected to a scanner and are simply exploring this option.

You can have Photoshop Elements automatically fix red eyes in your scanned image by clicking the checkbox for Automatically Fix Red Eyes. *This option is also available in the Photo Downloader when using the Advanced dialog box.*

Get photos and videos by searching

If you have photos and videos in different locations on your hard drive, but aren't exactly certain of the location, you can have Photoshop Elements search for them.

1   Select File > Get Photos and Videos > By Searching.

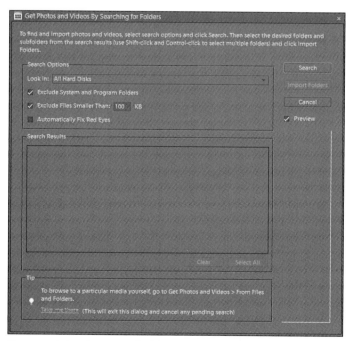

You can search through your entire hard drive or in specific folders to add images to Photoshop Elements.

2   Set search options such as location, exclusion size, and automatic red eye fix from the Search Options section.

3   Press the Search button to have Photoshop Elements search your hard drive for any folder containing photo and video files. If you do not want Photoshop Elements to perform this search at the time, press Cancel and go to the next section, "Setting a Watch Folder."

4   When the search is complete, select the folders that you would like to import photos from, then press Import Folders.

To select more than one folder, press the Ctrl key while clicking the folders.

Setting a Watch Folder

Manually adding individual photos and videos to Photoshop Elements can be a time-consuming process. To make this process easier, you can set a Watch Folder. This action allows the program to automatically import any new files that are found in the specified folder, such as the default Pictures folder used by Windows. Note that the Watch Folder feature is not available on the Mac OS version of Photoshop Elements; only the Windows version.

1   Choose File > Watch Folders.

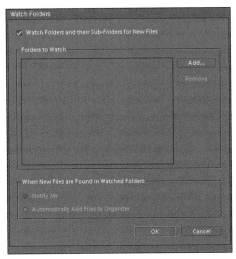

Setting a Watch folder makes it easy to import images.

2   Press the Add button and browse to find the folder you want to add to the Watch list. You can add multiple folders if you want.

3   Press OK if you have chosen a Watch folder, or Cancel if you do not want to set up a Watch folder.

Adding files and folders to the Organizer

In cases where you already have photos on your computer, you simply need to add them to the Organizer. In this example, you'll use the files provided on the DVD that accompanies this book.

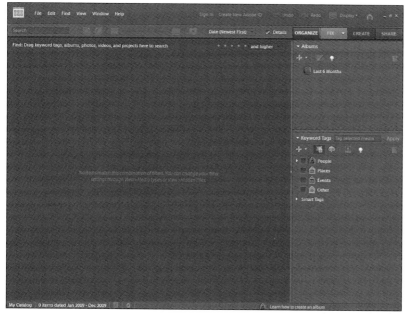

The Organizer is empty until content is imported.

1   Choose File > Get Photos and Videos > From Files and Folders. In the Get Photos and Videos from Files and Folders dialog box that appears, navigate to the Lessons folder that you copied to your computer from the DVD.

2   Select the Lessons folder and press the Get Media button. The photos begin to load into the Organizer.

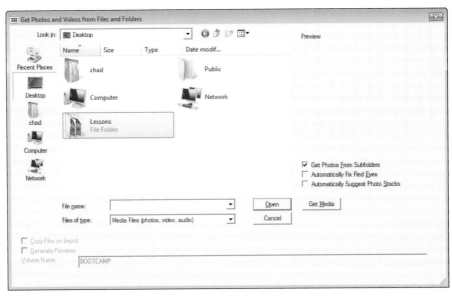

You can select a single folder and import all photos from it, and any subfolders as well.

3   A dialog box appears, asking if you would like to import the keywords that are attached to the photos. Click Select All to import all keywords and all the lesson keywords, and press OK. Keywords help you organize your images and are discussed in more detail in later lessons.

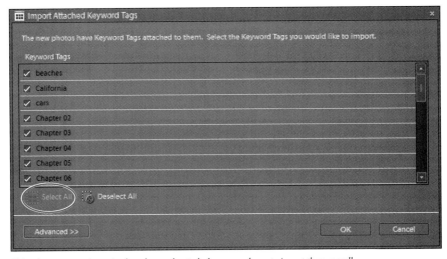

If the photos you are importing have keywords attached, you can choose to import them as well.

After you import images, only the imported images are displayed. A warning dialog box appears, informing you that the only files you are currently viewing in the Organizer are those that were just imported. Click the Don't show again *checkbox, if you'd prefer that this dialog box didn't pop up each time you import media. Press* OK *to close the dialog box.*

4   By default, the images displayed in the Organizer are categorized by date. Choose View > Show File Names to add the filenames to the display. If there is a checkmark next to *Show File Names*, the feature is already enabled. Choosing *Show File Names* when it is already selected disables the feature.

If the filenames still don't display in the Organizer after choosing View > Show File Names, *drag the thumbnail slider to the right until the filenames appear.*

Getting a still image from a video frame

Adobe Photoshop Elements can import video clips as well as photographs and other images. Although Photoshop Elements is not designed to do video editing, it can manage video clips either imported from some cameras, created using video software such as Adobe Premiere Elements, or that you obtained from friends and family. It can also take a single frame of a video clip and save it as a still image. Let's see how Photoshop Elements can be used to do this.

1   Make sure that you've imported the Lessons folder, as discussed in the "Adding files and folders to the Organizer" section earlier in this lesson.

2   From the Organizer, choose View > Media Types and uncheck all options except for *Video*. This hides everything in the Organizer that is not a video file. You should see one file remaining in the Organizer, called *Claire Bike Ride.avi*.

Hiding and showing media types makes it easy to see only certain media types with which you want to work. This is only one method of refining what you see in the Organizer. In the next lesson, you'll see how applying keywords and tags to your media can streamline this process as well.

3 Choose Edit > Deselect to make sure that you don't have any files selected in the Organizer, then press the arrow on the right side of the Fix tab in the upper-right corner of the workspace. From the drop-down menu, choose Quick Photo Edit (). This loads the Editor Workspace, which is used to extract a still frame from a video clip. The features of the Editor Workspace are covered in more detail in Lesson 2, "Organizing Your Photos."

Choose Quick Photo Edit.

4 Choose File > Import > Frame from Video.

The Frame From Video dialog box allows you to choose a video clip and grab still images.

5 In the Frame From Video dialog box, press the Browse button, and navigate to the Lessons folder that you copied to your hard drive. Select the file named *Claire Bike Ride.avi* and press Open.

6   The video clip that you selected is displayed within the Frame From Video dialog box. Use the player controls below the video clip to play, pause, stop, go forward, and go backward in the video. When the desired clip is visible, press the Grab Frame button or press the Spacebar on your keyboard to grab a still frame of the video. You can grab as many frames as desired.

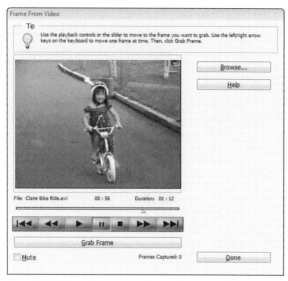

Press the Grab Frame button or press the Spacebar on your keyboard while the video is playing to grab still frames from the video.

7   When you have grabbed the desired number of frames, press Done.

8   All your clips appear in the bin at the bottom of the Editor workspace. When you are finished, close each file from the bin by selecting each file in the bin and pressing the Close button in the main window of the Editor. You will be prompted to save files upon closing them. Save them to the Lessons folder making sure that the *Include in the Organizer* checkbox is checked.

9   Press the Organizer button (▦) in the menu bar at the top of the workspace. You will probably only see the original video clip at this point because the other media types are still hidden. Choose View > Media Types and make sure there is a checkmark next to all the listed options. This ensures that you can see everything in the Organizer. All the images that you grabbed from the video clip should now be visible in the Organizer. If you can't see all of the images, choose View > Refresh or press F5 on your keyboard to have the Organizer to refresh the view of the images.

Workspaces

Workspaces are different environments built into Photoshop Elements that allow you to perform different tasks on your pictures. Photoshop Elements utilizes two main workspaces: the Organizer and the Editor. Each workspace launches as its own individual application. When you are in the Organizer workspace, which is the default workspace after importing images into Photoshop Elements, you can press the Fix tab in the upper right corner of the Organizer workspace and then press the Edit Photos button in the Task pane to launch the Editor workspace. Conversely, if you are in the Editor workspace, you can switch to the Organizer workspace by pressing the Organizer button (⊞) in the menu bar at the top of the screen.

Organizer basics

Because the Organizer workspace is the default workspace after importing your photos, most of your initial time will be spent here getting your photos, well, organized! In Lesson 2, "Organizing Your Photos," you'll discover in greater detail how you can organize and find photos that you've imported into Photoshop Elements, but for now, you'll look at some of the basics.

Creating an album

The concept of albums in Photoshop Elements is pretty straightforward. In fact, at some point you've probably created albums the old-fashioned way, by taking photos that were shot with a traditional film camera and developed, then putting them into an album book. You did this to keep your photos organized.

Albums in Photoshop Elements are very similar to those albums that you created in the past, only now they are digital. Albums allow you to organize photos that are related. For example, it might be an event, person, or group. You can also create Album Groups, which can organize multiple albums into a unique category or group. You can organize your photos any way you like, and albums make the process easy. Let's see how!

1   Make sure that the Organizer workspace is active and that all your images are being displayed by choosing View > Media Types and ensuring that there is a checkmark next to each option listed. This displays all the photos that have been imported into the Organizer.

2   Choose View > Show File Names to display each image's filename.

3   Choose Date (Newest First) from the Media Browser Arrangement drop-down menu at the top of the workspace to sort the images by date.

4   Scroll down toward the bottom of the Organizer and click once on the photo named *IMG_0840.JPG* to select it. Now hold down the Shift key on your keyboard and click once on the photo named *IMG_0903.JPG*. This selects the photos chosen, and all the photos in between them.

Hold down the Shift key and click to select a range of photos.

5   Press the Create new album or album group button (✚) in the Albums panel and choose New Album. The Album Details panel appears.

6 In the Album Name text field, type **AIRSHOW** and press Done. A new album is now displayed in the Albums panel.

The Album Details panel allows you to give your album a name.

7 To view the files in the new album you just created, click once on the *AIRSHOW* album. This displays only the photos of that album in the Organizer. When an album is active, it becomes highlighted in the Albums panel, and the album name appears in the upper left corner of the main Organizer window after the word Find.

8 To stop viewing a particular album, click the album again to display all photos.

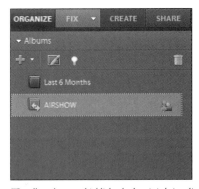

The album becomes highlighted when it is being displayed.

9 Hold down the Ctrl key and click on all the images of planes flying in the air. Ctrl+clicking allows you to select non-contiguous photos in the Organizer.

10 Press the Create new album or album group button in the Albums panel and choose New Album. Name this album **Planes in flight** and press Done. Albums provide an efficient means for organizing your photos. Now you'll create an album group to further organize the albums you've created.

11 Press the Create new album or album group button in the Albums panel and choose New Album Category. Name this category **July 2008 Airshow**, and press OK

12 Click and drag the two albums you've created, and drop them on top of the *July 2008 Airshow* album category. The albums are now contained within the category.

Drag and drop the albums on top of the album category for further organization.

How to get help

As you explore and work with Photoshop Elements, you're bound to have questions. Fortunately, help is close at hand. Below are some useful resources for obtaining help when you need it.

Photoshop help

Adobe Photoshop Elements provides detailed and searchable help that can be accessed quickly and easily by choosing Help > Photoshop Elements Help or Help > Organizer Help depending on if you're currently in the Editor or Organizer workspace, respectively. You can also access help from either workspace by pressing the F1 key on your keyboard. If you are connected to the Internet, you are directed to Adobe's on-line help, which contains the most up-to-date information available. If you do not have an Internet connection, Photoshop Elements directs you to a local copy of the help files that still contains a plethora of information but may not be completely current. Answers to your questions are only a click away.

Support Center

You can access the Photoshop Elements Support Center online at *www.adobe.com/support/ photoshopelements/*. The Support Center contains current information related to support issues that other users have had and what their solutions are. The Support Center also contains How-to videos demonstrating features of Photoshop Elements.

The Inspiration Browser

Adobe has released a service called *Photoshop.com* that allows you to upload and store photos online to share with friends and family. Photoshop Elements integrates with this service. When you sign up for this free service, you are provided with additional features in Photoshop Elements not otherwise available. Refer to Lesson 6, "Sharing Your Photos," for more information about *Photoshop.com*.

If you return to the welcome screen by pressing the welcome screen button (⌂) in the Organizer, there will be an area on the lower left side of the welcome screen to sign into your *Photoshop.com* account. Upon signing in, new options are displayed on the welcome screen. Press the Tips and Tricks link in the lower-right corner of the Welcome Screen to open the Adobe Elements Inspiration Browser. The Inspiration Browser contains tutorials posted by users like you who have found new and creative ways of using Photoshop Elements software. You can even post your own tutorials showing new ways of using Photoshop Elements that you've discovered.

The Inspiration Browser.

Self study

Now that you have had some practice importing photos into the Organizer, you can see how useful it is for organizing all your images. Practice on your own by importing your own photos using the various methods covered in this lesson and organizing them into albums. The more organized you are with your photos, the easier it is to locate them.

Review

Questions

1   Where are the four places from which you can get photos and videos?

2   How can you select a range of non-contiguous photos to add to an album in the Organizer?

3   Which workspace must be used to extract a still image from a video clip?

Answers

1   You can get them from a camera or card reader, a scanner, files and folders, and by searching your hard drive.

2   Ctrl+click any image in the Organizer.

3   The Editor workspace.

What you'll learn in this lesson:

- Understanding the Organizer workspace
- Analyzing and reviewing photos
- Creating a Smart album
- Tagging your photos and adding keywords

Organizing Your Photos

Photoshop Elements offers an intuitive way to label and catalog your pictures for quick and easy access when you need them.

Starting up

Within the Photoshop Elements Organizer: You will work with several files from the Lessons folder in this lesson. Make sure that you have copied the Lessons folder from the supplied DVD to your hard drive. In order to access these files in the Organizer, you need to import them. See "Adding files and folders to the Organizer" on page 11. Additionally, if you want Photoshop Elements to automatically detect when images are added to your library folder, you need to set it as a Watch Folder. See "Setting a Watch Folder" on page 10. To make selecting files a little easier, you can limit the display to only images used in each lesson. In the Keywords panel, select the specific lessons keyword from the imported keywords submenu.

Within the Photoshop Elements Editor: The Photoshop Elements Editor defaults to the last panel layout that you used. Before starting, make sure your tools and panels are consistent with the examples presented in these lessons by resetting the panel locations, by choosing Window > Reset Panels or press the Reset Panels button (⟳) in the Options bar.

See Lesson 2 in action!

Use the accompanying video to gain a better understanding of how to use some of the features shown in this lesson. The video tutorial for this lesson can be found on the included DVD.

Understanding the Organizer workspace

The Organizer is the heart of Adobe Photoshop Elements. You can use the Organizer to find, organize, and share your photos and media files. The Organizer's Photo Browser allows you to view thumbnails of any photo, video, and .pdf file that you have imported. To gain even more control over the photos that you view, you can use the Timeline to view and sort by date, or the Keyword Tags panel to view photos by keyword, and the Albums panel to view photos categorically by event or subject based on albums that you've created. The Properties panel and the Options bar allow you to view pertinent information and make basic changes to your photos quickly and easily. The Organizer is divided into several different areas.

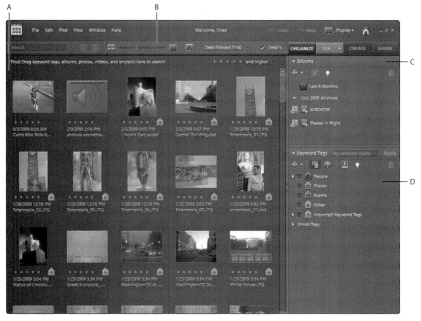

A. Photo Browser. B. Options bar. C. Albums panel. D. Keyword Tags panel.

Photo Browser

The Photo Browser is the main work area of the Organizer. Use the Browser to view and locate thumbnails of the photos, video clips, and audio files in your catalogs. You can select items in the Photo Browser to attach tags to them, add them to projects, or edit them.

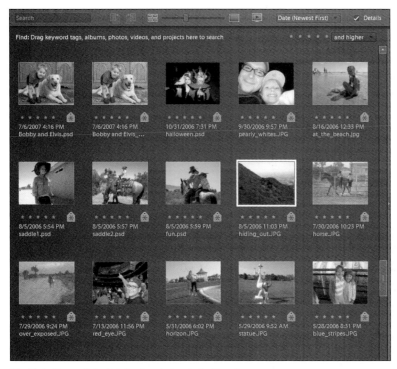

The Photo Browser is the hub for all work done in the Organizer.

Options Bar

The Options bar provides efficient ways to view your photos in the Photo Browser. The Search box offers a way to search for photos by filename, keyword, caption and other criteria. The rotate icons allow you to rotate images into their proper orientation. The thumbnail slider controls the size of the image thumbnails that are being viewed. The View, Edit, Organize in Full Screen button (▶) allows you to add keywords and make edits to your photos in full screen mode. The Media Browser Arrangement drop-down menu on the right side of the Options bar controls how photos are sorted by date, either newest first or oldest first. Finally the *Details* checkbox, when checked, displays additional information about the photo beneath each thumbnail.

The Options bar allows you to easily organize and search for your images in the Photo Browser.

Timeline

Photoshop Elements automatically organizes all your photos in the Photo Browser Timeline, even if the photos are not tagged. The Timeline is divided into months and years, and you can view images from a particular month or year by clicking that month or year in the Timeline. Choose Window > Timeline to turn this feature on or off.

The Timeline allows you to view the images in the Photo Browser chronologically.

Properties

The Properties panel, also located under the Window menu, is used to add and view additional information about your photos that is not available in the Photo Browser. Dimensions, captions, notes, file size, and location can all be viewed here.

The Properties panel adds information to the image that can include details and descriptions.

Albums

The Albums panel shows all the different photo albums that you have created to organize your photos. The default album shows all images that have been created in the last six months. Albums allow you to organize your photos in a variety of different ways. Think of the traditional photo albums that you may have created using photographic prints. You can create albums that group photos of a specific event together. For example, you might create an album to organize all the pictures you took at a friend's wedding, at a child's birthday party, or in a specific timeframe.

As with traditional photo albums, Photoshop Elements albums are used to organize photos so that you can group similar subjects together.

Keyword Tags

The Keyword Tags panel allows you to add keyword tags to your photos. Once applied to an image, keywords allow you to quickly sort through a wide range of images to display only what you wish to view.

Keywords are an organizational tool that makes finding the images you are looking for much easier.

Analyzing photos in the Organizer

After importing photos into the Organizer using one of a variety of methods covered in Lesson 1, "Importing Your Photos into Adobe Photoshop Elements," the next step is to analyze the photos that you've shot with your digital camera.

Rotating photos

During the process of taking pictures with your digital camera, you may have rotated your camera. When you import these photos into Photoshop Elements and view them in the Organizer, they appear rotated. This makes it difficult to view the images. You may find yourself tilting your head to the side to get a better view, which is just not an ergonomic way to view the photo! Fortunately, Photoshop Elements makes it easy to fix this problem.

1   In the Organizer, type **utah** in the Search text field in the Options bar at the top of the workspace. This filters the images to those that contain *utah* in the name of the file.

2   Notice that all these images have been composed in a portrait orientation but they appear rotated within the Organizer. Select the first photo, then press the Rotate Left button ( ) in the Options bar. This rotates the selected photo counter-clockwise in the Organizer.

Press the Rotate Left button in the Options bar
to rotate the image counter-clockwise.

3   Select the second photo and Shift+click the last photo to select the remaining photos, then press the Rotate Left button in the Options bar.

   Now that the images are being displayed in the proper orientation, you can continue reviewing your photos.

4   Press the Show All button at the top of the Photo browser to view the entire catalog in your Organizer.

Hiding photos

Not every photo you take will be a good photo. Photography is a process that involves many variables that can cause a photo to not make the cut. Whether it's an overexposed or underexposed image, or your nephew ran in front of the camera just as you hit the shutter release, or your finger was partially covering the lens when you snapped the shot, any number of things can cause a photo to be inferior. Your job is to weed out the bad ones and leave the good ones. Let's see how Photoshop Elements can make this process a snap!

1 In the Organizer, type **sunset** in the Search text field at the top of the workspace. Eight sunset images are displayed in the Photo Browser because the word *sunset* is contained in the names of these files.

2 Double-click on the first image, *sunset-1*, to display it in single photo view. This gives you a more accurate view of the quality of the photo. This image has a mailbox post and a street sign in the foreground which are undesirable. Although you could fix this using the tools provided in Photoshop Elements, it's not the best photo and you may not want to keep it.

3 Choose Edit > Visibility > Mark as Hidden. The *sunset-1* photo disappears from view in the Photo Browser, and the next photo is displayed.

It's important to understand that when you hide a photo from view, the photo is exactly that, hidden. You haven't deleted anything at this point. You've simply decided that you may not want that photo and have hidden it for review at a later time. At that point, you may decide to delete the photo.

4   This photo, *Sunset-2.jpg*, suffers from the same problem. There's a big mailbox in the foreground that really stands out and detracts from the image. Choose Edit > Visibility > Mark as Hidden. Photoshop Elements hides the photo from view. Use the down arrow on your keyboard to continue navigating through the images that are displayed in the Photo Browser.

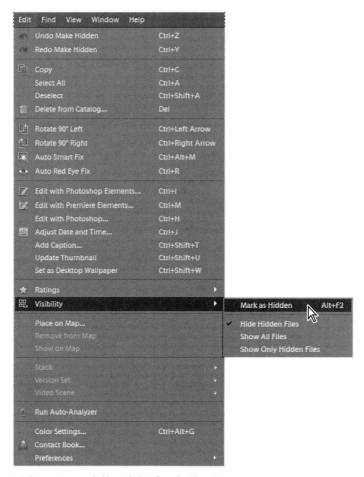

Marking an image as hidden to hide it from the Photo Browser.

5   Mark *Sunset-3* and *Sunset-4* as hidden, as well. The filenames appear in the lower-left corner of the Photo Browser. These images also have objects in the foreground that are distracting. The rest of the images don't look too bad, and so they remain visible.

6   Press the Small Thumbnail Size button (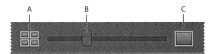) in the Options bar to view the images as thumbnails. You can drag the slider to the right of the Small Thumbnail Size button to resize the thumbnails for easier viewing.

A   B   C

A. Small Thumbnail Size button. B. Thumbnail slider.
C. Single Photo View button.

Reviewing and removing hidden photos

After you mark photos as hidden, you may want to go back and review those photos. You may decide that they're not so bad after all, or you may confirm that they aren't good shots and decide to delete them.

1   Choose Edit > Visibility > Show Only Hidden Files. This displays all the images that are currently hidden in the Organizer. Each photo that has been marked as hidden is displayed with a Hidden icon ().

Each photo that has been marked as hidden displays
with a Hidden icon in the lower-left corner of the image.

2   Double-click on the first thumbnail to display the photo in Single Photo view. The first two images are definitely bad. Use your down arrow key to navigate to the *Sunset-3* photo. This image contains characteristics that you like and can probably be recovered. Choose Edit > Visibility > Mark as Visible to put the image back into the visible category. Repeat this process for the *Sunset-4* image.

3   Press the Small Thumbnail Size button to display the hidden photos as thumbnails. These images are definitely not keepers, and so there's no point in allowing them to occupy hard drive space on your computer.

4   Select the first thumbnail, then Shift+click the second thumbnail to select it as well. Choose Edit > Delete Selected Items from Catalog or press the Delete key on your keyboard. The Confirm Deletion from Catalog dialog box appears. This dialog box is telling you that these photos will be removed from the catalog and will no longer be managed by Photoshop Elements. Make sure that you click the *Also delete selected item(s) from the hard disk* checkbox; otherwise, the photo files will still occupy storage space on your hard drive.

5   Press OK.

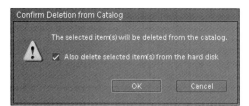

Make sure to check the box to Also delete selected item(s) from the hard disk *so that the deleted photos no longer occupy space on your hard drive.*

6   The Organizer is currently not displaying any images because in step 1, you set Photoshop Elements to only display the hidden files. Choose Edit > Visibility > Hide Hidden Files to display the photos that are visible and match the search criteria for *sunset*.

Renaming photos

Digital cameras are notorious for using obscure file-naming conventions to name photos. It's not uncommon to see a naming format like *IMG_01234.jpg*. This tells you nothing about the photo, and although the use of keywording and tagging (covered later in this lesson) can help to more clearly identify images, it's often helpful to rename the image to something more relevant, such as after the event or subject.

1   Make sure you are still viewing the sunset images by typing **sunset** in the Search text field, and press the Small Thumbnail Size button (⊞⊞) in the Options bar at the top of the workspace in the Organizer.

2   Select the first thumbnail, then Shift+click the last thumbnail to select all the images currently being displayed.

Although the filenames for these photos describe the sunset in the photo, you'll rename them to be even more descriptive. Photoshop Elements makes this easy and can batch renamed files instead of having to rename photos individually.

3   Choose File > Rename. The Rename dialog box appears.

4   Because there are multiple photos selected, the Rename dialog box displays a Common Base Name text field to use as the base text for every photo. Type **Northeast Sunset** in the Common Base Name text field.

With multiple photos selected, the Rename dialog box asks for a base name, then appends a number to each image automatically.

5   Press OK. Notice that every image has been renamed to *Northeast Sunset* but is appended with a consecutive number to differentiate each photo.

If you do not see the file names for the images, first check under the View menu and make sure there is a check mark next to Show File Names and Details. If these options are checked and you still do not see the file names, then drag the Adjust size of thumbnail slider to the right until the file names appear.

If you prefer renaming photos individually, the process is the same. However, the Rename dialog box asks you for a name for only the photo that is selected instead of a range of images.

Moving photos

Photoshop Elements manages photos that reside on your computer's hard drive. Even when you import images from a camera, card reader, or scanner, the files are copied from the device to a specific location on the hard drive of your choosing. To simplify file management, it's often useful for all your photos to reside in one common location. However, sometimes you may have imported photos from a folder on your desktop or another location. In these cases, you may want to move those images to the common location on your hard drive. Photoshop Elements simplifies this process by moving the files for you when directed. If you were to move the files using the Explorer in Windows, Photoshop Elements would lose track of the files and display them as missing because it could no longer locate the source file. Let's see how easy it is to move files in Photoshop Elements.

1   Press the Show All button at the top of the Photo Browser to display all the images in the current catalog.

2   Locate and select two photos, called *redeye* and *redeye-just the faces*. A quick search for redeye in the Search text field will display these photos. All the images in the Photo Browser currently reside in the Lessons folder that you imported in the Startup section of this lesson. You'll now move these two redeye photos to a different location on your computer.

3   Choose File > Move. The Move Selected Items dialog box appears. This dialog box shows the selected images that it is about to move, as well as their current location on your computer.

4   Press the Browse button, then navigate to and select your *Pictures* folder. Click the Pictures folder to make that folder active.

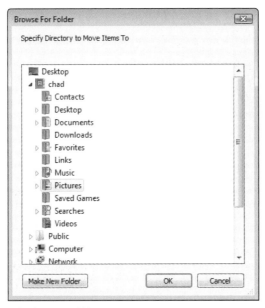

Select the Pictures folder.

In some versions of Windows, this folder is called My Pictures.

5   Press the Make New Folder button and name it **Lesson 2 Images**. Press OK in the Browse for Folder window.

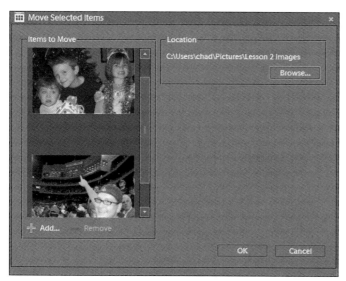

The Move Selected Items dialog box allows you to specify where to move the photos.

6   Press OK. The images are moved to the new location on your hard drive.

7   To confirm the new location of the images, select one of the *redeye* images, right-click it, then choose Show Properties. The folder path at the bottom of the Properties dialog box reflects the new location that you chose in step 5. Close the Properties dialog box.

You can see how easy Photoshop Elements makes the process of managing your images. It's important to remember that moving your files manually using Windows causes Photoshop Elements to lose the connection to your images and to display a missing image warning, forcing you to relink the images. Using the Photoshop Elements interface is much more seamless and robust.

Reviewing photos

Once you've eliminated the photos that you definitely don't want, you can review the photos that remain. This can include grouping similar photos together or viewing photos side by side.

Compare photos side by side

When you have several photos of the same subject, it's often difficult to evaluate them in a simple thumbnail view. Photoshop Elements allows you to view photos in a side-by-side view to make it easier to evaluate and rate your photos.

1   Type **sunset** in the Search text field in the Options bar at the top of the workspace to display only the sunset images.

2   Select the first thumbnail, then Shift+click the last thumbnail to select all the images being displayed. You can also press Ctrl+A (Windows) or Command+A (Mac OS) on your keyboard after clicking the first photo to select all the visible photos.

3   Press the Display icon (■) in the menu bar at the top of the workspace, and choose Compare Photos Side by Side, or press F12 on your keyboard.

4   By default, the photo on the left is highlighted. Press the left and right arrow keys on your keyboard to move through the photos.

5   When you find an image that you like, click the photo on the right side to select it and use the left and right arrow keys on your keyboard to navigate through the photos. This allows you to easily compare photos to each other.

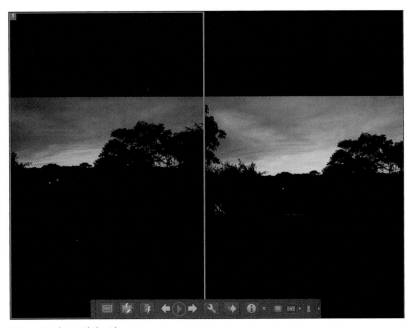

Comparing photos side by side.

6   In this side-by-side view, you can also rate images. Select either photo (left or right) that is being displayed. Position your cursor at the left of the screen to activate the QuickEdit panel (it hides after your mouse is idle) and click a star at the top to give it a rating from one to five. Star ratings toggle on and off as you click on them.

7   Press the Full Screen View button (■) in the Options bar at the bottom of the screen to expand each image to fill your screen. You can also rate photos in this view using the QuickEdit panel and navigate from photo to photo using the left and right arrow keys on your keyboard or by using the left and right buttons in the Options bar.

8   Press Esc on your keyboard to exit Full Screen mode or the side-by-side view.

Stacks

When you have several images of the same subject or event, or images that look a lot alike, it becomes a bit daunting to look at in the Organizer. All the images look the same and they also occupy a lot of room when they are displayed. Stacks allow you to group similar photos together to make browsing photos easier, but you can see the contents of a stack easily at any time.

1   Type **farm** in the Search text field in the Options bar to display all the farmland images.

2   Select the first image, then Shift+click the last image to select them all.

3   Choose Edit > Stack > Stack Selected Photos. The selected photos are condensed into a stack.

4   Click the triangle to the right of the stack thumbnail to expand the stack. To collapse the stack again, click the triangle to the right of the stack thumbnail.

The expanded stack.

5   If you decide later that you don't want the photos grouped in a stack, select the collapsed stack and choose Edit > Stack > Unstack photos to release them.

Organizing using albums

Photoshop Elements provides a variety of ways to use albums when organizing your photos. Additionally, you can use different types of albums to organize your photos depending on your particular need.

Creating a new album

Like physical photo albums, Photoshop Elements allows you to organize different pictures together into collections. For example, you could create a collection of all the photos of your trip to Disney World, or your nephew's tenth birthday party, or, as you will do in this example, a collection of Washington D.C. photos.

1 Press the Show All button in the Organizer to display all images. Make sure there are no images selected in the Organizer by clicking in the gray area between the photos. Press the Create new album or album category (✚) in the Albums panel, and choose New Album.

2 In the Album Details panel, type **Washington** in the Album Name text field. Click to deselect the checkmark for *Backup/Synchronize* (this option is not available in the free trial version if you are using it), and press Done. The new album appears in the Album list. You could add images to the album at this step, but for this exercise you will add images later.

Albums in Photoshop Elements function like traditional albums.

3 You are now going to apply it to the photos in the Organizer. Click the album and drag it onto the photo named *Lincoln Memorial*. The photo is added to this album, and the Album icon () appears under the photo.

The Album icon in the image indicates that the photo is a part of an album.

4 Click and drag the Washington album to the following photos: *Capitol Building, Washington Monument at Night, Washington Monument, White House, Washington DC Street Scene*, and *Statue of Lincoln*.

To ease the process of applying an album to photos, you can do searches in the Search text field to limit the displayed photos.

5 To view only photos in the new *Washington* album, select the album name in the Albums panel.

6 To view all your images, press the Show All button at the top of the Photo Browser or click the *Washington* album a second time.

Once again, if you do not see the icon for the album, adjust the size of the thumbnail slider to the right until the album icon appears.

Creating album categories

Album categories provide yet another level of organization when working with albums. Sometimes you may want to group multiple albums into a common category to make viewing and organizing more logical. In the following steps, you'll create another album and then organize the albums into a category.

1   In the Organizer, type **farm** in the Search text field just below the menu bar. This lists all the photos in the Organizer that contain the word *farm* in the filename.

Filtering the display of images by using the Search text field.

2   You should have four photos displayed in the Photo Browser at this point. If the stack from the earlier exercise is collapsed, then leave it, if it is not, click the arrow to the right of the stack to collapse it. Click the stack to select it.

3   Press the Create new album or album category button (✚) in the Albums panel, and choose New Album.

4   In the Album Details panel, type **Farmland** in the Album Name text field. Click to deselect the checkmark for *Backup/Synchronize*, then press Done.

     You will now move the *Washington* and *Farmland* albums into an Album group to further organize your albums.

5   Press the Show All button at the top of the Photo Browser to display all the photos in the Organizer, then click in the gray area between photos to ensure that no photos are currently selected.

6   Press the Create new album or album category button in the Albums panel, and choose New Album Category. In the Album Category Name text field, type **My Vacation**, then press OK.

Creating an album category and giving it a descriptive name.

7 In the Albums panel, click the *Washington* album, then drag and drop it on top of the *My Vacation* album category. Repeat this for the *Farmland* album.

The albums appear nested within the album category.

You can now see that the Washington and Farmland albums are *nested* inside the *My Vacation* album category, providing you with flexible organization of your albums. Selecting each album displays the contents of that album, and selecting the album again displays all the photos.

Creating a Smart Album

Smart Albums take organization to the next level by adding intelligence to the process of creating albums. With Smart Albums, you can define parameters by which photos are automatically placed into an album. For instance, you can tell every photo with a certain keyword to be automatically moved to a specific Smart Album.

Keywords are only one parameter that can be defined; you can also use capture date, camera make, filename, and many other parameters. Smart Albums take the human error factor out of creating albums, what's more, these Smart Albums are dynamic, which means that if you import any new files into the Organizer that match your Smart Album's criteria, they are automatically added to that album. You can be as general or as specific as you want with Smart Albums; the only limitation is your imagination!

1 Press the Create new album or album category button (✚) in the Albums panel, and select New Smart Album.

2 In the Name text field, type **My Summer 2005 Airshow Photos**.

3   In the Search Criteria section, make sure that the *All of the following search criteria[AND]* radio button is selected. From the *Filename* search criteria drop-down menu, choose *Capture Date*. Leave the *Is* drop-down menu at its default and change the Date to *8/28/2005*. You can do this by highlighting the month, day and year one at a time to type the value, or use the up and down arrows to the right of the field or use the arrow keys on your keyboard to change the value.

4   Press the plus icon in the lower-right corner of the Search Criteria section to add another search criterion by which your photos will be added to the Smart Album.

5   From the *Filename* search criteria drop-down menu that appears, choose *Camera Make*. From the *Is* drop-down menu, choose *Contains*, and in the text field to the right, type **Canon**.

6   Press OK. Only the images that match the defined parameters are displayed in the Photo Browser.

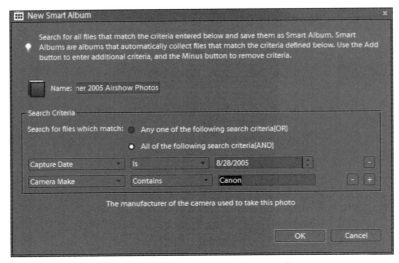

The search criteria that define which photos will be included in the Smart Album.

These parameters will find all images that were shot on 8/28/2005 and were taken with a Canon camera. You might ask yourself why you would choose parameters like this, and the reason could depend on the situation. But suppose, for example, that you went to this event with a group of people who were also taking photos at the event. You decide that afterwards you may like to share the photos with each other, but you'd like to know which photos you had taken. The search criteria defined above will find only images that were taken on the date specified with your camera (a Canon in this case). This ensures that you will always know which images were taken with your Canon camera. You could further refine the search criteria by choosing camera model for one of the search criteria and entering your exact camera model. This would be useful in the event that someone in your group was also using a Canon camera but a different model.

Tagging your photos

By tagging your images with ratings and keywords, you can quickly organize your photos and later locate just the images with the specific tags you are looking for. Film and photo paper are expensive, so in the old days of non-digital photography, you had to be very selective of which pictures you took and even more selective of which ones you printed. But with the proliferation of digital cameras and large-capacity hard drives, the number of photos taken and kept has increased dramatically. It might not be uncommon for you to have hundreds or even thousands of digital photos of family and friends on your computer at once. How you sort them so that you can find the precise picture you are looking for, when you need it, becomes a challenge. Some people rely on multiple folders inside one another with labels for the content of the photos and perhaps information about when they were taken. The problem with this approach is that it can take time to find specific images when you want them, and so the Organizer has a different way of doing it. In Photoshop Elements, you can forgo the multiple folders in favor of just tagging your images. We recommend that you tag and rate your photos immediately after you import them, while the subject or event is fresh in your memory. Creating this habit now will pay dividends many times over when you need to find your photos in the future. Photoshop Elements 8.0 adds enhanced tagging capabilities such as the Tag cloud that allows you to quickly view photos with a certain tag. In addition, Photoshop Elements 8.0 adds facial recognition that makes it incredibly easy to find pictures of a certain person within the Organizer.

Adding ratings

To make it easier to categorize your photos, the Photoshop Elements Organizer can be used to add stars to a photo. The star system runs from zero to five stars and you're the judge of which images get five star ratings!

1   Press the Show All button, then select the *redeye* photo in the Organizer.

2   This image already has a five-star rating. Change the rating to three stars by clicking on the third star below the photo. As you hover your cursor over the stars, they appear highlighted in yellow, if the image doesn't have a rating. Click the fifth star to return it to a five-star rating.

Set the star rating of the redeye *image.*

Adding keywords and categories

In addition to being able to add a star rating to an image, you can add keyword tags to your images to make sorting and searching easier. Photoshop Elements already has a few keywords ready to use, and when you imported the photos from the Lessons, their keywords were also imported. Now you are going to make your own keywords.

1   Scroll down and select the photo named *Hercules* in the Photo Browser. This is a photo of the head of a Greek statue located at the Metropolitan Museum of Art in New York City. Press the Rotate Left button (▣) located at the top of the Photo Browser to fix the orientation of the photo.

Orientation issues can be quickly fixed using the Rotate Left and Rotate Right buttons.

2 In the Keyword Tags panel on the right side of the workspace, press the Create new keyword tag, sub-category, or category button (✚) and choose New Category.

You can create new categories, sub-categories, and tags from the menu.

3 In the Create Category dialog box, type **Metropolitan Museum** into the Category Name text field and choose the green tag icon from the Category Icon section. Press OK.

The Create Category dialog box.

A new category is created in the Keyword tags list. Select the new *Metropolitan Museum* category.

4 Press the Create new keyword tag, sub-category, or category button, and choose New Keyword Tag.

5   In the Name text field, type **Sculpture**. In the Note text field, type **Photos of artwork taken at the Metropolitan Museum of Art in NYC**.

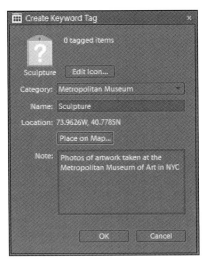

To create a new sub-category, you must have a category tag selected.

6   Press the Place on Map button and in the resulting dialog box, type **1000 Fifth Avenue, New York, New York 10028-0198**. Press the Find button. Photoshop Elements will look up the address and list possible matches. Select the suggested address and press OK. A dialog appears displaying features that are available when you've added a location to a keyword tag. Press OK twice to close all open dialog boxes.

Because you added a location to this keyword tag, the Map panel is displayed in the Organizer. We'll work with the Map panel later. Close the panel by pressing the X in the upper-right corner of the panel.

6   The new keyword tag is placed in the *Metropolitan Museum* category. Click and drag the new *Sculpture* tag over the image of Hercules, then release the mouse. The tag is now assigned to the image and indicated by the green tag in the lower-right corner.

You can add one or more keyword tags to any image.

7 Type **Greek** in the search text field at the top of the Photo browser. Click once on the image *Greek Sculpture_01* to highlight it.

8 Press the Shift key and click the image *Greek Sculpture_06* to select the images.

9 Click and drag the *Sculpture* tag to one of the selected images; the tag applies to all highlighted images. Press the Show All button to show all images in the Organizer.

People Recognition

Photoshop Elements 8.0 introduces a new feature called People Recognition. People Recognition analyzes images that you've imported and tries to detect people within each image. Once detected, People Recognition detects the same people in other images so they can be tagged and found very easily at a later date. Photoshop Elements guides you through several steps to help Photoshop Elements confirm when it has correctly identified a person within an image.

1 Make sure that you are displaying all photos in Organizer by clicking on the Show All button if it is visible.

2 View the photos by Date (Newest First) by choosing that option from the Media Browser Arrangement drop-down menu in the Options bar at the top of your screen.

3 Select the *kids_001.jpg* image in the Organizer then Shift+click the *kids_002.jpg* image to select both images. Click the Rotate Left icon in the Options bar to display the images in the correct orientation.

4 Select the *kids_001.jpg* image and click on the Start people recognition button (◼) in the Keyword Tags panel.

5 The People Recognition window displays with boxes around each person's face. You need to identify each person inside of this image. The box around the boy's face is currently highlighted. Click the "Who is this?" field and type **Gabe** in the text field and press Enter.

6   Select the box around the girl's face, click the "Who is this?" field and type **Claire** in the text field and press enter. The Keyword Tags panel now contains two new tags in the People category for the two people that you identified in the photo.

The People Recognition window is where you identify people within an image.

7   Double-click the box around the face of the boy in the image. A new window is displayed asking you to confirm which photos in the organizer are or are not Gabe.

8   The Unconfirmed tab should be active. If it is not selected, click it to make it active. The bottom portion of the window asks "Which of these are Gabe?" and displays images that it thinks are not Gabe with an X on top of the thumbnail. If any images are incorrectly identified, you can click the X to change the image to a confirmed image or click any confirmed image to put an X on the image. The image in the upper-left corner should be the only confirmed image in this case. Press Save.

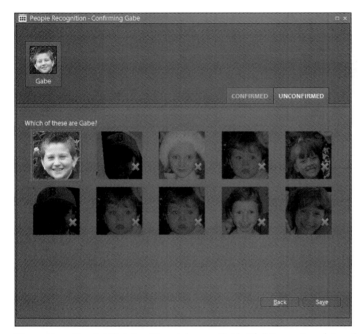

You need to confirm that Photoshop Elements has correctly identified the correct people in each image.

9   A dialog appears indicating that all the items with Gabe in them have been confirmed and asks if you want to find more people. Press No.

10 Back in the People Recognition window, click on the girl's face to make the box active, then double-click on the box to open the confirmation window. There should be only one confirmed image in the upper left corner of the confirmed window. Press the Save button, then press no when asked if you'd like to find other people. Press the Done button in the People Recognition window to close the window.

11 People Recognition is actually always at work in the Organizer. You'll notice that as you are viewing thumbnails of your images in the Organizer, the "Who is this?" field will appear when it detects a person within an image. You can click this field at any time to identify people within each photo. This is a very efficient way to tag images in Photoshop Elements.

People Recognition is constantly at work within the Organizer, providing a quick method for identifying people in your images.

12 Click the Find box directly to the left of the Claire tag in the Keyword Tags panel to display all images of Claire. Click the box again to display all images. Do the same for the Gabe tag in the Keyword Tags panel. Once people are identified within your images, it's a snap to view all images of that person!

Clicking the box directly to the left of one of the People tags in the Keyword Tags panel displays all images of that person.

Finding your photos

Here's where you reap the benefits of tagging and rating your photos. Without these components, the best you'll have to work from is the date that the photos were shot and possibly the filename, and that isn't always easy to remember. Let's see how tagging and rating those photos earlier in this lesson helps you to find those images easily.

Find photos by star rating

1   Make sure that there is no text in the Search text field of the Options bar, then press the Show All button, if it is visible. This displays all the photos in the catalog. If the Show All button is not available, it is because you are currently viewing all images in the Organizer.

2   In the upper-right corner of the Photo Browser is a star ratings filter. This allows you to show images with certain star ratings. Click the second star on the star ratings filter to display any image that is tagged as two stars or higher. You can also change the ranking menu to the right of the star ratings filter to *and higher, and lower,* or *only* to further refine which star-rated images are displayed.

Applying the star ratings filter displays only photos that match the chosen rating.

3   Click the second star on the star ratings filter to stop filtering the photos by star rating.

Find photos by keyword

Searching for photos by keyword tag allows more precise filtering of images. The keyword tags provide even more flexibility because you can create custom-named keyword tags as you did earlier in this lesson.

1   Make sure that there is no text in the Search text field of the Options bar, then press the Show All button, if it is visible. In the Keyword Tags panel, click the triangle to the left of the *Imported Keyword Tags* category to display the keywords available within that category.

2   Click the Find box located to the left of the *Washington D.C.* keyword tag to display all images that are tagged with this keyword.

Clicking the Find box to the left of a keyword tag displays all images tagged with that keyword tag in the Photo Browser.

3   Click the Find box again to stop filtering the photos using the *Washington D.C.* keyword tag.

4   If necessary, expand the *Metropolitan Museum* category by clicking the triangle to the left of its name. Click the Find box to the left of *Sculpture* to display all images that are tagged with this keyword.

5   Click the Find box again to stop filtering the photos using the *Sculpture* keyword tag.

Find photos using the keyword Tag Cloud

The keyword Tag Cloud is a new feature in Photoshop Elements 8.0. The Tag Cloud collects all the tags used in the Tags panel and rates the keyword based on how many images have that tag applied. The more often a tag is used, the larger the text for that tag will appear in the Tag Cloud.

1   Press the View Keyword Tag Cloud button (⬢) at the top of the Keyword Tags panel. All the tags that are applied to any images in the Organizer are displayed alphabetically in the Keyword Tags panel. Note that the text size of each tag varies. The more often a tag is used, the larger it appears in the Tag Cloud.

2   Click the Chapter 02 tag in the Tag cloud to display all images in the Organizer that have the Chapter 02 tag applied. In the bar at the very bottom of the Organizer, you can see that 24 items have been found.

3   Click the Claire tag in the Tag Cloud to display all images in the Organizer that have the Claire tag applied.

4   Click the View Keyword Tag Hierarchy button (▣) at the top of the Keyword Tags panel to display the Hierarchical list of keywords.

Self study

1   Create albums that match the theme of your personal photos and then add your photos to them.

2   Create and apply keyword tags that will allow you to sort the photos in the Organizer.

 If you created an album specifically for use with this book, you will need to switch to your own personal album before working on your own photos, you can then switch back to the album for this book before continuing with future lessons.

Review

Questions

1   What is the benefit of using stacks in Photoshop Elements 8.0?

2   Why is tagging your photos using keywords important in Photoshop Elements?

3   Why would you want to create and use albums in Photoshop Elements?

Answers

1   Stacks provide a way of organizing similar photos into a group. This helps when browsing images in the Organizer, as similar photos are grouped together, which eliminates the need to scroll through as many images.

2   If you tag photos using keywords, you gain the ability to search for images based on those keywords at a later point in time.

3   Photoshop Elements albums allow you to organize your photos just like traditional photo albums.

What you'll learn in this lesson:

- Understanding the Adobe Photoshop Elements Editor

- Auto correcting your photos

- How to resize and crop a photo

Fixing Common Photographic Problems

In this lesson, you will explore how Photoshop Elements can automatically correct or adjust most images in seconds. You'll also explore more advanced tools that allow you to correct red eye, or the sky, in an image. Finally, you'll discover how to rotate and crop an image.

Starting up

Within the Photoshop Elements Organizer: You will work with several files from the Lessons folder in this lesson. Make sure that you have copied the Lessons folder from the supplied DVD to your hard drive. In order to access these files in the Organizer, you need to import them. See "Adding files and folders to the Organizer" on page 11.

Within the Photoshop Elements Editor: The Photoshop Elements Editor defaults to the last panel layout that you used. Before starting, make sure your tools and panels are consistent with the examples presented in these lessons by resetting the panels. Do this by choosing Window > Reset Panels or by pressing the Reset panels button (↻) in the Options bar.

See Lesson 3 in action!

Use the accompanying video to gain a better understanding of how to use some of the features shown in this lesson. The video tutorial for this lesson can be found on the included DVD.

Welcome screen

If you're currently viewing the Welcome screen, press the Edit button ( ) to enter the Editor workspace. If you are currently in the Organizer, click the Fix tab in the upper-right corner of your screen and press the Edit Photos button or select an image and choose Edit > Edit with Photoshop Elements.

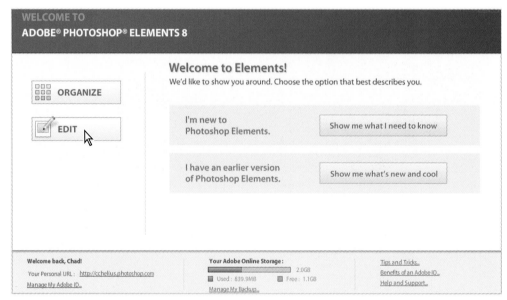

Choose the Editor from the Photoshop Elements Welcome screen.

Understanding the Editor workspace

In Photoshop Elements 8, adjustments to your photos are made in the Editor. If you want to crop, straighten, or color correct your images, the Editor is where this happens. It is the one-stop shop for all your photo correction and retouching needs.

A. Toolbox. *B*. Options bar. *C*. Project Bin. *D*. Panel Bin.

The default Editor interface is divided into four main areas: the Toolbox, the Options bar, the Project Bin, and the Panel Bin.

The Toolbox on the left side of the workspace stores all the tools you need to select, cut, paint, and correct your photos and can be viewed in a single or double column view by clicking on the double arrow (⏩) at the top of the Toolbox. The Options bar at the top of the workspace displays the selected tool options. The three tabs on the right side of the Options bar switch between the Edit, Create, and Share modes. Within the Edit tab is a drop-down that allows you to change between Full, Quick, and Guided modes. The Project Bin displays the images you are using. When you have multiple files open at once, the Project Bin provides a quick and efficient way to switch from one file to another. The Panel Bin on the right side of the workspace stores the Layers and Effects panels.

The Project Bin

Located at the bottom of the Editor, the Project Bin displays thumbnails of open photos. It's useful for switching between multiple open photos in your workspace. Choose Window > Project Bin to toggle the display of the Project Bin on and off.

The Panel Bin

The Panel Bin in the Editor lets you store multiple panels in a single area. The Project Bin provides fast access to your panels. By default, the Palette Bin appears on the right side of the workspace. Choose Window > Palette Bin to toggle the Palette Bin on and off.

Editing modes: Full, Quick, and Guided

At the right side of the Edit tab is a drop-down menu where you can choose between the three editing modes: Full, Quick, or Guided. You'll take a look at all three of these modes during this lesson, as you explore how easy it is to fix common photo problems that can occur in your images.

At the right of the Edit tab is a drop-down menu where, you can choose from the Full, Quick, or Guided editing modes.

Using Quick Fix

Quick Fix conveniently assembles many of the basic photo-fixing tools in Photoshop Elements. As you work in Quick Fix, you should limit the number of color and lighting controls that you apply to a photo. As a general rule, you use only one of the Auto controls on a photo. If that control doesn't achieve the desired look, press the Reset button and try another one. You can also adjust your image using the slider controls, whether you've used an Auto control or not. In this exercise, you'll duplicate and save one image as four different files, so that you can compare each of the auto fix features' effects on the same image.

1 Press the Organizer button (⊞) to view your photo library. If you are unable to see the filenames, choose View > Show File Names.

2 Locate and select *fishing.jpg*. Press the Fix tab at the right side of the Option bar and press the Edit Photos button in the Task pane.

Click the Fix tab in the Organizer, then press the Edit Photos button to open the image in the Editor.

3 Once the image opens, choose File > Save As. Navigate to the Lessons folder, and uncheck the *Save in Version Set with Original* checkbox in the Save Options Organize: section. Type **Smart Fix** in the Name text field and make sure the Format is set to JPEG; then press Save. In the JPEG Options dialog box, leave all settings at their defaults, and press OK to accept the current JPEG settings.

4 Choose File > Save As again, and type **Levels** in the Name text field. Choose File > Save As two more times and name the files **Contrast** and then **Color**.

5 In the Editor, choose File > Open, and navigate to the Lessons folder, and select *Smart Fix.jpg*; then press Open.

Using Auto Smart Fix

Auto Smart Fix is a very powerful feature for making quick corrections to your images. It analyzes a photo and makes corrections to common problems with contrast, color balance, and saturation. In this exercise, you will see how quickly you can clean up an image automatically using the Smart Fix feature.

1   Inside Edit mode, click the triangle on the right side of the Fix tab and choose Edit Quick from the drop-down menu. This opens the Quick Fix panel in the Panel Bin. In the Smart Fix section, press the Auto button.

The Smart Fix Auto button in the Quick Fix mode.

2   To view how this feature affects the image, you will need to see the before and after views. Beneath the image is the View drop-down menu. Choose Before & After – Horizontal from the drop-down menu, then press the Fit Screen button in the Options bar at the top of the screen.

The before and after images.

3   You may notice that the girl now has a more accurate skin tone. To better see the effects of this feature, you'll increase the amount of the Smart Fix. Drag the Amount slider in the Quick Fix panel section of the Smart Fix all the way to the right. The colors of the tree become more vivid. Notice that the entire color range of the image is adjusted, along with the contrast of the image. The Smart Fix feature has modified the lightest points in the image to make them whiter, while making the darker points blacker.

4   Choose File > Save to save your edits. If the Save As dialog box opens, press Save. If Photoshop Elements asks you to replace the current image, press Yes. Press OK when the JPEG Options dialog box appears.

Auto Levels

Auto Levels analyzes a photo, and corrects problems with brightness that are usually caused by the image being either underexposed or overexposed.

With Auto Levels, the darkest areas of the image become darker, while the lightest areas become lighter. In this exercise, you will see the effect that Auto Levels has on an image.

1   Choose File > Open, and select the *Levels.jpg* image from the Lessons folder. Press Open.

2   Use the keyboard shortcut Ctrl+0 (Windows) or Command+0 (Mac OS) to fit both previews on the screen.

3   In the Lighting section of the Panel Bin, press the Levels Auto button to initiate the automatic Levels command. You can already see how much darker some parts of the image have become.

4   At the bottom of the Lighting section of the Quick Fix panel are the following sliders: Lighten Shadows, Darken Highlights, and Midtone Contrast. Drag the Midtone Contrast slider to the right to darken the midtones (neither the lightest nor darkest areas) of the photo.

5   Once a change is made, two buttons appear at the top of the Lighting section: the Cancel Current Quick Fix Operation button (✖) and the Commit Current Quick Fix Operation button (✓). Once you are satisfied with the changes, press the Commit button.

Before and after using the Auto Levels command.

There is no right or wrong way for your images to look in this exercise. Use this exercise to learn about each option. Feel free to experiment with these features. Many times, the changes are very subtle, and because different images have their own individual characteristics, it will be necessary to experiment with the different adjustments to get the best results.

6   Choose File > Save to save your edits. If the Save As dialog box appears, press Save. If Photoshop Elements asks you to replace the current image, press Yes. Press OK when the JPEG Options dialog box appears.

Auto Contrast

Auto Levels and Auto Contrast have similar effects on an image. Often the effect is so similar that you can choose to use either tool in most situations. Auto Contrast corrects the lack of distinction between the light and dark areas of a photo.

1   Choose File > Open and select *Contrast.jpg* from the Lessons folder.

2   Use the keyboard shortcut, Ctrl+0 (Windows) or Command+0 (Mac OS), or press the Fit Screen button in the Options bar to fit both previews on the screen.

3   In the Lighting section of the Quick Fix panel, press the Contrast Auto button to initiate the Auto Contrast command. Notice how some parts of the image become much darker.

4   Drag the Darken Highlights slider to the right, to about 25, darkening the highlights of the photo. Notice that the lost contours of the girl's shirt reappear.

5   Once you are satisfied with your changes, press the Commit button (✓) at the top of the Lighting section.

Before and after using the Auto Contrast command.

6   Choose File > Save to save your edits. If the Save As dialog box opens, press Save. If Photoshop Elements asks you to replace the current image, press Yes. Press OK when the JPEG Options dialog box appears.

Correcting color automatically

Auto Color analyzes a photo and can correct common problems in color balance caused by the surrounding lighting conditions. For example, many buildings use fluorescent lights. While they may look white, fluorescent lights actually have a slight green tint, and this can create a green color cast in your photos. Similarly, a blue color cast can be created when you use an indoor camera setting when taking pictures outside.

1   Choose File > Open and select *Color.jpg* from the Lessons folder.

2   Use the keyboard shortcut, Ctrl+0 (Windows) or Command+0 (Mac OS), or press the Fit Screen button in the Options bar to fit both previews on the screen.

3   In the Lighting section of the Quick Fix panel, press the Color Auto button to initiate the Auto Color command. The trees in the image becomes brighter.

In the Color Section are two sliders: Saturation and Hue. Saturation makes colors either more vivid or muted, depending on which way you drag the slider. Hue changes the existing colors.

4   Drag the Saturation slider to the right to about 20. Notice how this punches the colors and makes them richer.

This image before and after using the Auto Color command and Temperature slider.

5   Once you are satisfied with your changes, press the Commit button (✓) at the top of the Color section.

The Balance section within the Quick Fix panel allows you to further enhance the colors in an image. Temperature makes the colors warmer (red) or cooler (blue) and Tint makes the colors either more green or more magenta.

6   Drag the Temperature slider to the left to cool the photo. Once you are happy with the adjustment, press the Commit button (✓) at the top of the Balance section.

7   Choose File > Save to save your edits. If the Save As dialog box opens, press Save. If Photoshop Elements asks you to replace the current image, press Yes. Press OK when the JPEG Options dialog box appears.

Comparing images in Full Edit View

You will now compare all four photos in Full Edit View to see what effect each command has on the image.

1 Press the arrow at the right of the Fix tab and choose Full Edit from the drop-down menu.

2 Press the Arrange button (▦) and press the Tile All in Grid button, the second choice in the first row, to display each image in its own window.

3 Press the Arrange button again and choose Match Zoom and Location at the base of the list so that all photos are at the same magnification and position in their respective windows.

Use shortcuts to Zoom All

If you hold down the Shift key while you zoom using the Zoom tool (⬭), it zooms in on all open images at the same time. If you hold the Shift+Alt keys together while using the Zoom tool, it zooms out on all the open images at the same time.

Using the Navigator

The Navigator panel is a tool for monitoring an image; it also makes it easy to zoom and scroll in the image. The usefulness of the panel is that you can keep the current tool active, and, at the same time, zoom in and out of your image. Dragging the red frame to the area you want to see allows you to quickly scroll around the image, and is quicker and more efficient than trying to use the vertical and horizontal scroll bars. In this next exercise, you will work with controlling the Navigator.

1 Choose Window > Navigator to open the Navigator panel.

The Navigator panel.

2   Click an image to select it, then use the slider in the Navigator panel to adjust each image. After adjusting the images, review the results.

Dragging the slider to the right will make the red square smaller. When you do this and place your cursor in the middle of the square you will see a hand icon (✍) displayed. Click and hold to drag the square around the image to reposition the viewing area. This is especially effective when retouching an image at a high zoom percent. Instead of zooming out of the image to see where you are, in order to move to a different spot, you can utilize the Navigator's thumbnail and red square to guide you to a different spot.

Another useful navigation tool is to select the Hand tool (✍) and click an image to make it active. If you hold down the Shift key while dragging on that active photo, all four images will be repositioned consistently!

All four images are tiled to the screen.

3   Now save all four documents. Choose File > Save As. In the Save As dialog box, change the filename to **(current filename)_working** and the format to Photoshop. Press Save and then press OK in the dialog box that appears. Repeat for all open photos.

4   Choose File > Close All. If asked if you want to save the changes, press No.

The Guided Edit mode

Using the Guided Edit mode is like having your own guide walk you through the steps to improve your images. It helps you accomplish common photo tasks quickly and easily, and provides you with explanations during the process. Guided Edit mode also gives you number values while using sliders, which allows you to make more precise changes. The Guided Edit section is located in the Edit tab drop-down menu in the Editor. In this exercise, you will fix an image that is too dark (underexposed), and also fix an image that is too light (overexposed). For more on exposure, refer to Lesson 4, "Adjusting Exposure."

The Guided Edit options.

Fixing an underexposed or dark image

1 Press the Organizer button (≡) at the top of the workspace on the menu bar. The Organizer opens.

2 Locate the file named *under_exposed.jpg*, and select it. The image is too dark, and you'll use Guided Edit mode to correct the image. Click the Fix tab at the top of the workspace, then click the triangle to the right of the tab and choose Guided Photo Edit from the menu that appears. Guided Edit panel asks you how you would like to change this image.

Choose Guided Photo Edit from the drop-down menu.

3 In the Lighting and Exposure section in the Guided Edit panel, choose Lighten or Darken. The Guided Edit panel changes to reflect the Lightening and Darkening options.

4 You can click the Auto button to see if Photoshop Elements can automatically fix the file for you. You'll see that the image actually gets darker. This image needs some additional help. Undo the Auto change by pressing the Reset button located toward the bottom of the panel. Now you can use the sliders to manually lighten the photo.

There are three sliders in the Lighten and Darken section. The first slider lightens the shadows, or the dark area, of an image. The second slider darkens the highlights, or the lightest part, of an image, and the third slider affects the medium to bright parts of the image, which is everything in between light and dark.

5 Drag the Lighten Shadows slider to 24, or type **24** in the text field to the right of the slider. The image now regains color from the shadows.

6 Leave the Darken Highlights settings at their defaults, and drag the Midtone Contrast slider to the left to decrease that value to -9, or type **-9** in the text field to the right.

7   To compare the changes you made to the original image, press the After Only button at the bottom of the Guided Fix panel. You can now see both images using Before and After – Horizontal.

Before and after the Lightening options.

8   Press Done once you are happy with the changes.

9   Choose File > Save. In the Save As dialog box, type **under_exposed_working** in the Name text field and change the format to Photoshop. Press Save.

10 Choose File > Close. If you are asked to save changes, press No.

You can now see how Guided Edit mode helped lighten this underexposed image. Don't worry, no fish were harmed in the making of these images. It was strictly a catch-and-release fishing expedition.

Fixing an overexposed or light image

1   Press the Organizer button (⊞) at the top of the workspace. This reveals the Organizer.

2   Locate the *over_exposed.jpg* file, and select it. The image is too light, and you'll use Guided Edit mode to correct the image. Press the arrow on the right side of the Fix tab and choose Guided Photo Edit from the menu that appears.

3   In the Lighting and Exposure section of the Guided Edit panel, choose Lighten or Darken. The Guided Edit panel now changes to reflect the *Lighten or Darken a Photo* options.

4   You can click the Auto button to see if Photoshop Elements can automatically fix this file for you. Although the Auto feature effectively fixes the image, you'll correct this image by using the sliders. Undo your Auto change by pressing the Reset button located toward the bottom of the panel. Now you can use the sliders to manually darken the dull, muted photo.

5   Drag the Lighten Shadows slider to 2, or type **2** in the text field to the right. You can now see that the shadow areas are lighter.

6   Drag the Darken Highlights slider to 10, or type **10** in the text field to the right; this increases the bright areas of the photo.

7   Drag the Midtone Contrast slider to the right to increase that value to 8, or type **8** in the text field to the right.

You have successfully corrected an overexposed image.

Before and after using the Darkening options.

8   Press Done once you are happy with the changes.

9   Choose File > Save. In the Save As dialog box, type **over_exposed_working** in the Name text field and change the format to Photoshop. Press Save.

10   Choose File > Close. If asked to save the changes, press No.

Using Full Edit mode

Unlike the Quick and Guided Edit modes in which you have a limited number of tools to use, in Full Edit mode you can use all the tools that Photoshop Elements has to offer. It is the most powerful photo correcting mode in Photoshop Elements. You can make selections using the selection tools, add type, and access and use the Layers panel. Instead of destructively editing a photo by changing the original image, you can also select a portion of the photo and use adjustment layers. Refer to Lesson 4, "Adjusting Exposure" for more on adjustment layers. In this exercise, you will use the Full Edit mode to remove a color cast, and also to correct skin tones.

1 Press the Organizer button (▦) at the top of the workspace in the menu bar. This reveals the Organizer.

2 Locate and select the *wonder.jpg* file. The image is too blue, and you'll use Full Edit mode to correct the image. Press the arrow to the right of the Fix tab and choose Full Photo Edit from the menu that appears, or use the keyboard shortcut, Ctrl+I (Windows) or Command+I (Mac OS).

This image has a bluish color cast.

Removing a color cast

A color cast is an unwanted color shift in an image. In this exercise, the image has a color cast of blue due to the poor lighting conditions at the time that the photo was taken. You'll use the Remove Color Cast command to correct this photo.

1   From the Menu bar, choose Enhance > Adjust Color > Remove Color Cast.

Choose Remove Color Cast from the menu.

2   Once the Remove Color Cast dialog box appears, your cursor becomes an eyedropper. You can use this eyedropper to select any white, black, or gray in the image, and this feature automatically removes the color cast. Click the gray part of the wall behind the children to automatically remove the bluish tint.

3 Press OK to apply this change.

The color cast is removed.

4 Choose File > Save. In the Save As dialog box, type **wonder_working** in the Name text field and change the format to Photoshop. Press Save.

5 Choose File > Close. If you are asked to save the changes, press No.

Correcting skin tone

This next image has a blue color cast to it. Instead of using the Remove Color Cast command, you will use the Adjust Color for Skin Tone command. Because there is a skin tone in this image, Photoshop Elements can remove the color cast for you by letting you adjust the skin color.

1 Press the Organizer button (▦) at the top of the workspace. This reveals the Organizer.

2 Locate and select the *skin_tone.jpg* file. The image is too blue, and you'll use the Full Edit mode to correct the image. Press the arrow to the right of the Fix tab and choose Full Photo Edit from the menu that appears, or use the keyboard shortcut, Ctrl+I (Windows) or Command+I (Mac OS).

3   Choose Enhance > Adjust Color > Adjust Color for Skin Tone.

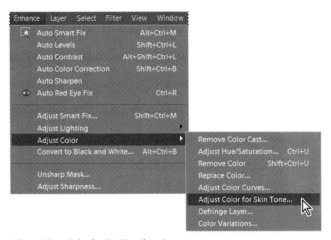

Choose Adjust Color for Skin Tone from the menu.

4   Once the Adjust Color for Skin Tone dialog box opens, your cursor becomes an eyedropper. You can use this eyedropper to select any skin tone in the image, and this feature automatically removes the color cast and tries to make the skin look more natural. Click the girl's nose to automatically remove the blue tint. Click other areas of the photo to experiment with this tool. You also have a slider for the skin color; you can choose to make it more tan, and also change the blush, which adds or takes away red from the image. There is also a Temperature slider. Drag the Temperature slider up (to the right) to make this image warmer.

The color cast is removed using Adjust Color for Skin Tone.

To compare what the image used to look like versus what it currently looks like, click the Preview check box on and off.

5   Press OK once you are happy with the changes.

6   Choose File > Save. In the Save As dialog box, type **skin_tone_working** in the Name text field and change the format to Photoshop. Press Save.

7   Choose File > Close. If asked to save the changes, press No.

Photomerge Exposure

When taking pictures, it's often difficult to get the desired exposure on camera. You see, the human eye can see a much wider range of tones than a camera can see. This often leads to images that are either too dark or too light because the camera can't capture the range from darks to lights in the same picture. Photoshop Elements 8.0 introduces a new feature called Photomerge Exposure. This feature can actually combine two or more images with varying exposures into one image that contains the best tonal ranges from the combination of exposures. To get the best results with this feature, you must do a little pre-planning by taking photos at different exposure values when taking a picture (a minimum of two photos is required). In addition, although you can get decent results holding the camera by hand, you'll get the best results when you use a tripod.

1   Press the Organizer button (▦) at the top of the workspace in the Menu bar. This reveals the Organizer.

2   Type **too** in the Search text field at the top of the Organizer to filter the images displayed to those that contain *too* in the filename. Two images are displayed.

3   Click the first image to select it, then hold down the Shift key on your keyboard and click the second image to select it as well.

Both images are selected in the Organizer.

4   With both images selected in the Organizer, choose File > New > Photomerge Exposure.

The Editor opens and processes both images displaying the merged image with the Photomerge panel active in the Panel bin. Photomerge has two modes: Simple Blending and Smart Blending. Simple blending is a quick one step process that merges the photos where the Smart blending is a more advanced blending giving you adjustment options.

5   Maker sure that the Smart Blending radio button is selected and drag the Highlight Details slider to about 90 and the Shadows to about 70. Feel free to experiment with the sliders to see the different effects that can be achieved. Press the Done button at the bottom of the Photomerge panel when you are finished.

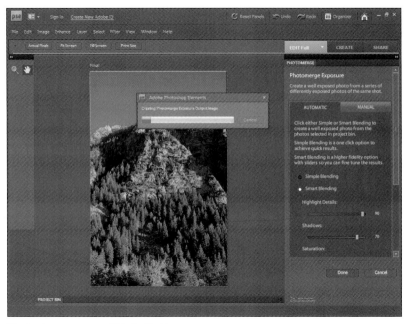

The two images are processed into the final image.

6   When the final output image is finished processing, you'll have your merged image. Choose File > Save. In the Save As dialog box, type too_perfect in the file name field and choose Photoshop from the format drop-down menu. Press the Save button.

7   Click the Organizer button at the top of the Editor workspace. The Organizer is revealed. Notice that all three images have been put into a Version Set.

8   Expand the Version Set by clicking on the arrow at the right side of the thumbnail and you'll see the merged image, the too_light and the too_dark images.

The Toolbox

Photoshop Elements is a tool-rich program, and there are tools for accomplishing nearly any task. There are more than 40 tools available in the panel, and they are grouped together based on similarity. Tools with similar names and functions are stored together in tool groups.

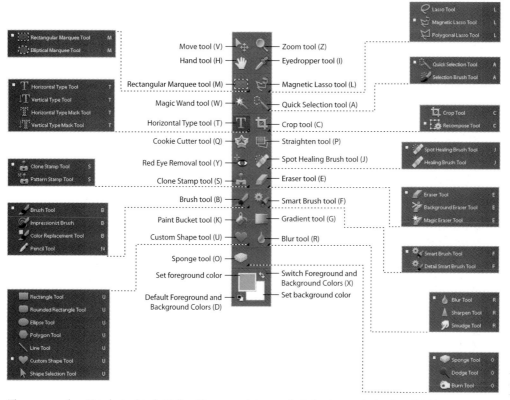

There are more than 40 tools stored in the Toolbox. Key commands to access the tools using your keyboards are listed in parentheses ( ).

Using tools

In this next exercise, you will use several tools in order to become more familiar with changing brush sizes or selections.

Red Eye Removal tool

The Red Eye Removal tool analyzes a selection by searching for red spheres, and removes any red reflections it finds. It converts the red in the pupils to a neutral black color. The red eye phenomenon is almost always visible in photographs taken at night with a flash. It is actually caused by light reflecting off the back of the eyes. Many cameras now come with a red eye reduction feature, which causes the flash to go off twice, once right before the picture is taken and a second time to actually light the picture. The first flash causes the subject's pupils to contract, which significantly reduces red eye.

1   Press the Organizer button (▦) at the top of the workspace in the menu bar. This reveals the Organizer.

2   Locate and select the *red_eye.jpg* file. The image contains an image of a man with red eye. You will use the Red Eye Removal tool to remove the red from his eyes.

Before using the Red Eye Removal tool.

3   Press the arrow to the right of the Fix tab and choose Full Photo Edit from the menu that appears, or use the keyboard shortcut, Ctrl+I (Windows) or Command+I (Mac OS).

4   Choose the Zoom tool (🔍) from the Toolbox, then click the person's face to zoom in. If you zoom in too far, you can hold the Alt (Windows) or Option (Mac OS) key and click to zoom out.

You can also use the Navigator to zoom in and out.

5   Choose the Red Eye Removal tool (👁) from the Toolbox.

6   Click and drag a selection around the first eye. If it doesn't work on the first pass, try it again.

7   Select an area around the second eye to instantly remove the red from it.

After using the Red Eye Removal tool.

8   Choose File > Save. In the Save As dialog box, type **red_eye_working** in the Name text field and change the format to Photoshop. Press Save.

9   Choose File > Close. If you are asked to save the changes, press No.

Whitening teeth

In this exercise, you will use the Smart Brush tool to whiten someone's teeth. You will also discover how to make a good selection and use an adjustment layer.

1   Press the Organizer button (▦) at the top of the workspace. This reveals the Organizer.

2   Locate and select the *pearly_whites.jpg* file. The image contains a little girl whose teeth are about to be whitened.

3   Press the arrow to the right of the Fix tab, then choose Full Photo Edit from the menu that appears, or use the keyboard shortcut, Ctrl+I (Windows) or Command+I (Mac OS).

4   Choose the Zoom tool (🔍) from the Toolbox, then click the person's face to zoom in.

5   Choose the Smart Brush tool (🖌) from the Tools pane. The Smart Brush tool panel opens. Scroll to the bottom of the list and choose Very Pearly Whites as the Brush style.

This is the Smart Brush tool options panel.

6 Click and drag the brush on the teeth, being careful not to select outside the teeth. If you need a smaller brush, choose a smaller brush size, or use the slider to choose a smaller diameter from the Brush drop-down menu in the Options bar. Don't worry if you selected too much; you'll fix the selection in the next step.

Changing the brush size.

 You can also use the [ ] bracket keys on the keyboard to change the brush size.

Notice the small toolset that appears above the selection. The first brush is for starting a new selection from scratch. The second brush lets you add to a current selection, and the third brush lets you subtract from a selection.

7 Choose the third Subtract from selection brush. Adjust your brush size if needed, then subtract from the selection so that only the teeth remain selected.

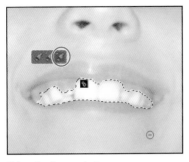

Subtracting from a selection.

8   Once you are happy with the selection, choose the Move tool (⊕) from the Toolbox. Notice that a new layer has been added to the Layers panel. This is an adjustment layer. Select the Background layer so that you don't have to see the selection; you can just view the changes the adjustment layer has made. Notice the visibility icon (👁) to the left of the adjustment layer. This icon allows you to toggle the visibility of the layer on and off. You can edit this adjustment layer at any time. For more on adjustment layers, refer to Lesson 4, "Adjusting Exposure."

The finished whiter teeth.

9   Choose File > Save. In the Save As dialog box, type **pearly_whites_working** in the Name text field and change the format to Photoshop. Uncheck the *Save in Version Set with Original* checkbox. Press Save.

Because an adjustment layer was used, the original image has not been modified.

10   Choose File > Close. If you are asked to save the changes, press No.

Enhancing blue skies

In this exercise, you will use the Smart Brush tool to make the sky in the photo appear more blue. You'll first choose the correct Smart Brush option, then make a selection.

1   Press the Organizer button (🎞) at the top of the workspace. This reveals the Organizer.

2   Locate and select the *blue_sky_jumper.jpg* file. The image contains a little girl jumping, and you will change the way the sky looks using the Smart Brush tool.

3   Press the arrow to the right of the Fix tab and choose Full Photo Edit from the menu that appears, or use the keyboard shortcut, Ctrl+I (Windows) or Command+I (Mac OS).

4   Choose the Smart Brush tool (🖌) from the Toolbox. The Smart Brush tool panel appears. Scroll to the top of the list and choose Blue Skies as the brush style.

Choose Blue Skies.

5   Click and drag the brush on the sky, being careful not to select the trees. If you need a bigger brush, choose a bigger brush size or use the slider to choose a bigger diameter from the Brush drop-down menu in the Options bar. Don't worry if you selected too much; you'll fix that in the next step.

Making the selection.

6   If necessary, select the third, Subtract from selection, brush. Adjust your brush size if needed, and subtract from the selection, so that only the sky remains selected. Don't worry about being too precise; you'll adjust that later.

7   You may have noticed that the image has a selection but there has been only a minor color change. This is because the adjustment layer you are currently working on has an automatic blending mode of Color Burn applied to it. Blending modes describe the way layers blend or interact with each other. In the Layers panel, change the blending mode to Multiply, and the effect is more visible.

Modifying the selection.

8   You can still see a rough edge around the selection. You will blur that edge by feathering it so the edge is less noticeable. Press the Refine Edge button in the Options bar at the top of the screen. Type **32.3** in the Feather text field or move the slider to the right to the desired amount. Press OK.

Applying a feather in the Refine Edge dialog box.

9   Once you are happy with the selection, choose the Move tool (⊹) from the Toolbox. Notice that a new adjustment layer has been added to the Layers panel. Select the Background layer so that you don't have to see the selection; you can just view the changes the adjustment layer has made. Notice that you made the sky more blue and it fades into the trees instead of having a solid edge. Toggle the visibility on the Blue Skies 1 layer by pressing the visibility icon (👁) to the left of the layer.

The image with the enhanced sky.

10 Choose File > Save. In the Save As dialog box, type **blue_sky_jumper_working** in the Name text field and change the format to Photoshop. Press Save.

11 Choose File > Close. If you are asked to save the changes, press No.

Sharpening

Using Unsharp Mask corrects common focus problems, such as blurriness caused by an improperly focused or jostled shot. As with any sharpening effect, the more distortion there is in an image, the lower the likelihood that it can be corrected. Sharpening should always be the last step in the correction process. In this exercise, you will sharpen an image.

1 Press the Organizer button (⊞) at the top of the workspace. This reveals the Organizer.

2 Locate and select the *fishing.jpg* file.

3 Press the arrow to the right of the Fix tab and choose Full Photo Edit from the menu that appears, or use the keyboard shortcut, Ctrl+I (Windows) or Command+I (Mac OS).

Before using Unsharp Mask.

4 Choose Enhance > Unsharp Mask from the menu bar.

5 In the Unsharp Mask dialog box, type **175** in the Amount text field. Type **1** in the
Radius text field and **5** in the Threshold text field. To see how the sharpening is affecting
different areas of the image, click inside of the preview window in the Unsharp Mask
dialog box and drag to expose other areas of the image. In addition, if you click in the
preview window and hold your mouse button down, you'll see the image before the
sharpening is applied. Release the mouse button to see the sharpening. This is a nice way
to see a before and after view of the image.

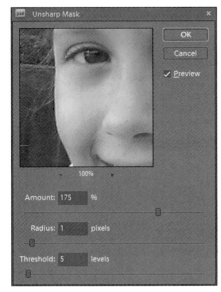

The Unsharp Mask settings.

Press OK. Notice how much sharper this made the image. Another way to see the effect of sharpening is to click the Undo and Redo buttons at the top of the screen to toggle back and forth. It's easiest to see the effects of sharpening when viewing an image at 100% magnification. Simply select the Zoom tool in the Toolbox and click the 1:1 button in the options bar.

After applying Unsharp Mask.

6   Choose File > Save. In the Save As dialog box, type **fishing_working** in the Name text field and change the format to Photoshop. Press Save.

7   Choose File > Close. If asked to save the changes, press No.

Unsharp Mask defined

Unsharp masking is a traditional film compositing technique used to sharpen edges in an image. The Unsharp Mask command corrects blurring in the image, and it compensates for blurring that occurs during the resampling and printing process. Unsharp Mask is recommended as a last step for your images, whether they will end up printed or online. A good place to start is to set the Amount to 150, the Radius to 1 or 2, and the Threshold to 10, then adjust as needed. The Amount determines how much the contrast of pixels is increased. The Radius determines the number of pixels around the edges that are affected. The Threshold determines how different the brightness values of pixels should be before they are considered edge pixels.

Cropping images

Cropping an image allows you to remove unwanted, excess area from around your photo. Sometimes it is simply a matter of removing unimportant elements; at other times, it may be a matter of correcting an excess fringe or border around your photo. It's always best to compose your shot on camera, however the crop tool allows you to correct or enhance the composition of your photo after the shot was taken.

1   Press the Organizer button (▦) at the top of the workspace. This reveals the Organizer.

2   Locate and select the *statue.jpg* file. The image needs to be cropped.

3   Press the arrow to the right of the Fix tab and choose Full Photo Edit from the menu that appears, or use the keyboard shortcut, Ctrl+I (Windows) or Command+I (Mac OS).

4   Choose the Crop tool (◪) from the Toolbox. Click and drag to make a selection around the girl and the statue. You can adjust the crop area by dragging on the side, top, bottom, or corner points to adjust the crop.

Making a selection with the Crop tool.

5   Double-click the image to apply the crop or click the green checkbox to apply the crop to the image.

6   Choose File > Save. In the Save As dialog box, type **statue_working** in the Name text field and change the format to Photoshop. Press Save.

7   Choose File > Close. If you are asked to save the changes, press No.

Rotating images

Photoshop Elements gives you the ability to control almost everything about your images, from color and tone, to orientation and size. Rotating and resizing images is a quick and easy process.

1   Press the Organizer button (▦) at the top of the workspace. This reveals the Organizer.

2   Locate and select the *horizon.jpg* file. The image needs to be cropped and rotated.

3   Press the arrow to the right of the Fix tab and choose Full Edit from the menu that appears, or use the keyboard shortcut, Ctrl+I (Windows) or Command+I (Mac OS).

4   Choose the Crop tool (🔲) from the Toolbox. Make a selection around the mother and daughter. You can rotate the crop area by placing your cursor just outside a corner point. Notice how the cursor changes to a circle with two arrows on the unclosed ends.

5   Rotate the crop area so that the two middle points on the left and right of the image match up with the horizon line. With the crop area selected, you can also click in the middle of the crop area and drag it to reposition the crop area on the photo.

Rotating a crop.

6   Double-click the image or click the green checkmark at the bottom of the crop area to apply both the rotate and crop in one step. Leave the file open for the next exercise.

The finished cropped and rotated image.

Resizing images

There will be times when you need to resize either the width and height of your documents, or adjust the pixel resolution. The Image Size dialog box allows you to do both of these things. The Image Size dialog box is divided into two main areas: Pixel Dimensions and Document Size. Pixel Dimensions shows the number of pixels that make up the image. For web graphics, the pixel dimensions are more relevant than the document's actual printing size. Document Size shows the resolution information, as well as the actual physical size of the image. Pixel Dimensions can be changed when the *Resample Image* checkbox is checked. In this exercise you will make an image smaller so that you can e-mail it to someone.

1   Select Image > Resize > Image Size. The Image Size dialog box allows you to change the printable size and resolution of your images.

2   Select the *Resample Image* checkbox at the bottom of the dialog box. If the image doesn't resample when you decrease the resolution, the file size will grow. You want to shrink both the physical dimensions and the file size.

3 Type **72** in the Resolution text field, type **4** in the Document Size Width text field, and change the Resample Image option to Bicubic Sharper. Note that the file size is reduced dramatically.

Bicubic sharper uses an algorithm that yields good results when reducing the size of an image. Whenever an image is resampled, some quality is lost. Bicubic sharper helps to minimize this loss in quality.

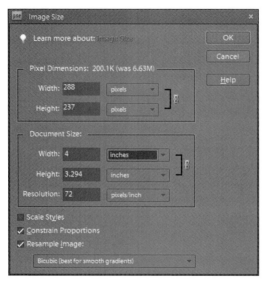

The new image size settings showing the reduced file size.

4 Press OK.

5 Choose File > Save. In the Save As dialog box, type **horizon_working** in the Name text field and change the format to Photoshop. Press Save.

6 Choose File > Close. If asked to save the changes, press No.

The image could now be sent as an e-mail attachment, as it is much smaller. Sharing images is covered in more detail in Lesson 6, "Sharing Your Photos."

Recompose

Photoshop Elements 8.0 takes resizing images to a new level with the Recompose tool. The recompose tool analyzes an image and tries to detect elements of importance. Think of the recompose tool as a way of internally cropping your photo! Let's take a look at how this tool works.

1   Press the Organizer button (▦) at the top of the workspace in the Menu bar. This reveals the Organizer.

2   Type **0920** in the Search text field at the top of the Organizer to filter the images displayed to those that contain *0920* in the filename. One image of planes flying is displayed. Click the image to select it.

3   Click the arrow to the right of the Fix tab and choose Full Photo Edit from the drop-down menu.

4   Click and hold the Crop tool (🔲) and choose the Recompose tool (🔲). Press OK when the Recompose dialog box appears. Note that handles appear on every side and every corner of the photo.

The image prior to using the Recompose tool.

5   Select the handle on the right side of the photo and drag to the left, to about 75% of its original size. Notice how the planes themselves are not actually scaling but the space between them is. The planes are actually closer together now. Click the green checkmark at the bottom of the image to commit the change.

6 Click and hold the Recompose tool and choose the Crop tool.

7 Drag a crop area around the new (smaller) image area. Click the green checkmark at the bottom of the image to commit the crop.

8 Choose File > Save. Type **IMG_0920_recomposed** in the File name text field and choose Photoshop from the Format drop-down menu. Uncheck the *Save in Version Set with Original* checkbox and press Save.

The recomposed image.

9 Continue practicing with other images. As your images get more complex, you may need to assist Photoshop Elements in determining the important and non-important areas of the image. You'll notice when you choose the Recompose tool that protect and remove brushes appear in the options bar. You can use these brushes to paint over areas that can be removed and over areas that need to be protect or not scaled.

The protect and remove brushes tells Photoshop Elements what can be removed and what needs to be protected.

Congratulations, you have completed the lesson.

Self study

1   Select the teeth of the man in the image file, *pearly whites.jpg*, and refine the edge with a feather so that the edge is less sharp. Make sure you zoom in so that you can really see it.

2   Try using Unsharp Mask on different photos in this lesson and see how well it sharpens the images.

3   Open *statue.jpg* and fix the horizon line using the Crop tool.

4   Open *skin_tone.jpg* and try to fix the image using the Remove Color Cast command.

5   Open *statue.jpg* and *horizon.jpg* and practice changing the sky color. Also try different blending modes on the Sky adjustment layer.

Review

Questions

1   When should you apply sharpening?

2   What is a good sharpening amount to start with?

3   What should you click with the eyedropper while using the Remove Color Cast command?

4   After drawing an area with the Crop tool, what must you do to apply the crop?

Answers

1   At the very end of the image editing process.

2   A good value to start with when using the Unsharp Mask filter is 150 for the Sharpening amount.

3   A white, black, or grey portion of the image.

4   Click the red checkmark or press the Enter (Windows) or Return (Mac OS) key on your keyboard to commit the crop.

What you'll learn in this lesson:

- How to fix exposure problems with blending modes

- How to use adjustment layers

- Creating and working with layers

- How to correct a selected part of an image

Adjusting Exposure

With Photoshop Elements, you can go beyond the automatic fixes that the program provides and use layers and blending modes to correct your images. You can also use adjustment layers for your changes. When you save the file in the native Photoshop format (.psd), your layers are retained, and none of your changes permanently modifies the image.

Starting up

Within the Photoshop Elements Organizer: You will work with several files from the Lessons folder in this lesson. Make sure that you have copied the Lessons folder from the supplied DVD to your hard drive. In order to access these files in the Organizer, you need to import them. See "Adding files and folders to the Organizer" on page 11.

Within the Photoshop Elements Editor: The Photoshop Elements Editor defaults to the last panel layout that you used. Before starting, make sure your tools and panels are consistent with the examples presented in these lessons by resetting the panel locations. Do this by choosing Window > Reset Panels or pressing the Reset Panels button (↻) at the top of the workspace.

See Lesson 4 in action!

Use the accompanying video to gain a better understanding of how to use some of the features shown in this lesson. The video tutorial for this lesson can be found on the included DVD.

Welcome screen

If you're currently viewing the welcome screen, press the Edit button (✐) to enter the Editor workspace. If you are currently in the Organizer, press the Editor button (✎) at the top of the workspace and choose Full Photo Edit from the drop-down menu to the right of the Fix tab.

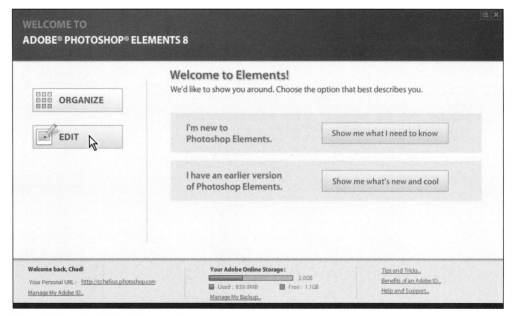

Choose Edit from the Photoshop Elements welcome screen.

Understanding exposure

Exposure is a measure of the amount of light allowed to reach the film or CCD (for digital phtography) of a camera when a photo is taken. If a digital photo is underexposed, it is too dark; Digital images that are overexposed are too light. In this exercise, you will explore an alternative way of fixing exposure problems in your images.

Exposure adjustments with blending modes

In Lesson 3, "Fixing Common Photographic Problems," you fixed exposure problems by using the auto-correction features. In this lesson, you will use a different technique to get the same effect. You will first adjust an underexposed image, then you will fix an overexposed image. The edits you make in this lesson will not modify the underlying image.

Improving underexposed images

The first things to discuss in this lesson is what layers are, and what blending modes are. You will start by learning the difference between Multiply and Screen blending modes.

1   Press the Organizer button (▦) to view the Lessons. If you can't see the filenames, choose View > Show File Names.

2   Locate and select *fishing2.jpg*. Press the arrow icon to the right of the Fix tab, then choose Full Photo Edit from the drop-down menu, or use the keyboard shortcut, Ctrl+I (Windows) Command+I (Mac OS).

The fishing image.

Layers

Layers are like transparent sheets of clear film stacked on top of one another. When artwork is placed on different layers, it can be moved and edited independently. You can paint on or erase parts of a layer; erasing creates a transparent area where you can see the layers below. The Layers panel allows you to manage layers; from here you can create, lock, and hide them.

1   If the Layers panel is not visible, choose Window > Layers to show the Layers panel.

The Layers panel in Photoshop Elements.

2   Select the layer named *Background*, Press the panel menu button (-≡) at the top of the panel, and choose Duplicate Layer.

3   The Duplicate Layer dialog box opens. Leave the settings at their defaults and press OK.

The Duplicate Layer dialog box.

You should now have two layers.

Blending modes

Blending modes in layers control how pixels in an image are affected by other layers. The two most basic blending modes are Multiply and Screen.

The Multiply blending mode takes a looks at the color information in the layers below and multiplies the base color by the blend color. The result is always a darker image, because multiply loses the white in the image.

The Screen blending mode looks at each layer's color information and multiplies the inverse of the layers below. The resulting image is always lighter, because the Screen blending mode loses the black of the image.

You are going to apply the Screen blending mode to the Background copy layer to lighten the image.

1   In the Layers panel, make sure the *Background copy* layer is selected, then change the blending mode from Normal to Screen at the top of the Layers panel. The result is an instantly lighter photo.

The image after changing the blending mode.

To see how this blended layer has affected the image, press the visibility icon (👁) next to the Background copy layer to hide the layer. Press the visibility icon again to show the layer.

2   Choose File > Save. In the Save As dialog box, type **fishing2_working** in the Name text field and change the format to Photoshop. Press Save.

3   Choose File > Close. If asked to save the changes, press No.

Improving faded or overexposed images

Because of lighting conditions, photos can appear too bright, or washed out. They are considered overexposed, because too much light was allowed into the camera. In this exercise, you will use the Multiply Layer blending mode to darken a washed-out image.

1   Press the Organizer button (▦) to open the Organizer and view your photo library. If you can't see the filenames, choose View > Show File Names.

2   Locate and select *horse.jpg*. Press the arrow button to the right of the Fix tab and choose Full Photo Edit from the drop-down menu.

The horse image before editing.

3   Select the Layer named *Background*, Press the panel menu button (•≣), and choose Duplicate Layer.

4   The Duplicate Layer dialog box opens. Leave the settings at their defaults and press OK.

5 In the Layers panel, make sure the *Background copy* layer is selected, then choose Multiply from the Blending mode drop-down menu.

The image after selecting the Multiply blending mode.

The result is a darker photo. However, this is too dark. You can reduce the effect a bit by lowering the opacity of the current layer, adjusting how much of the effect is applied.

6 Use the Opacity drop-down menu that is located to the right of the Blending mode drop-down menu at the top of the Layers panel to adjust how much of the effect you want to apply to the photo. Type **65** into the Opacity text field or move the slider to 65.

Adjusting the Opacity of the blended layer.

To see how this blended layer has affected the image, press the visibility icon (👁) to the left of the *Background copy* layer to hide it. Press the visibility icon again to show the layer.

Feel free to try other blending modes during this exercise to see how each blending mode affects the image. To easily cycle through blending modes, use the keyboard shortcut, Shift++(plus key) or Shift+-(minus key).

7   Choose File > Save. In the Save As dialog box, type **horse_working** in the Name text field and change the format to Photoshop. Press Save.

8   Choose File > Close. If asked to save the changes, press No.

Making adjustments manually

Not every image can be adjusted automatically. Some images need more attention than others. In this exercise, you will learn how to manually adjust brightness and contrast, as well as shadows and highlights. You will also learn how to read a Histogram to adjust both Levels and Curves of an image. In this exercise, you'll duplicate and save one image as four different files, so that you can compare what each feature does to an image.

1   Press the Organizer button (▦) at the top of the workspace to view your photo library. If you can't see the filenames, choose View > Show File Names.

2   Locate and select *wicked_surprised.jpg*. Press the arrow to the right of the Fix tab and choose Full Photo Edit from the drop-down menu.

The wicked_suprised image.

3   Once the image is open, choose File > Save As. Navigate to the Lessons folder. Type **Brightness Contrast** in the Name text field and click the *Save in Version Set with Original* checkbox to uncheck it. Press Save. In the JPEG Options dialog box, press OK to accept the current JPEG settings.

4   Choose File > Save As again and type **Shadow Highlight** in the Name text field; then press Save. Choose File > Save As two more times and save the files as **Levels2** and **Curves**. Close any open images in the Editor when you are finished.

5   Choose File > Open. Navigate to your Lessons folder and select *Brightness Contrast.jpg*. Press Open.

Adjusting brightness and contrast manually

The Brightness/Contrast command helps you adjust an image that does not use its entire tonal range. Images that are too dark can be made brighter. This often throws off the contrast of the image, which can also be adjusted in this window.

1   Choose Enhance > Adjust Lighting > Brightness/Contrast. No changes are made yet.

2   Drag the Brightness slider to the right to 65, or type **65** in the Brightness text field, to brighten the image.

3   To bring back some shadows, increase the contrast to 30 by dragging the Contrast slider to the right, or by typing **30** in the Contrast text field. To get a quick view of your adjustments, click to check, and then uncheck the *Preview* checkbox to compare before and after versions.

Adjusting brightness and contrast.

4   Choose File > Save to save your edits. If the Save As dialog box opens, press Save. If Photoshop Elements asks you to replace the file, press Yes, then press OK when the JPEG Options dialog box appears.

After adjusting the brightness and contrast.

Adjusting shadows and highlights manually

Shadows and Highlights allows you to lighten shadows, darken highlights, and also adjust the midtone contrast. In this exercise, you will work on a different version of the same image.

1   Choose File > Open. Navigate to your Lessons folder and select *Shadow Highlights.jpg*; then press Open.

2   Choose Enhance > Adjust Lighting > Shadows/Highlights. Shadows are lightened by 25 percent by default.

3 Notice that the image now has a dull, bluish-gray appearance. Increase the midtone contrast to +30 to regain some contrast inside the image by moving the slider to the right, or by typing **30** in the Midtone Contrast text field.

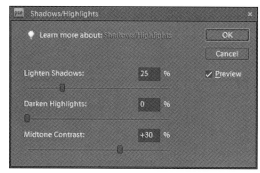

The adjusted Shadow/Highlight settings.

4 Choose File > Save to save your edits. If the Save As dialog box opens, press Save. If Photoshop Elements asks you to replace the file, press Yes, then press OK when the JPEG Options dialog box appears.

The image after Shadow/Highlights is applied.

Making tonal adjustments using Levels

The Levels command allows you to look at a histogram showing you where most of the tones in an image are located. You can control the darkest and the lightest portions of the image and all the midtones in between. In the last two exercises, you corrected the shadows, highlights, brightness, and contrast, but you never really removed the blue color cast. Now, you'll fix the contrast of this photo using Levels, you'll also remove the blue color cast.

Histogram

The Histogram panel indicates the tonal balance of your image. It can tell you whether the image contains enough detail in the shadow, midtone, and highlight areas. Choose Window > Histogram to toggle the Histogram panel on and off. If the Histogram option is not available, that is because the Histogram panel is only available in Full Edit mode. If necessary, choose Full Edit, then choose Window > Histogram to open the panel.

The Histogram panel shows the tonal balance of the image.

1   Choose File > Open. In the Open dialog box, navigate to the Lessons folder and select
    the file named *Levels2.jpg*. Press Open. You can see that most of the tonal information
    from this photo is on the left side of the histogram. This means that the image is lacking
    the brightness which would be displayed on the right side of the histogram. You can
    close the histogram for now; you'll be seeing it again when you learn about Levels.

The image before the Level changes.

2   Choose Enhance > Adjust Lighting > Levels. In the Levels dialog box, there are three
    sliders at the bottom of your histogram; the two end sliders control white and black, and
    the middle slider controls the colors in between. Drag the white slider to the left, to 178,
    which brings it to the bottom of the first peak displayed in the histogram. You have now
    made all the tones that exist from 178 to 255 white, brightening the photo.

3   To further lighten the photo, drag the middle slider to the left, to 1.19. If you were to drag the middle slider to the right, it would darken the image.

The adjusted Levels settings.

4   The image is starting to look better but you still need to correct for the blue color cast. At the top of the dialog box, use the Channel drop-down menu to choose the Blue channel. Drag the middle slider to the right to .75 to decrease the blue in the image.

The final image after removing color from the Blue channel.

5   Press OK to commit the changes. Choose File > Save to save your edits. If the Save As dialog box opens, press Save. If Photoshop Elements asks you to replace the file, press Yes, then press OK when the JPEG Options dialog box appears.

Making tonal adjustments using Curves

Curves allow you to have pinpoint control over the appearance of the shadow, midtone, and highlight areas in your image. The most straightforward use of Curves is to enhance the contrast in an image, but the controls available with Curves allow you to do far more than that. The Curves dialog box allows you to correct both highlights and shadows, as well as midtone contrast and brightness, but unlike Levels, it does not allow you to adjust individual channels.

1   Choose File > Open. In the Open dialog box, navigate to the Lessons folder and select the file named *Curves.jpg*. Press Open.

2   Choose Enhance > Adjust Color > Adjust Color Curves. Select the Increase Contrast style on the bottom left side of the panel. The image becomes darker.

3   Drag the Midtone Brightness slider to the right to increase the midtone brightness.

4   Drag the Midtone Contrast slider slightly to the left to increase the contrast of the image. There are no set numbers in this window, so feel free to experiment with all the different sliders. When you are finished, press OK.

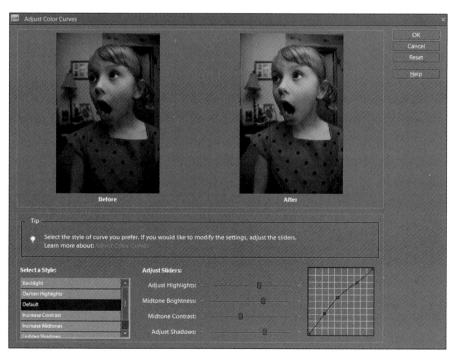

Changing the color curve.

5 Choose File > Save to save your edits. If the Save As dialog box opens, press Save. If Photoshop Elements asks you to replace the file, press Yes, then press OK when the JPEG Options dialog box appears.

Comparing images in Full Edit view

You will now compare all four photos in Full Edit view to see the what effect each command has on the image. Make sure you still have all four files open; if not reopen them.

1 Press the arrow to the right of the Edit tab and choose Edit Full from the menu.

2 Press the Arrange button (▦) and choose the Tile All in Grid option. This tiles the images into four separate boxes in the workspace.

You can now compare what each command did to these files. The edits you made on these documents were destructive. There is no way of turning off any of the features you just used. The histograms for these images show how image data was lost. Because of this, you would want to run any of these commands only one at a time. You will learn about adjustment layers which allow you to make similar adjustments, but are non-destructive.

3 Choose File > Close All. If you are prompted to save any changes, press No.

Using adjustment layers

There is a non-destructive way to make corrections to your image. Adjustment layers, instead of making changes to the actual image, create a new layer and allow that layer to control the tonal range or color of all the layers below it. If you decide you don't like an adjustment, you can just discard the layer, and you are back to the original image. In this exercise, you will create an adjustment layer and save the image as a .psd file.

1 Press the Organizer button (▦) at the top of the workspace. This reveals the Organizer.

2 Locate and select the file named *at_the_beach.jpg*. The image is too dark, and you'll use a Levels adjustment layer to edit it. Press the arrow to the right of the Fix tab at the top of the workspace and choose Full Photo Edit from the drop-down menu.

3 Choose Layer > New Adjustment Layer > Levels. In the New Layer dialog box, type **Levels Adjustment** in the Name text field, then press OK.

It's always a good idea to name layers and adjustment layers as you create them. It gives you a better indication of what layers you've created, and helps you understand their purpose.

4   The Levels dialog box opens as in previous exercises, but you'll notice that a new adjustment layer has been created for you.

5   Grab the middle slider in the Levels dialog box and drag it to the left to lighten the image. Drag the slider to 1.65.

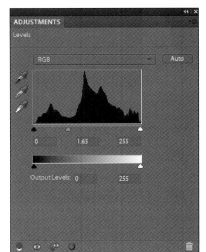

The adjustment layer and Levels dialog box.

6   To turn the effect off, press the visibility icon (👁) to the left of the adjustment layer.

7   If you'd like to go back and adjust any settings, double-click the gears icon (⚙) to enter the Levels dialog box.

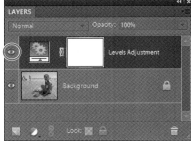

Adjustment layer visibility turned off.   *Adjustment layer visibility turned on.*

8   In order for Photoshop Elements to store these layers, the image should be saved in the Photoshop (.psd) format. Choose File > Save As. Navigate to your Lessons folder, change the format to Photoshop, then press Save.

9   Choose File > Save As. Navigate to your Lessons folder, change the format to .jpg, then press Save, then press OK in the JPEG Options dialog box. You'll save a version of this image in another file format to understand the importance of file formats when manipulating files.

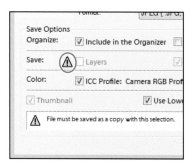

Notice the warning icon that appears next to the Layers option.

10   Choose File > Open, navigate to the Lessons folder and select *at_the_beach copy.jpg*, then press Open. Notice how adjustment layers were not saved in the .jpg format. If your windows are tiled, you will need to click on each window to bring it to the front in order to examine the Layers panel. Turn tiling off by pressing on the Arrange button (▦) and choosing Consolidate All.

11   Choose File > Close to close the file *at_the_beach copy.jpg*. You can see that the adjustment layer is included in the .psd file.

You can also save images in the .tiff format to retain your layers.

12   Choose File > Close to close the file *at_the_beach.psd*.

Correcting selected parts of an image

Sometimes you need to change only parts of an image. In this exercise, you will create an adjustment layer that affects only a certain color, then you'll learn how to make selections, save them, put them on a new layer, and edit them individually.

Hue/Saturation adjustments

For this exercise, you will change a girl's green striped shirt to blue stripes using the Hue/Saturation command located under Adjustment Layers.

1   Press the Organizer button (⊞) at the top of the workspace. This reveals the Organizer.

2   Locate and select the file named *blue_stripes.jpg*. You'll adjust the color of this image using a Hue/Saturation adjustment layer. Press the arrow to the right of the Fix tab at the top of the workspace and choose Full Photo Edit from the drop-down menu.

The blue_stripes.jpg *image.*

3 Choose Layer > New Adjustment Layer > Hue/Saturation. When the New Layer dialog box opens, press OK to accept the default settings.

Inside the Hue/Saturation dialog box, you can change colors in your images. The default is set to edit the Master, or all the colors. You can change this to any other color, and use the Eyedropper tool (🖋) to select a color, and change the hue, saturation, and lightness of that color.

4 Choose Greens from the Edit drop-down menu and select the first eyedropper icon at the bottom of the Hue/Saturation adjustment panel. As you move the cursor over the image, you can see that the cursor is now an eyedropper. Click one of the green stripes of the girl's shirt.

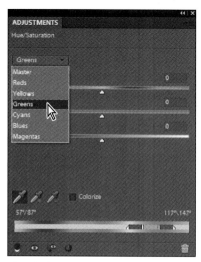

The Edit drop-down menu.

5   The Hue slider controls the color, the Saturation slider controls the amount of that color, and the Lightness slider controls the light and dark values. Move the Hue slider to +124. The stripes turns blue. Have fun with this image and experiment dragging the Hue slider to different values. There is no other green in this image except for a small bow tie on the other girl's shirt, so the rest of the image is not affected. Press OK when you are finished.

The image after modifying the hue and saturation.

6   Choose File > Save. In the Save As dialog box, type **blue_stripes_working** in the Name text field and change the format to Photoshop. Press Save.

7   Choose File > Close. If asked to save the changes, press No.

Working with selections

In this section, you will discover how to make selections, save selections, and move selections to a new layer. You will also use blending modes and adjustment layers to fix individual parts of the image.

1   Press the Organizer button (⊞) at the top of the workspace. This reveals the Organizer.

2   Locate and select the file named *hiding_out.jpg*. The image is too dark in the foreground, and too light in the background. Press the arrow to the right of the Fix tab at the top of the workspace and choose Full Photo Edit from the drop-down menu.

Using the Quick Selection tool

The Quick Selection tool makes selections for you based on color and texture. You can click with this tool to make selections, or you can also click and drag to paint a selection. The selection you make doesn't have to be exact because the Quick Selection tool automatically and intuitively creates a selection.

1   Choose the Quick Selection tool (✎) from the Toolbox. Click and drag over the sky and the valley up to the edges of the rocks to select the background. Press and hold the Alt key and the tool changes from select to deselect. If necessary, drag the tool and remove any unwanted areas of the selection.

The selection.

Saving selections

You can spend quite a bit of time making selections, so it makes sense to save selections in case you need to access them again. If you save the file as a .psd or a .tiff, selections are saved in the file. You will now save this selection so that you can use it later on.

1   Choose Select > Save Selection.

2   In the Save Selection dialog box, type **Background** in the Name text field and press OK.

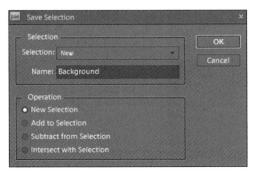

Naming a saved selection.

Moving selections to a new layer

You will now bring this selection onto a new layer by itself so that you can use a blending mode to clean it up.

1   Choose Edit > Copy, then choose Edit > Paste.

You can also use Ctrl+J (Windows) or Command+J (Mac OS) or choose Layer > New > Layer via Copy to move your selection to a new layer.

A new layer added to the Layers panel.

2   A new layer, named *Layer 1*, has been made for you. To darken the selection and blend Layer 1 with the Background layer, select Layer 1 and choose Multiply from the Blending mode drop-down menu. The color of the valley is more vivid, and its tonal range now contains the shadows that were previously missing.

3   To view what effect this has on the Background layer, press the visibility icon (👁) next to Layer 1. Now you will correct the rest of the image. You will use a selection that you saved, invert the selection, and make an adjustment layer.

4   Choose Select > Load Selection.

5   In the Load Selection dialog box, make sure *Background* is selected and click the *Invert* checkbox so that the selection selects the opposite of the original selection, then press OK. Your selection is now back and active.

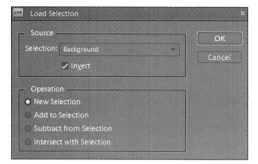

Loading a selection.

6   Choose the *Background* layer by clicking on it. This way, Photoshop Elements realizes that you're on the Background layer before you make the adjustment layer. A mask will be made that affects only the selected area.

The foreground before the Levels dialog box is opened.

7   Click the Create new fill or adjustment layer icon (🍩) at the bottom of the Layers panel and choose Levels.

Creating a new adjustment layer.

9   In the Levels Adjustment panel, click the white slider and drag it to the left to a value of 115, or type **115** in the white text field in the Input levels section.

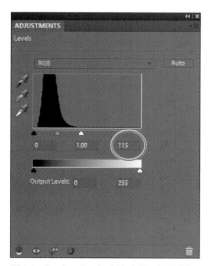

This is what the value should look like for RGB.

10 The image still looks too blue. Choose Blue from the Channel drop-down menu. Drag the middle slider to .90 to decrease the blue.

Modifying the Blue channel.

11 Now the image looks too yellow. You will now go into the Green channel to fix it. Choose Green from the Channel drop-down menu. Drag the middle slider to the right to .93 to decrease the yellow in the image. If you'd like to review the changes, toggle the visibility icon of the Levels 1 or Layer 1 layers to review your work. Notice the mask icon on the Levels layer. Any time you make a selection prior to choosing an Adjustment layer, a mask is created from the selection to isolate the affected area without changing the area outside the selection.

12 Choose File > Save. In the Save As dialog box, type **hiding_out_working.jpg** in the Name text field and change the format to Photoshop. Press Save.

Saving in the JPEG format will remove the saved selection from the file. If you want to keep a working file with the selection you should save it as a .psd file.

This is the foreground after adjusting the levels.

13 Choose File > Close. If asked to save the changes, press No.

Self study

1 Open the file named *blue_stripes.jpg*, make a Hue/Saturation adjustment layer, select the girl's red sweatshirt, change the Edit from Master to any color, then try to change the hue. Notice how many colors in the document are affected.

2 Make a selection using the Quick Selection tool around the red sweatshirt in *blue_stripes.jpg*; then make a Hue/Saturation adjustment layer to see how the adjustment layer affects only the selection.

3 Open *at_the_beach.jpg*. Make a selection of the girl, copy and paste her onto a new layer, and use a blending mode on that layer to lighten her. Then do the same for the background in the image.

4 Adjust the *hiding_out.jpg* file by either moving both selections to new layers, then fixing them. Or try to use adjustment layers for both of the selected parts of the image.

Review

Questions

1 In the Layers panel, what does the icon that controls layer visibility look like?

2 What is the shortcut for moving a selection to a new layer?

3 Why should you use adjustment layers?

4 What file format saves both selections and layers?

5 Name a web file format that doesn't support layers.

Answers

1 The icon for layer visibility looks like an open eye.

2 The shortcut is Ctrl+J (Windows) or Command+J (Mac OS).

3 The advantage of using adjustment layers is that you can discard or disable the layer to remove the adjustment, or you can further refine it at a later time non-destructively.

4 A .psd or .tiff file.

5 A .jpg or .gif file.

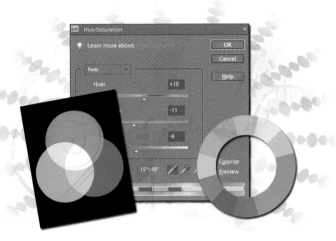

What you'll learn in this lesson:

- Fundamentals for understanding color

- How to choose a color adjustment method

- How to adjust color globally in a photo

- How to use selections to adjust color in specific areas of a photo

Adjusting Color

Photoshop Elements has tools for easily adjusting the color and tonal range of your photos. You can adjust entire photos using global controls, or specific areas using selections. In this lesson, you'll learn to adjust color using different methods.

Starting up

Within the Photoshop Elements Organizer: You will work with several files from the Lessons folder in this lesson. Make sure that you have copied the Lessons folder from the supplied DVD to your hard drive. In order to access these files in the Organizer, you need to import them. See "Adding files and folders to the Organizer" on page 11.

Within the Photoshop Elements Editor: The Photoshop Elements Editor defaults to the last panel layout that you used. Before starting, make sure your tools and panels are consistent with the examples presented in these lessons by resetting the panel locations. Do this by choosing Window > Reset Panels or by pressing the Reset panels button (↻) in the Options bar.

See Lesson 5 in action!

Use the accompanying video to gain a better understanding of how to use some of the features shown in this lesson. The video tutorial for this lesson can be found on the included DVD.

Welcome screen

If you're currently viewing the welcome screen, press the Edit button (✐) to enter the Editor workspace. If you are currently in the Organizer, click the arrow to the right of the Fix tab and choose > Full Photo Edit from the drop-down.

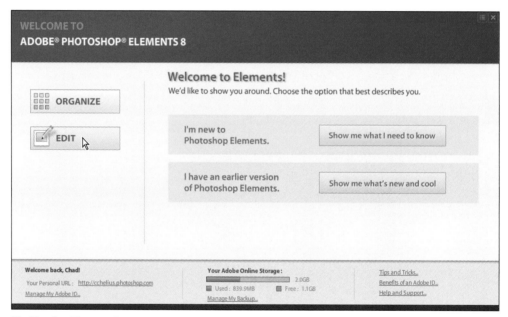

The Photoshop Elements welcome screen.

Understanding color

Two different color models are used to adjust color in Photoshop Elements. The HSB (hue, saturation, and brightness) model is based on the way the human eye sees color. The RGB (red, green, and blue) model is based on the way computer monitors display color. The color wheel is another tool that helps you understand the relationships between colors. Photoshop Elements offers four image modes that define the number of colors displayed in an image: RGB, bitmap, grayscale, and indexed color.

HSB color

The human eye perceives color in terms of three characteristics—hue, saturation, and brightness (HSB).

Hue

Hue refers to the color reflected from or transmitted through an object. It is measured as a location on a color wheel, expressed as a degree between 0 and 360. In most cases, hue is defined by the name of the color, such as red, orange, or green.

Saturation

Saturation is the strength or purity of the color. Sometimes called *chroma*, it refers to the amount of gray in proportion to the hue, and is measured as a percentage from 0 (gray) to 100 (fully saturated). On a color wheel, saturation increases from the center to the edge.

Brightness

The brightness value is the relative lightness or darkness of the color. It is usually measured as a percentage from 0 (black) to 100 (white).

In Photoshop Elements, you can use the HSB model to define a color in the Color Picker, but you cannot use the HSB mode to create or edit images.

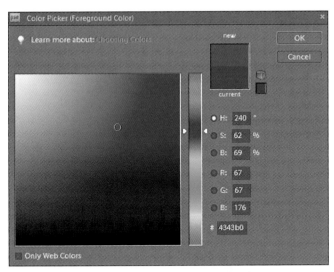

Use the HSB controls in the Adobe Color Picker to select colors.

RGB model

Most of the visible spectrum of color can be recreated by mixing red, green, and blue (RGB) light in varying amounts. These three colors are often called the *additive primaries*, because when added together, they produce white light. Where two colors overlap, they create cyan, magenta, or yellow, or *subtractive primaries*.

RGB color is commonly used in lighting, video, and computer monitors. Your monitor, for example, displays color by transmitting light through red, green, and blue phosphors.

The default mode of new Photoshop Elements images and images from your digital camera is RGB.

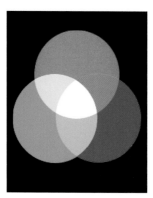

Additive colors (RGB) are added together to create white light.

Color wheel

Using a color wheel is a good way to gain a better understanding of the relationship between colors. Looking at the wheel, you'll see that directly across from each additive primary (red, green, blue) is its complement: red/cyan, green/magenta, and blue/yellow.

Further, each subtractive primary (cyan, magenta, yellow) is made up of two additive primaries. It does not, however, contain any of its complement. So, if you increase the concentration of a primary color in your image, you reduce the concentration of its complement.

For example, cyan is composed of blue and green light, but there is no red light in cyan. When adjusting cyan in Photoshop Elements, you change the color values in the red color channel. By adding red to your image, you subtract cyan from it.

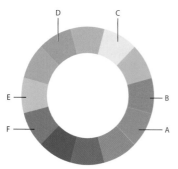

Using a color wheel helps you understand the relationship between colors.
A. Magenta. B. Red. C. Yellow. D. Green. E. Cyan. F. Blue.

About image modes

Image modes define the number of colors that can be displayed in an image. They can also affect the file size of the image. Photoshop Elements offers you four image modes: RGB, bitmap, grayscale, and indexed color.

Image modes define the color capability of an image.

Bitmap mode

Bitmap uses one of two color values (black or white) to represent the pixels in an image. Images in bitmap mode are called 1-bit images because they have a bit depth of 1.

Grayscale mode

Grayscale uses up to 256 shades of gray. Every pixel in a grayscale image has a brightness value ranging from 0 (black) to 255 (white). Grayscale images are 8-bit images.

Indexed Color mode

Indexed Color uses up to 256 colors. In this mode, Photoshop Elements builds a color lookup table (CLUT), which stores and indexes the colors in the image. If a color in the original image does not appear in the table, the program chooses the closest one, or simulates the color using available colors. By reducing the number of colors used, indexed color can reduce file size while maintaining your image's quality. Indexed-color images are 8-bit images, and are often used in web pages.

Limited editing is available in Indexed Color mode. For more comprehensive editing control, you should convert temporarily into RGB mode.

Switching image modes

When you choose a color mode in the Editor (using the Image > Mode command), you are changing the color values in the image. Although you might want to convert into a different mode for several reasons, it's best to keep the following in mind:

* For the most control over editing, work in RGB mode as often as possible.

* Save a backup copy before converting so that you can edit the original version of the image after the conversion.

* If you have images that utilize layers, the images are flattened automatically when you convert them into bitmap or indexed-color mode, because these modes do not support layers.

Comparing methods of adjusting color

Photoshop Elements provides several tools and commands for fixing the color and tonal range of your photos. You can work in one of three workspaces, depending on the requirements of your image.

Choose an editing workspace based on your experience and needs.

Understanding Edit Guided

Edit Guided leads you through the tasks of color correction. If you are new to digital imaging or not yet comfortable with Photoshop Elements, you can use this method to increase your understanding of the process.

Understanding Edit Quick

Edit Quick conveniently assembles many of the basic photo-fixing tools in Photoshop Elements. If you have limited knowledge of digital imaging, Quick Fix is a good place to start adjusting photos.

Understanding Edit Full

Edit Full contains lighting and color-correction commands, as well as tools for fixing image defects, making selections, adding text, and painting on your images. If you've worked with images before, you'll find that the Full Edit method provides the most flexible and powerful image-correction workspace.

When working in Full Edit, you can make adjustments directly to the image pixels, or you can use adjustment layers to make nondestructive, editable adjustments. Some tools automatically create an adjustment layer for the correction you're applying. See "Using adjustment layers" in Lesson 4, "Adjusting Exposure," for more information.

Adjusting tonal range in Full Edit

Setting an overall tonal range allows for the most detail possible throughout the image. In this exercise, you'll use Edit Full to adjust the tonal range of an image.

1   Press the Organizer button (▦) in the menu bar at the top of the Edit workspace. This reveals the Organizer.

2   Locate and select the file named *Bobby and Elvis*. Press the arrow to the right of the Fix tab in the menu bar at the top of the Organizer workspace and choose Full Photo Edit from the drop-down menu, or use the keyboard shortcut Ctrl+I (Windows) or Command+I (Mac OS).

Before fixing the color in this image, you'll create a backup copy.

Making a duplicate of a file

1   Once the image opens in Full Edit, choose File > Save As.

Save a duplicate copy of your image before
you begin to adjust color.

2   The Save As dialog box opens. Navigate to the Lessons folder and click the *Save in Version Set with Original* checkbox to uncheck it. Make sure Format is set to Photoshop. Name the file **Bobby and Elvis_work** and press Save.

Restoring shadow and highlight detail

You should begin correcting an image by adjusting the values of the extreme highlight and shadow areas in the image (also known as the tonal range).

1 In the Editor, choose Enhance > Adjust Lighting > Shadow/Highlights. Make sure the *Preview* checkbox is checked.

2 Drag the Lighten Shadows slider to the left so that it reads 10 percent. Lighten Shadows brightens the dark areas of your photo and reveals more of the shadow detail that was captured when you took the image.

3 Drag the Darken Highlights slider to the right so that it reads 10 percent. Darken Highlights darkens the light areas of your photo and reveals more of the highlight detail that was captured when you took the image. Pure white areas of your photo don't have any detail and aren't affected by this adjustment.

4 Drag the Midtone Contrast slider to the right so that it reads +25 percent. Midtone Contrast adds or reduces the contrast of the middle tones. You should use this slider if the image contrast doesn't look right after you've adjusted shadows and highlights. Press OK.

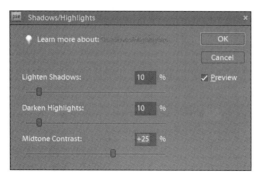

Use the Shadows/Highlights dialog box to improve tonal detail in the image.

You've restored depth to the tonal range of the image by improving the detail in its shadows and highlights.

To reset the image to how it looked when you opened the dialog box, uncheck the Preview *checkbox, or hold down Alt (Windows) or Option (Mac OS) and press the Reset button while the Levels dialog box is open.*

5 Keep the image open as you will use it in the next exercise.

Correcting color in Full Edit

Sometimes adjusting the tonal range brings out a color cast in an image. A color cast is an undesired color shift in a photo. For example, a photo taken indoors with a flash might contain more blue than it should.

In Lesson 3, "Fixing Common Photographic Problems," you removed a color cast automatically. In this exercise, you'll have more control over the process as you remove a slight blue cast from your image in Full Edit.

Correcting color casts using Color Variations

You can make color and tonal adjustments in the Color Variations dialog box by comparing and choosing different thumbnail variations of the photo.

 You can't use the Color Variations command with images in Indexed Color mode.

1   Choose Enhance > Adjust Color > Color Variations. The two preview images show the original image (Before) and the adjusted image after you've made changes (After).

2   Select Midtones in section 1 to choose the area of the image you want to adjust.

3   Drag the Adjust Color Intensity slider in section 2 to control the intensity of the adjustment that you'll make when clicking a button in section 3. Dragging the slider to the left decreases the amount of adjustment, and dragging to the right increases the amount of adjustment to be applied. Drag the slider slightly to the left.

4   Click the Increase Red button in section 3 to remove the slight blue cast in this image. Each time you click a button, the After thumbnail is updated.

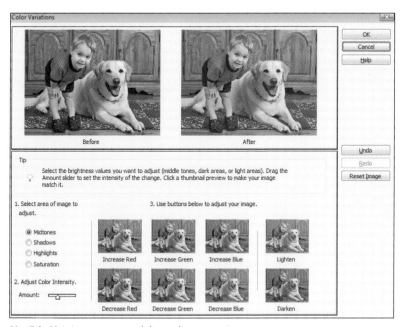

Use Color Variations to compare and choose adjustment options.

5   When you're satisfied with the results, press OK to apply the adjustments to your image.

6   Choose File > Save. Keep the image open as you will use it again in the next exercise.

Removing a color cast using Levels

As you become more comfortable with color correction and the RGB color model, you might want to try selectively editing channels using Levels.

1   Choose Enhance > Adjust Lighting > Levels.

2   Choose a color channel to adjust from the Channel pop-up menu. In this exercise, you'll choose Green to remove green from (and add magenta to) the image.

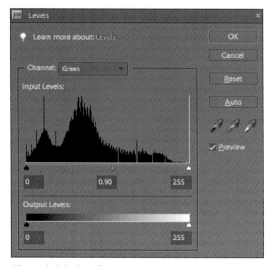

The Levels dialog box allows you to remove a color cast by adjusting individual color channels.

3   Drag the middle input slider to the right until it reads 0.90. Some of the coldness of the image is removed as green is removed and magenta is added. Press OK. (Your histogram may differ from the screen shot in the book.)

Adjusting color curves in an image

The Adjust Color Curves command adjusts highlights, midtones, and shadows in each color channel of an image. You can also compare and choose different tonal presets by selecting from the list of styles in the Select a Style box.

1   In the Editor workspace, confirm that **Bobby and Elvis_work** is still open and visible.

2   To adjust a specific image area or layer, select it with one of the selection tools. If no selection is made, the adjustment applies to the entire image. (See "Making Selections" later in this lesson.)

3   Choose Enhance > Adjust Color > Adjust Color Curves.

4   In the Select a Style box, choose Default as the type of adjustment to apply.

5   Experiment by dragging the Adjust Highlights, Midtone Brightness, Midtone Contrast, and Shadows sliders. Note the changes in the tone curve to the right of the sliders.

Adjust Color Curves automatically adjusts tonal range in each color channel of an image.

6   When you're satisfied with the adjustment, apply the adjustment by pressing OK.

7   Choose File > Save.

Adjusting color saturation and hue

You can use the Hue/Saturation command to adjust the hue (color), saturation (purity), and/or lightness of an entire image or of individual colors in an image.

The Hue slider can be used to change the range of colors in a portion of an image. You can use the Saturation slider to make colors more vivid or more muted.

Use Hue/Saturation to adjust color, purity, and lightness of an image.

Changing color saturation or hue

1   With the *Elvis* and *Bobby_working.psd* file still open Choose Enhance > Adjust Color > Adjust Hue/Saturation.

The two color bars in the dialog box represent the colors in their order on the color wheel. The upper bar shows the color before the adjustment; the lower bar shows how the adjustment affects all hues at full saturation.

2   In the Edit drop-down menu, choose Master to adjust all colors at once.

3   For Hue, enter a value of, or drag the slider to, +5 to remove red from your photo.

The slider values reflect the number of degrees of rotation (from –180 to +180) around the color wheel. A positive value indicates clockwise rotation, and a negative value indicates counterclockwise rotation.

4 For Saturation, enter a value of, or drag the slider to, -15 to decrease the color saturation in your photo.

5 For Lightness, enter a value of, or drag the slider to, -5 to decrease the lightness in your photo. Press OK.

Adjusting saturation in specific areas

Scrubbing with the Sponge tool changes the color saturation of an area. You'll use it to restore saturation to a specific area of your photo.

Increasing saturation by scrubbing with the Sponge tool

1 Select the Sponge tool (◉) from the Toolbox

2 In the Options bar, set the Brushes to Soft Round 27 pixels.

3 Set the Mode to Saturate. This mode boosts the color's saturation.

4 Set the Flow to 5 percent. This sets the rate of saturation change.

The Sponge tool settings in the Options bar.

5 Drag with the sponge over the boy's face, and note the return of some warmth to this area of the photo. Each time you overlap an area that you painted with the sponge, that area is saturated by another 5 percent. This is the reason for setting flow percentages at lower numbers, so you can layer your painting in order to avoid too harsh a result.

Making selections

Selections define the editable pixels in a photograph. They allow you, for example, to darken one area in a photo without affecting the rest. Selections can be made with either a selection tool or a selection command. A selection outline surrounds the selection, and can be hidden. You can edit the pixels inside a selection border, but you can't access pixels outside the selection outline until you deselect the selection.

Selections define the editable areas in a photo.

The importance of selections

Photoshop Elements provides selection tools for different kinds of selections. For example, the Rectangular Marquee tool selects square and rectangular areas, the Magic Wand tool can select an area of similar colors with one click, and freeform selections can be made with one of the Lasso tools. Further, you can smooth the edges of a selection with feathering and anti-aliasing.

About the selection tools

Selection tools can be found in the Toolbox, which is located, by default, on the left side of the workspace.

Rectangular Marquee tool, Elliptical Marquee tool

Magic Wand tool

Lasso tool, Polygonal Lasso tool, Magnetic Lasso tool

Quick Selection tool

Smart Brush tool

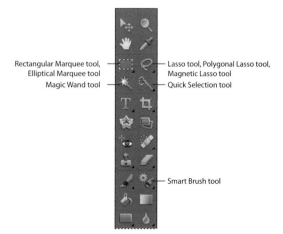

Photoshop Elements provides you with different selection tools for different selection needs.

The **Rectangular Marquee** tool draws square or rectangular selections.

The **Elliptical Marquee** tool draws round or elliptical selections.

The **Lasso** tool draws freehand selections.

The **Polygonal Lasso** tool draws multiple straight-edged segments of a selection.

The **Magnetic Lasso** tool draws a selection that automatically snaps to edges you drag over in the photo.

The **Magic Wand** tool selects pixels of similar color with one click.

The **Quick Selection** tool automatically makes a selection based on color and texture when you click or click-drag an area.

The **Selection Brush** tool automatically selects or deselects the area you paint, depending on whether you're in Selection or Mask mode.

The **Smart Brush** tool applies color and tonal adjustments and effects to a selection. The tool automatically creates an adjustment layer for non-destructive editing.

In this exercise, you'll use one of these tools, the Selection Brush tool, to work with selections.

Using the Selection Brush tool

You can make selections in two ways using the Selection Brush tool: in Selection mode, by painting over the area you want to select, or in Mask mode, by painting out areas you don't want to select using a transparent overlay.

You can also start with a rough selection made with another selection tool, and then fine-tune your selection with the Selection Brush tool. Also, you can add to or subtract from the selection by choosing from the Selection brush tool options.

Choose from Selection Brush tool options to fine-tune your selection.
A. Add to selection. B. Subtract from selection. C. Brush drop-down menu.
D. Brush size. E. Mode. F. Hardness.

1   Select the Selection Brush tool (✐) from the toolbox. If necessary, click and hold on the Quick Selection tool (✎) in the toolbox and select the Selection Brush from the list of nested tools that appears.

Next, you'll set Selection Brush tool options in the Options bar at the top of the workspace.

2   By default, the tool is set to Add To Selection. (To subtract from the selection, you would click Subtract From Selection in the Options bar.)

3   Choose the Hard Round 13 pixels brush from the Default Brushes drop-down menu.

4   Increase the brush size to 20 pixels by dragging the Size slider to the right or by clicking on the word Size and dragging to the right.

5 From the Mode drop-down menu, choose Selection to add a selection to the image.

6 Set the brush tip's hardness to a value of 100 percent for a crisp edge on your selection.

7 Click and drag in your photo to select the boy in the image. Don't worry if you select too much, you will edit your selection in the next steps.

8 From the Mode drop-down menu, choose Mask to switch to Mask mode. The red overlay shows areas that are masked, or not currently selected. You can use mask mode to remove areas from your selection.

9 Paint out any areas that you've selected in error.

10 Choose Selection from the Mode menu to return to the Selection mode.

Subtract from a selection while in Mask mode.

Add to or subtract from a selection

You can add to or subtract from an existing selection to adjust selection borders.

1   Choose any Selection tool, and hold down Shift (a plus sign appears next to the pointer) to add to the selection, or hold down Alt (Windows) or Option (Mac OS) (a minus sign appears next to the pointer) to subtract from a selection. Then select the area to add or subtract and make another selection.

2   In the Options bar, click *Add To Selection* or *Subtract From Selection* and make another selection.

Add to or subtract from a selection using settings in the Options bar.

Smoothing selection edges with anti-aliasing and feathering

Anti-aliasing and feathering are terms that refer to smoothing the hard edges of a selection. Anti-aliasing smooths the jagged edges of a selection by softening the color transition between edges and background pixels. Because only the edge pixels change, no detail is lost.

1   Select the Lasso (◠), Polygonal Lasso (◺), Magnetic Lasso (◿), Elliptical Marquee (○), or Magic Wand tool (◣).

2   In the Options bar, notice that Anti-alias is selected by default. It is best to keep this on for most selections.

Blur the edges of a selection by feathering

You can smooth the hard edges of a selection by feathering. Feathering builds a transition between the selection and surrounding pixels. This blurring can cause some loss of detail at the edge of the selection.

You can create a feathered selection with the Elliptical Marquee, Rectangular Marquee, Lasso, Polygonal Lasso, or Magnetic Lasso tool. You can also add feathering to an existing selection by using the Select menu.

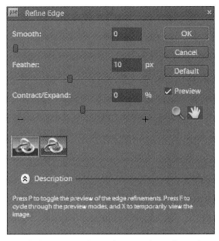

Add feathering to a selection by using the Refine Edge Command

Define a feathered edge for an existing selection

1   If necessary, use the Selection Brush tool to reselect the boy in your photo.

2   Choose Select > Refine Edge. The Refine Edge dialog box allows you to preview your selection and control its appearance.

3   Type **10** in the Feather text field. This defines the width of the feathered edge.

4 Press the Custom Overlay Color button (■) to display your selection as a mask. When this is on, you can actually see what the edge of your selection looks like. Press OK.

When using Custom Overlay Color, the default color is red. In some photos, this may be difficult to see. Double-click the Custom Overlay Color button to and click the red color to display the color picker where you can choose a more appropriate color.

The Custom Color Overlay button allows you to view the edge of your selection.

After feathering is applied, you will not see much of a visual change in the selection appearance. A feathered edge is noticeable when merging the selected area with another part of the image or when placed in another image. You will see the effects of the feathered edge later in the exercise.

Saving selections

When you save a selection, you can edit that area of your photo at a later time. You can also work on other parts of the photo before loading the saved selection.

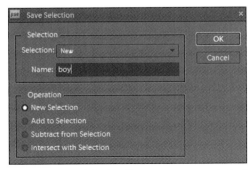

The Save Selection dialog box allows you to save your selection for later editing.

1   With your selection of the boy active, choose Select > Save Selection.

2   In the Save Selection dialog box, choose New from the Selection drop-down menu.

3   Type **boy** as the name for the selection in the Name text field, then press OK.

4   Choose Select > Deselect or use the keyboard shortcut Ctrl+D (Windows) or Command+D (Mac OS) to hide the selection.

     You have saved the selection of the boy, and next will add it to a new selection.

Modifying a new selection with a saved selection

New selections can be modified by replacing, adding to, or subtracting saved selections from them.

1   Use the Selection Brush tool (✐) to make a selection for the dog in your photo. Don't worry too much about where the dog appears behind the boy, just estimate where the dog's body would appear.

2   Choose Select > Load Selection.

3   In the Load Selection dialog box, choose the selection of the boy you made earlier from the Selection drop-down menu.

4   Select *Add to Selection* to add the current selection (of the dog) to the saved selection (of the boy).

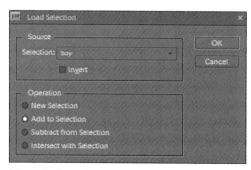

The Load Selection dialog box allows you to add to, subtract from, or intersect with a new selection.

You should see a selection of both the boy and his dog, which you'll now invert to select the background.

5   Press OK to load the selection.

Inverting a selection

When you invert a selection, Photoshop Elements changes the unselected areas into selected areas, and protects the pixels you previously selected.

1   With the boy and dog selected, choose Select > Inverse.

This command is commonly used to select an object that appears against a solid-colored area. You can select the solid color using the selection tool of your choice, and then choose Select > Inverse.

Invert a selection using the Select > Inverse command.

You'll now convert the background of your photo to black and white, to add emphasis to the boy and his dog.

Converting to Black and White

When you use the Convert to Black and White command, you can compare and choose from image styles that reflect the content of your image, and then use the intensity sliders to adjust the conversion.

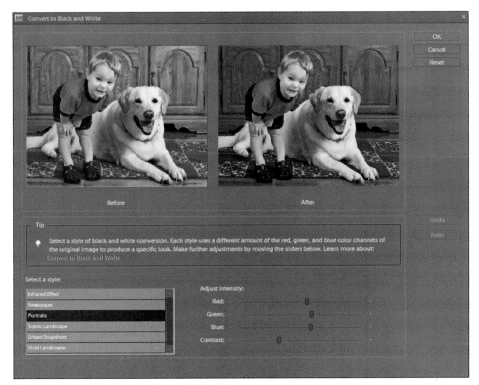

Control conversion in the Convert to Black and White dialog box.

1   Confirm that the background of your photo is selected. If you do not select an area or layer, the entire image is converted.

2   Choose Enhance > Convert to Black and White.

3   Select the *Portraits* style option, as it reflects the content of your image.

4   Experiment by dragging the Adjustment Intensity sliders to adjust red, green, blue, or contrast in the black and white background.

These sliders won't colorize your image; instead, they include more or less information from the original color channels in the new black and white image.

5   To convert the background to black and white, press OK.

6   Choose File > Save. Keep the file open as you will use it in the next exercise.

Adding color to areas of an image

You can colorize an entire image, or select areas to colorize with different colors.

 If the image you are coloring is in grayscale mode, convert it into RGB by choosing Image > Mode > RGB Color in the Editor.

Colorize areas of a photo with the Colorize *option.*

1 In the Editor, confirm that the background of your image is still selected.

2 Choose Enhance > Adjust Color > Adjust Hue/Saturation.

3 Select *Colorize*. If the foreground color isn't black or white, Photoshop Elements converts the image into the hue of the current foreground color. The lightness value of each pixel does not change.

4 Use the Hue slider to select a new color. Use the Saturation slider to experiment with the saturation amount. Press OK.

Saving and exporting images

About saving images and file formats

When you've finished adjusting an image in the Editor, you'll need to save it, or you'll lose your changes. To preserve all image data, you should save regular images in Photoshop (PSD) format. Multiple-page creations are always saved in Photo Project (PSE) format. These formats don't compress your image data.

Although your digital camera may save photos in JPEG format, it's better to use the PSD format rather than resave a photo in JPEG format. Every time you save in JPEG format, the image data is compressed, causing some data to be lost. The only disadvantage of saving in PSD format is that the file size increases significantly because the file is not compressed.

With Photoshop Elements, you can save images in several file formats, depending on how you plan to use them. See the sidebar on page 150 for more information.

1   Choose File > Save As.

2   Change options like the filename or format, set any of the following file-saving options, then press Save.

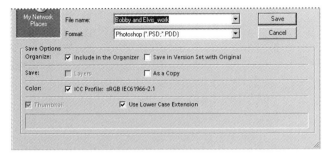

Explore the options available in the Save As dialog box.

- *File name* defines the filename of the saved image.

- *Format* defines the file format of the saved image.

- *Include in the Elements Organizer* includes the saved file in your catalog so that it displays in the Photo Browser. This option is unavailable for file formats that are supported in the Editor but are not supported in the Organizer.

- *Save in Version Set with Original* saves the file, then adds it to a version set in the Photo Browser to keep the different versions of the image organized, but only if *Include in the Organizer* is selected.

- *Layers* preserves all layers in the image. In some formats, all layers are flattened. To preserve layers, select another format.

- *As a Copy* saves a copy of the file while keeping the current file open. The copy is saved to the folder containing the currently open file.

- *ICC Profile* embeds a color profile in the image for various formats.

- *Thumbnail* saves thumbnail data for the file. This option is available when the *Ask When Saving* option for Image Previews is set in the Preferences dialog box.

- *Use Lower Case Extensions* writes the file extension in lowercase.

File formats for saving

Photoshop Elements can save images in the following file formats:

BMP: A standard Windows image format.

CompuServe GIF (Graphics Interchange Format): Commonly used to display graphics and small animations in web pages. GIF is a compressed format designed to minimize file size and transfer time.

JPEG (Joint Photographic Experts Group): Used to save photographs, JPEG format retains all color information in an image but compresses the file size by selectively discarding data.

JPCX: A bitmap format widely supported on a variety of platforms.

PSD (Photoshop): The standard Photoshop Elements format for images. You should generally use this format for edited images to save your work in a single-page file.

PSE (Photo Project Format): The standard Photoshop Elements format for multiple-page creations. You should generally use this format for photo projects to save your work in a multiple-page file.

Photoshop PDF (Portable Document Format): A cross-platform and cross-application file format. PDF files accurately display and preserve fonts, page layouts, and both vector and bitmap graphics.

Photoshop EPS (Encapsulated PostScript): Used to share Photoshop files with many illustration and page-layout programs.

PICT: Used with Mac OS graphics and page-layout applications to transfer images between applications. PICT is especially effective at compressing images with large areas of solid color.

Pixar: Used for exchanging files with Pixar image computers.

PNG (Portable Network Graphics): Used for lossless compression and for displaying images on the Web.

Photoshop Raw: Used for transferring images between applications and computer platforms when other formats don't work.

Scitex CT: Used in the prepress industry.

TGA (Targa): Designed for systems using the Truevision video board. When saving an RGB image in this format, you can choose a pixel depth of 16, 24, or 32 bits per pixel and RLE compression.

TIFF (Tagged-Image File Format): A flexible bitmap image format supported by most paint, image-editing, and page-layout applications. Most desktop scanners can produce TIFF files.

In addition, Photoshop Elements can open files in several other older formats: PS 2.0, Pixel Paint, Alias Pix, IFF format, Portable Bit Map, SGI RGB, Soft Image, Wavefront RLA, and ElectricImage.

Self study

1   Try converting the image to Indexed Color mode and observe any color shifts.

2   Experiment with different Brightness/Contrast values to bring out more detail in the photo.

3   Use the Magnetic Lasso selection tool to select the dog in the image.

4   Convert the entire image to black and white and add color to the boy's clothes selectively.

5   Try saving the photo file in different file formats, and note the different results.

Review

Questions

1   What is the advantage of adjusting color in the Full Edit workspace?

2   What does the Sponge tool do?

3   Why are selections important in the color adjustment process?

Answers

1   Full Edit contains lighting and color-correction commands, as well as tools for fixing image defects, making selections, adding text, and painting on your images.

2   The Sponge tool selectively saturates and desaturates color in an image.

3   Selections isolate pixel areas for more specific editing of color.

What you'll learn in this lesson:

- Share images and order prints online
- Create Photo Mail and e-mail attachments
- Order photo books, and other products from online providers
- Print photos, contact sheets, and picture packages with your home printer

Sharing Your Photos

Photoshop Elements makes it easy for you to share and print your images You can post photos online, or e-mail them to family and friends, have photos professionally printed by online providers, or print them at your convenience on your home printer.

Starting up

Within the Photoshop Elements Organizer: You will work with several files from the Lessons folder in this lesson. Make sure that you have copied the Lessons folder from the supplied DVD to your hard drive. In order to access these files in the Organizer, you need to import them. See "Adding files and folders to the Organizer" on page 11.

Within the Photoshop Elements Editor: The Photoshop Elements Editor defaults to the last panel layout that you used. Before starting, make sure your tools and panels are consistent with the examples presented in these lessons by resetting the panel locations. Do this by choosing Window > Reset Panels or by pressing the Reset panels button (⟳) in the Options bar.

See Lesson 6 in action!

Use the accompanying video to gain a better understanding of how to use some of the features shown in this lesson. The video tutorial for this lesson can be found on the included DVD.

Welcome screen

If you're currently viewing the welcome screen, press the Organize button (⚏) to enter the Organizer workspace.

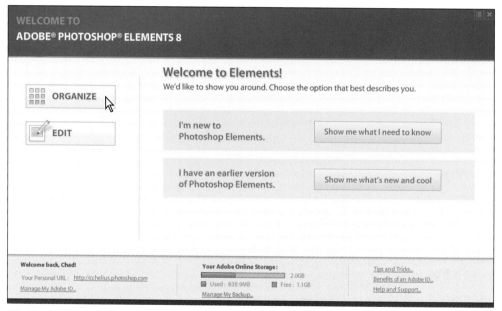

The Photoshop Elements welcome screen.

Sharing photos

After you've imported, organized, and edited photos on your desktop, you'll want to share them with family and friends. With Photoshop Elements, you can allow others to view your photos through an interactive online album, or through e-mail that you send. You can also print photos on your own printer, order professionally printed photos, or put your photos on a CD or DVD. In this exercise, you'll learn how to share photos from the Organizer.

In the Editor, you can also share photos that you've edited or have open in the Project Bin.

Creating an online album

The Online Album Wizard provides step-by-step guidance for adding, deleting, and arranging photos, choosing a layout template, and sharing your files. Later in this exercise, you will be prompted to sign in with your Adobe ID. If you wish, you can sign in now by pressing the Sign In option at the top of the workspace. If you do not have an Adobe ID, press the Join Now button and create one in order to proceed with the exercise.

The Online Album Wizard lets you arrange photos. It does not allow you to edit them.

1   You'll be sharing photos from the Photos to Share folder within the Lessons folder. These images were already imported into the Organizer when you added the Lessons folder in Lesson 1, see "Adding files and folders to the Organizer," if you skipped this step. Type **share** into the search text field at the upper-left of the Organizer workspace to isolate the sixteen images for this lesson.

2   In the Organizer, click to select 10 photos that you'd like to include in your online album.

3   Click the Share tab to select the way you want to share photos.

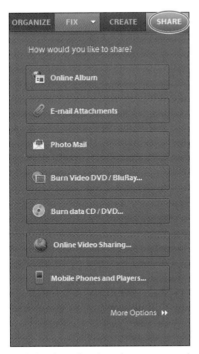

Click the Share tab to choose how you want to share photos.

4   Press Online Album to open the Online Album Wizard in the Organizer and click the *Create New Album* radio button.

5   Under Share To, specify one of the following sharing options for your online album:

- *Photoshop.com* (U.S. only) allows you to share your albums online.

- *Export to CD/DVD* allows you to burn your online album files onto a disc for full-screen playback on a computer.

- *Export to FTP* allows you to upload the files to a web server.

- *Export to Hard Disk* allows you to save the files locally on your hard drive.

6   Choose Photoshop.com and press Next.

7   If you work with album categories, choose the appropriate category from the drop-down menu.

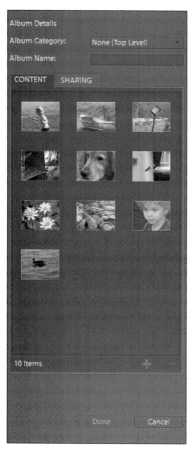

Use the Online Album Wizard to customize your online album.

8   Type **Summertime** in the Album Name text field.

9   Select two more photos in the Organizer and then press the Add Selected Items button (+). You can also drag photos from the Organizer into the Items area.

10   Select one of the photos you just added to the Items area and then press the Remove Selected Items button (–) to remove it from the album.

11   Drag the thumbnails to arrange them in the order that you want them to appear. When you place your cursor over a thumbnail you will see a hand icon (🖑). As you drag the thumbnail, the other thumbnails shift slightly to indicate the placement of the one you are dragging.

12   Press the Sharing tab at the top of the panel. Photoshop Elements builds an album preview for you.

Photoshop Elements builds an album preview for you.

13   Double-click the different templates available at the top of the screen. As you choose different templates, a Slideshow Settings window appears in the main slideshow window. Enter a Title and Subtitle of your choice. Click the *Include Sound Effects* checkbox if you'd like sound effects played in your slideshow. You can also change the background color from this window.

14 When you are finished entering information into the Slideshow Settings window, you can press the Show/Hide Slideshow settings button (🖼) located above the template thumbnails to hide the window.

The Slideshow Settings window.

15 Click the *Share to Photoshop.com* checkbox. You will be prompted to sign in with your Adobe ID. If you do not have an Adobe ID, you will need to press the Create New Adobe ID button and create one in order to proceed with the exercise.

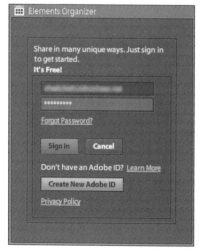

Sign in with your Adobe ID

Sharing options for online albums

The options in the Sharing tab allow you to control whether your new online album is public or private and also lets you control whether viewers are allowed to download photos, or order prints from your images. Photoshop Elements also lets you automatically send e-mail to people on your contact list to notify them that a new album has been shared on *Photoshop.com*.

Choose your sharing options in the Online Album Wizard.

In the Online Album Wizard, you can set the following sharing options:

- Clicking the *Display in My Gallery* checkbox makes your online album viewable by other *Photoshop.com* members.

- The Message text field allows you to add a descriptive message to your online album.

- Select the people who can view your gallery in the Send E-mail To box. You can also press the Edit Recipients in Contact Book button (📖) if you want to add another name and e-mail address to the list.

1   Under Allow Viewers to, select any of the following options:

   •   *Download Photos* allows recipients to download photos from your online album.

   •   *Order Photo Prints* allows recipients to order photos from printing services connected with Adobe.

2   Make sure that you've chosen an e-mail address or you've checked the *Display in My Gallery* checkbox, then press Done. A message appears, stating that the album is being uploaded.

Photoshop Elements uploads your album to Photoshop.com.

Stop sharing an online album

If at any time you'd like to stop sharing your online album, you can do so easily:

1   Click the Organize tab, and in the Albums panel, click once to highlight the album you are sharing.

2   Press the Stop Share button (⊕) to the right of the album name.

3   In the Stop Share Album dialog box, press OK.

You can stop sharing an album at any time.

Sharing photos by e-mail

Photoshop Elements makes it easy to share photos by e-mail. You can either attach individual photos to an e-mail using your e-mail client, or use Photo Mail to embed a photo in an e-mail.

Attaching a photo to an e-mail

This feature allows you to send photos as individual e-mail attachments. You can specify the size of the photo, and also convert images to JPEG format if necessary.

Before sending your files, it's best to do the following:

- **Set your e-mail preferences.** You can change the image size and compression settings so that photos download quickly without significant loss of detail. You can also choose to save files to a folder on your hard drive to facilitate manually attaching them to e-mail.

- **Set up your contact book.** You can address e-mail messages ahead of time, and keep track of those you've shared photos with. Keep in mind, however, that you can always address the e-mail from inside your e-mail client. You can choose Edit > Contact Book to add contacts.

After this setup is complete and you've created an e-mail, all that's left to do is to send it and share your photos with friends and family.

1   Select a photo in the Photo Browser, click the Share tab, and then press the E-mail Attachments button.

If this is the first time you're e-mailing a photo, Photoshop Elements asks you to confirm the e-mail client you want to use.

2   To add more photos to the e-mail, select them in the Photo Browser, then press the Add button (✚). Please keep in mind that there is a limit on the size of e-mail attachments. This limit varies but is usually somewhere between 5-10 MB.

You can also remove items by selecting them in the list, and then pressing the Remove button (➖).

3   Select an option from the Maximum Photo Size drop-down menu, and use the Quality slider to adjust image clarity. Images that are smaller in physical size and lower in quality will have a smaller file size. Since your Internet Service Provider may have a limit on the size of file attachments in e-mail, these are very important options to pay attention to.

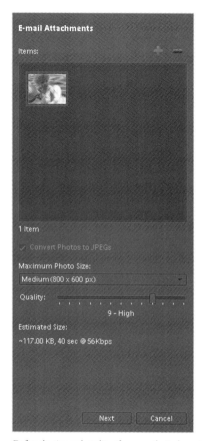

Define the size and quality of an e-mail attachment.

4   Press Next. Enter a descriptive or personalized message in the Message text field.

5   Select e-mail recipients (from your contacts) by clicking names in the Select Recipients section.

You can also choose not to select any recipients at this time, and instead enter the addresses when the e-mail message appears.

Add a message to your e-mail and send it to your selected recipients.

7 Press Next. The e-mail application specified in the Sharing Preferences opens. If Photoshop Elements doesn't support your preferred e-mail client, use it instead to attach the file manually. When you are finished with the e-mail, return to Photoshop Elements.

If you are using the Adobe E-mail service as your e-mail client, before you can send an e-mail you will be asked to verify the e-mail address you want to use. This verification process needs to be completed only once.

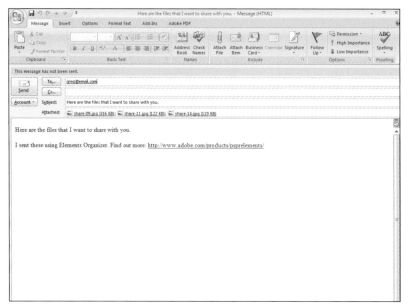

Your e-mail is created with attachments and message included.

Sending a photo using Photo Mail

Photo Mail provides you with a wizard that helps you to embed your photos in the body of an e-mail message, complete with your choice of custom layouts, called stationery. You can choose from a variety of stationery themes, backgrounds, frames, and borders, among other options.

After you select your stationery, Photoshop Elements automatically converts all images to the JPEG format and generates the e-mail.

You can send Photo Mail through Microsoft Outlook, Outlook Express, or Adobe E-mail Service.

To send a photo using Photo Mail, follow these steps:

1   Select a photo in the Photo Browser, press Share, then press Photo Mail.

2   If this is the first time you're e-mailing a photo, confirm your choice of e-mail client and then press Next.

3   Click the *Include Caption* checkbox if you'd like to include any captions that you've added to your photos in the final email. You can also drag the image thumbnails to change the order that the photos appear in the final email. Press Next.

4   Type a message in the Message text field that you'd like to appear in the sent e-mail and then select recipients for the e-mail by doing one of the following:

   •   Select names (from your contacts) in the Select Recipients list.

   •   Alternatively, add recipients to your contact book by selecting the *Edit Recipients In Contact Book* option, and press OK. The recipient appears in the Select Recipients list. Click the Next button.

5   In the Stationery & Layouts Wizard, choose a stationery style. There are multiple categories from which to choose. Then press Next Step, and fine-tune the layout by experimenting with Photo Size, Layout, Text, Borders, and the Padding Color and Border Color. In order for changes to the Padding Width and Border Width to preview, you must press the Apply Borders button.

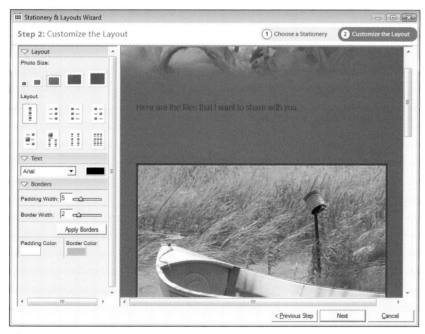

Choose a stationery to customize your Photo Mail layout.

6 Press Next. Photoshop Elements opens your default e-mail application, and allows you to send Photo Mail. When you are finished with the e-mail, return to Photoshop Elements.

Your Photo Mail is created with the stationery you specified.

Setting up Adobe E-mail Service

If you use a web-based e-mail client such as Google's Gmail or Yahoo Mail, you can also use the Adobe E-mail Service to send Photo Mail directly to recipients. The first time you use Adobe E-mail Service, you must register and provide e-mail verification.

You must have a valid e-mail address and an Internet connection to use Adobe E-mail Service.

To send Photo Mail using Adobe E-mail Service, follow these steps:

1   Choose Edit > Preferences > Sharing, and select Adobe E-mail Service from the E-mail Client drop-down menu.

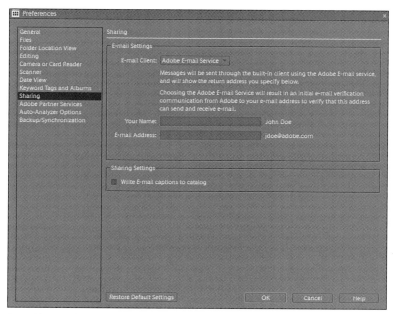

Use Adobe E-mail Service to send Photo Mail directly to recipients.

2   Type your name and e-mail address in the designated text fields. Press OK, if you are prompted to do so.

3   The first time you use Adobe E-mail Service, a verification e-mail is sent to the address you just specified. In the body of the e-mail, there is a Sender Verification code. When you are prompted to enter the code, copy and paste it from the e-mail into the dialog box, and then press OK.

  4 As soon as your e-mail is verified, press OK.

Now, whenever you're connected to the Internet, you can send e-mail directly from Photoshop Elements.

Using the Quick Share panel

The Quick Share panel may be the simplest way to e-mail photos to recipients. After you create a list of recipients, you can just drag photos onto the list in the Quick Share panel. This saves you the time and effort of entering contact information each time you want to share photos.

Sharing photos using online services

Online services let you order prints, photo books, and other photo products on the Internet. There is no charge to join a service, but you need a valid e-mail address to receive correspondence, and a credit card number to place an order.

The online services available to you depend on your location. For example, online ordering services differ between North America and Asia. The options available change dynamically to show what's available in your area, and updates when new services become available. As of this writing, Kodak and Shutterfly are the online print partners that you can order prints from directly within Photoshop Elements.

 Users of Photoshop Elements in the United Sates can share photos with their Photoshop.com *account. At this time,* Photoshop.com *membership is only available in the United States.*

Ordering prints

Photoshop Elements allows you to order professionally printed photos and have them mailed to designated recipients. You should, however, make any desired changes to photos before ordering prints, as the online services do not allow you to enhance photos.

  1 Make sure that you are in the Create tab, and, in the Photo Browser, select the photos you want to order.

2 Choose File > Order Prints and choose the service you'd like to use to order your prints, or press the Photo Prints button in the Create panel and choose your desired service from the Create panel. Photoshop Elements 8 offers the choice between Shutterfly and Kodak. Both of these services offer free accounts, but you must have an existing account to use these services from within Photoshop Elements 8.

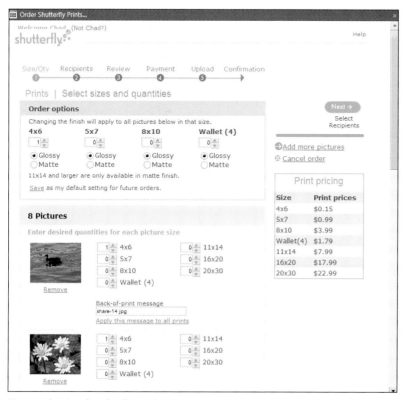

You can order prints through online services.

 If this service is available in your area, you can also choose Photo Prints from the Create tab. If you have not signed up for Shutterfly or Kodak EasyShare, you will have to complete the form before you continue. If you choose not to join at this time, close the Order Prints window and proceed to the next exercise.

3   Specify the size and number of each photo you want to order, and then click Next.

4   Select where to send the prints, then press Next.

5   Confirm your order details, and add more recipients if desired. Press Next.

6   Choose a shipping method and coupon information (if applicable), and then press Next.

7   Enter your credit card information. Then press Place Order to order your prints.

Ordering a printed photo book

With Photoshop Elements, you can order a professionally printed photo book and have it delivered to designated recipients or you can print a photo book on the printer attached to your computer. Your photo book can contain various numbers of photos on each page of the photo book. You should, however, make any desired changes to photos before ordering a photo book, as some online services do not allow you to enhance photos.

1   In the Photo Browser, select the photos you want to use. Photo projects (in PSE format) can also be used to order photo books.

2   In the Create tab, choose Photo Book and choose a service from the available options. In this example, the Kodak Gallery was chosen. If you select a Shutterfly option, your photos are uploaded to the Shutterfly web site and the photobook creation process occurs using the Shutterfly web site. Because the Kodak Gallery was chosen, you are redirected to the Elements Editor and the photobook layout process occurs there.

Choose Photo Book from the Create tab.

3 Rearrange the order of photos in the Project Bin to choose a title page photo. By default, the first photo in the Project Bin is always the title page photo. Press Next.

Kodak printed photo books have a cover that is designed to show a single centered photo on the title page. For best results, make sure your title page (or first page) has a single centered photo.

4 Choose a layout option (either *Random Photo Layout* or *Choose Photo Layout*).

5 Choose a theme. As you click on the thumbnail for each theme, a larger window appears giving you a better view of what the theme looks like.

6 Specify additional options:

   • *Auto-Fill With Project Bin Photos* fills the photo book with photos from your Project Bin.

   • *Include Captions* inserts captions with your photos.

   • *Number of Pages* determines how many pages your photo book will have. The minimum is 20 pages and the maximum is 80.

7 Press Create to view your photo book.

Customize your photo book with various layout options.

8 Customize your photo book by doing any of the following:

   • To resize or rotate a photo, drag a corner of the bounding box.

   • To add or remove photos, press the Add a Page or Delete a Page buttons. You can also right–click (Windows) or Ctrl+click (Mac OS) to add or remove pages.

   • Click Show Print Guides to see how the photo book will be printed.

   • Select a background for each spread in the Content panel and click apply to apply the background to the spread.

9 Right-click a photo and choose Position photo in Frame. Drag the slider above the photo to scale the image within the frame and/or drag the corner handles while holding down the shift key to manually scale the image within the frame. Press the commit button (✓) when you are finished.

Resizing the photo within the frame.

10 Press Order. Your photo book is converted to a PDF file. The Photo Book is prepared for ordering. Depending on the speed of your computer, this process could take several minutes.

11 When the Adobe Photoshop Services browser opens, log in to your Kodak account using your username and password by clicking the Sign In link. If you do not have a username and password, you can create one from this screen.

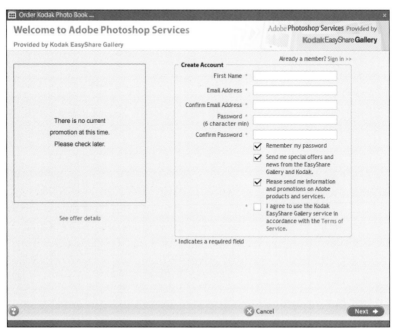

Order photo books from the Adobe Photoshop Services browser.

If you are already a member, click the Sign In link in the upper-right corner of the dialog box, type your e-mail address and password, and press Next.

11 Specify the cover material and quantity, and then press Next.

12 Type in your location information, and then press Next.

13 Confirm your order details, and add more recipients if desired. Press Next.

14 Choose a shipping method and coupon information (if applicable), and then press Next.

15 Type in your credit card information. Press Place Order to order your photo book.

 When getting photo projects ready for photo books, think about how the images will appear in printed format. Also, consider how books are structured when deciding which photos should go on each page. And for best results, you should always preview your projects before ordering books to make sure photos are optimally placed, cropped, and framed.

Printing photos

Photoshop Elements enables you to print your photos in many different, and convenient, ways. As you've seen, you can have your photos professionally printed by online providers, or you can print your photos at your convenience with your home printer. You can print individual photos, thumbnails of each photo (called a contact sheet), or a page of one or more photos printed at various sizes (called a picture package). If you are so inclined, you can even flip the image to print T-shirt transfers.

Additionally, you can print the projects you've created in Photoshop Elements, like photo albums, cards, and calendars. Some of these projects can even be ordered from online print services. Let's first take a look at the Print Photos interface.

Printing photos in the Organizer

When you're in the Organizer, the Print Photos dialog box is divided into three sections: one shows a list of photos you're printing, another shows a print preview, and the third allows you to set the options for your print job. When you change a print option, Photoshop Elements automatically updates the preview. If you're printing multiple pages of photos, the pages appear as thumbnails in the dialog box. You can use the Navigation buttons to move back and forth between these pages.

1 Select photos in the Photo Browser.

2 Choose File > Print or press the Photo Print button in the Create tab of the Task Pane, then press the Print with Local Printer button.

3   Choose a printer from the Select Printer drop-down menu. You can also press the Show Printer Preferences button (▤) to set your print options.

4   Choose Individual Prints from the Select Type of Print drop-down menu.

5   Choose a size from the Select Print Size drop-down menu.

If you choose a print size small enough to fit more than one image on a single page, you can also choose One Photo Per Page.

6   Type a number in the Print x copies of each image section.

7   Select *Crop To Fit* if you want to fit the individual image to your desired print layout. The image is scaled and cropped to reflect the aspect ratio of the print layout. Otherwise you can click on each image in the layout and use the Rotate buttons and the Scale slider at the bottom of the layout to adjust how each image appears.

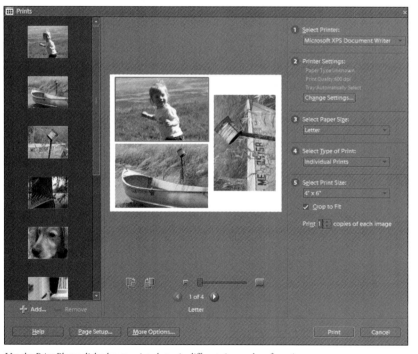

Use the Print Photos dialog box to print photos in different sizes and configurations.

8   Click More Options to choose from, or change, these additional settings:

- *Iron-on Transfer (inverts image)* is used for printing T-shirt transfers.

- *Trim Guidelines* prints guidelines on all edges of the photo to facilitate trimming.

- *Border* allows you to define the border's thickness by entering a value in the Border text field.

- *Max Print Resolution* sets the resolution, by default, to 220 ppi to speed up printing.

- In the Color Management section, you can choose a printer profile from the Print Space drop-down menu. If you have an ICC profile for your printer and paper combination, you can choose it from the menu. See "About color management" on the next page.

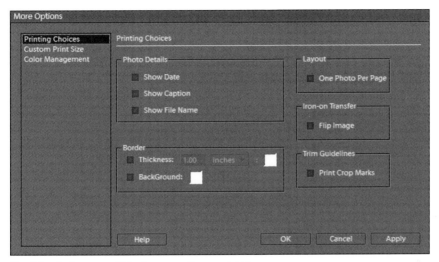

Press More Options to set additional parameters for your print job.

9   Press OK.

About color management

Color management helps you to achieve consistent color among digital cameras, scanners, computer monitors, and printers. Each of these devices reproduces a different range of colors, called a *color gamut*. As you move an image from your digital camera to your monitor, and finally to a printer, the image colors shift. This shift occurs because every device has a different color gamut and thus reproduces the colors differently.

Color management translates the image colors so that each device can reproduce them in the same way, and the colors you see on your monitor will be close to the colors in your printed image. All colors may not match exactly, because the printer may not reproduce the same range of colors as the monitor.

Managing color with profiles

Profiles describe the color spaces of the input device and the document. Using the profiles' descriptions, the color management system identifies the document's actual colors. The monitor's profile tells the color management system how to translate the numeric values into the monitor's color space. Using the output device's profile, the color management system translates the document's numeric values into the color values of the output device, so the actual colors are printed.

Profiling devices

For color management to work, you must profile your devices or use an ICC profile created by the device's manufacturer.

Capture devices

Profiling can be useful for capture devices such as digital cameras or scanners. You may want to profile a scanner or digital camera, if you want to accurately reproduce the colors in scanned transparencies or digital captures, and reduce your color correction workload in Photoshop Elements.

Monitors

Calibrating and profiling your monitor is important. If you are using a laptop or other LCD monitor, you can use the profile provided by the manufacturer. If you own a colorimeter and corresponding software to create profiles, you can use those profiles in Photoshop Elements. Keep in mind that in order for monitor profiling to work accurately, the lighting environment where you use your monitor must stay consistent.

Printers

Profiling your inkjet printer will generally give you better results, although you can make excellent prints without a printer profile by using the controls in your printer driver. Many printer manufacturers provide ICC printer profiles on their web sites. You need a separate profile for each printer, ink, and type of paper. You can also have profiles made for your favorite combination of ink and paper.

When you work on a photo and save it, Photoshop Elements can embed (tag) an ICC profile that reflects the colors on your computer monitor or the device that produced it. Embedding profiles with an image makes its color portable, so that different devices can translate its color values. For example, if you send the photo to your inkjet printer, the color management system reads the embedded profile and translates the color data using the printer's profile. Your printer can then use the translated color data to accurately translate its color into the selected media.

Adding photos using the Print Photos dialog box

You can add photos to a print job from within the Print Photos dialog box.

1   In the Print Photos dialog box, press the Add button (✚).

2   In the Add Photos dialog box, choose one of the following:

  • *Media Currently in Browser* shows photos currently visible in the Photo Browser.

  • *Entire Catalog* shows all photos in your catalog.

  • *Album* shows photos from a specific album. Choose an album from the drop-down menu.

  • *Keyword Tag* shows photos with a specific tag. Choose a tag from the drop-down menu.

  • *Only Show Media with Ratings* shows only those photos marked with the Favorites tag.

  • *Also Show Hidden Media* shows only those photos marked with the Hidden tag.

3   Click to select one or more photos. You can also click *Select All*, then press Add Selected Photos.

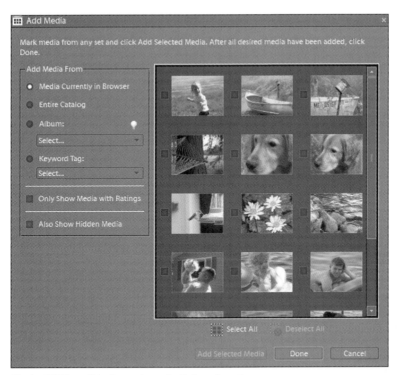

Use the Add Photos dialog box to view and add photos from other sources.

4   Press Done to close the Add Media window.

5   Press Print or Cancel.

Printing a contact sheet

With a contact sheet, you can conveniently preview photos by displaying a series of thumbnail images on one page.

1   In the Photo Browser, click to select several photos, and choose File > Print, or click the Print Photos button in the Create tab, then press the Print with Local Printer button.

2   Choose a printer from the Select Printer drop-down menu. You can also press the Change Settings button to set your print options, and choose a page size from the Paper Size drop-down menu.

3   From the Select Type of Print drop-down menu, choose Contact Sheet. All photos listed on the left side of the dialog box are automatically shown in preview.

4   To remove a photo, select it on the left side and press the Remove button (–).

5   For Columns, specify the number of columns (between 1 and 9) in the layout. The image size and number of rows adjust, based on your choice. If the images don't fit on a single page, more pages are added to accommodate them.

6   If multiple pages are created, use the Navigation buttons below the layout preview to move through the pages.

7   To adjust the rotation and cropping of the thumbnail images, use the Rotation buttons and Scaling slider below the layout preview.

8 To add text below each thumbnail, click the *Show Print Options* checkbox and select any of the following:

- *Date* includes the date embedded in the image.

- *Caption* includes the caption text embedded in the file's metadata.

- *Filename* includes the image's filename.

- *Page Numbers* prints page numbers at the bottom of each page, if multiple pages are required.

To print using color management, click More Options, and choose a profile from the Print Space menu. See "About color management" on page 176.

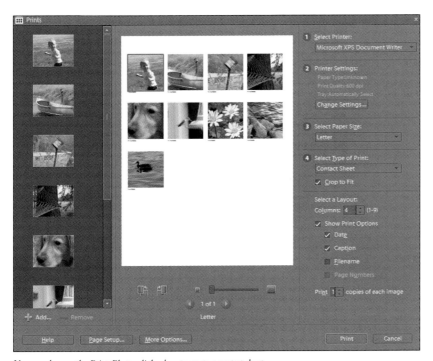

You can also use the Print Photos dialog box to create a contact sheet.

8 Press Print to print your contact sheet, or press Cancel to exit the dialog box without printing.

Printing a picture package

The Picture Package feature enables you to place multiple copies of your photos on a single page, in the same way that commercial portrait studios do. Photoshop Elements offers you a number of size and placement options to customize your picture package.

1   In the Photo Browser, click to select several photos, and choose File > Print, or click the Print Photos button in the Create tab, then press the Print with Local Printer button.

2   Choose a printer from the Select Printer drop-down menu. You can also press the Change Settings button to set your print options, and choose a page size from the Paper Size drop-down menu.

3   From the Select Type of Print drop-down menu, choose Picture Package. The first photo listed on the left side of the dialog box is automatically previewed.

4   Choose a layout from the Select a Layout drop-down menu.

5   Choose a border from the Select a Frame drop-down menu. One border will be used for the entire picture package.

6   Click the *Fill Page With First Photo* checkbox to print images on separate pages. When you choose this option, you can use the Navigation buttons below the preview to view each page.

7   Click the *Crop To Fit* checkbox to crop photos so that they fit the layout size or use the Rotate buttons and Scale slider at the bottom of the Layout.

8   You also have the option to replace a photo in the layout by dragging an image from the list on the left over an image in the layout preview, and then releasing the mouse button.

You can click the Add button and use the Add Photos dialog box to add photos to your picture package.

9   To print using color management, click More Options and choose a profile from the Print Space drop-down menu. See "About color management" on page 176.

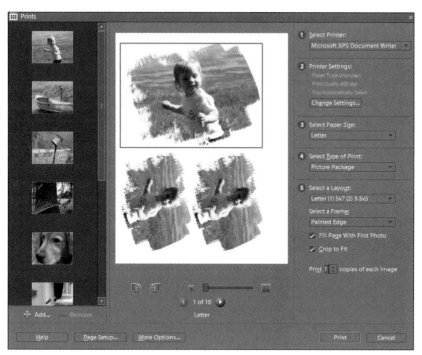

Print packages are also created from the Print Photos dialog box.

10   Press Print to print your picture package or press Cancel to exit the window without printing.

Setting page and printer options

If, when printing, you're not getting the desired results, try changing your page and printer options.

1   Choose File > Print and click on the Page Setup button at the bottom of the window.

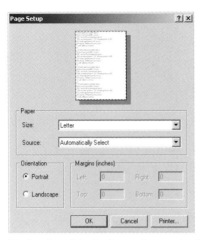

The Page Setup dialog box lets you change settings for printing.

2   When the Page Setup dialog box opens, press the Printer button and select a printer from the Name drop-down menu. To specify layout and paper options, press the Properties button. You can also press the Advanced button in the printer driver dialog box (if available) to set other printer options. Then press OK to close the dialog boxes.

The availability of the Advanced button and printer options depend on your printer, print drivers, and version of Windows.

3   Back in the Page Setup dialog box, specify paper size, orientation, and other desired options, and then press OK.

You may also want to change the measurement setting that defines the sizes you can choose from when you print or crop a photo.

Specifying measurement units for printing

1   In the Photo Browser, choose Edit > Preferences > General.

2   From the Print Sizes drop-down menu, choose either Inches or Centimeters/ Millimeters, and then press OK.

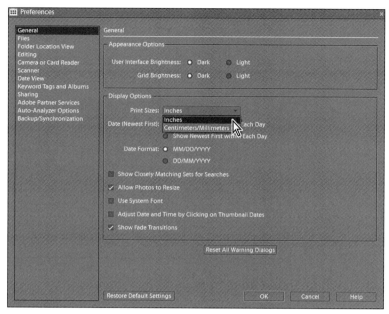

Changing your measurement units helps to define sizes for printing and cropping.

Backing up and synchronizing files

Backing up files is essential for protecting your valuable photo files. If your computer fails, files that have been backed up are safely stored on the destination volume of your choice, and can be restored into Photoshop Elements.

Backing up and synchronizing files to *Photoshop.com*

Photoshop Elements enables you to open a *Photoshop.com* membership account and back up your photos to *Photoshop.com* servers.

Currently, Photoshop.com *services are only available to Photoshop Elements users in the United States.*

Once you enable backups, Photoshop Elements uploads the albums you specify to *Photoshop.com*. In Photoshop Elements 8, you can backup individual Albums or all photos not contained in an Album.

Photoshop Elements also keeps the files on your computer synchronized with the files on *Photoshop.com*. Your albums on *Photoshop.com* are updated whenever you add, delete, or edit photos.

About synchronized albums on *Photoshop.com*

It is possible to add, delete, or edit photos in *Photoshop.com* after backing up your albums. But you should remember that Photoshop Elements synchronizes albums backed up to *Photoshop.com* with the respective albums on your computer. Therefore, if you edit a photo on *Photoshop.com*, the corresponding photo on your computer is updated with those edits. By the same token, if you edit to a photo on your computer, the backed-up photo on *Photoshop.com* is updated with those edits.

Photoshop Elements also synchronizes your albums when you add tags to files, as well as add or delete photos.

If you delete a photo from an album on your computer without deleting it from the catalog, the photo remains in your Photoshop.com *account.*

Starting backup or synchronization

1   Make sure that:

    •   You've registered for a *Photoshop.com* membership.

    •   Your computer is connected to the Internet.

    •   You've imported all the files you want to backup or synchronize into albums.

2   Choose Edit > Preferences > Backup/Synchronization.

3   In the Backup/Synchronization Preferences dialog box, choose *Backup/Sync Is On*.

4   Choose the Backup/Synchronization options according to what you want the services to do when backing up.

5   Choose the album or albums that you want to back up or synchronize.

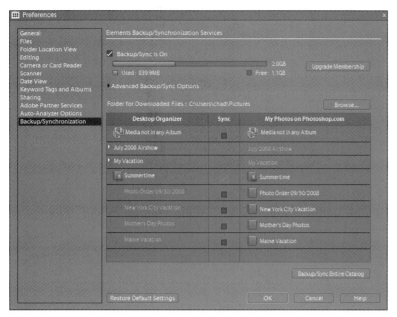

Set up Backup/Synchronization Services in the Preferences dialog box.

The progress bar in the upper-right corner of the dialog box shows how much space is used online while you backup or synchronize your albums.

 You can click Upgrade Membership to purchase more storage on Photoshop.com *if you reach the designated storage limit.*

6   Press OK. Photoshop Elements automatically backs up photos on your computer until you discontinue backup or synchronization.

 In Photoshop Elements 8, it's possible to keep multiple machines synchronized with the same albums. Simply create Albums with the same names on each installation of Photoshop Elements, then sync those albums to the same Photoshop.com account. Any changes made on one computer will be updated on the other.

Stopping and restarting backup or synchronization

Automatic backup and synchronization of files to *Photoshop.com* can be paused, restarted, or stopped at any time.

1   In the System Tray in Windows, right-click on the *Photoshop.com* Backup/ Synchronization Agent icon (▣). If Backup/Sync is off, the icon will not appear in the System Tray. The icon appears only when Backup/Sync is on.

2   Choose any of the following commands from the menu that appears:

- *Backup/Sync only when Idle* performs backup or synchronization when the computer is idle (that is, when you are not performing other tasks).

- *Backup/Sync Now* initiates a Synchronization immediately.

- *Pause Backup/Synchronization* stops automatic backup or synchronization temporarily.

- *Resume Backup/Synchronization* restarts your paused backup or synchronization.

- *Stop Backup/Synchronization* turns off backup or synchronization. When this command is chosen, it can only be restarted by selecting Backup/Sync Is On, inside the Backup/Synchronization Preferences.

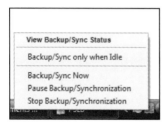

Pause or stop backup and synchronization in the Windows System Tray.

Exporting photos

You can also export photos to a folder on your hard drive for backup purposes. If you export a photo, the original remains protected in your catalog, and you can control the exported photo's size and file format.

1   In the Organizer, choose the photo or photos you want to export, and then choose File > Export As New File(s).

2   Specify any of the following options:

- File Type designates the file format for the exported photo. If you select *Use Original Format*, the file's current format is maintained.

- Size And Quality sets the pixel dimensions, file size, compression, and quality of the photo. This option is disabled if you choose Use Original Format as the file type.

You can't change the image size or quality when exporting using the Original Format file type.

- Location defines the folder in which the exported file is to be stored. You can click Browse to specify a different folder.

- Filenames allows you to set the name of the exported file. To use the current name of the photo, choose *Original Name*. To add a sequential number, select *Common Base Name* and type a name. If a filename already exists in the destination folder, Photoshop Elements modifies it to avoid overwriting an existing file.

Export photos as new files to back them up.

3   Press Export or Cancel.

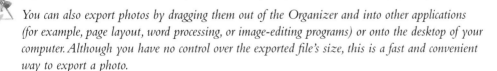
You can also export photos by dragging them out of the Organizer and into other applications (for example, page layout, word processing, or image-editing programs) or onto the desktop of your computer. Although you have no control over the exported file's size, this is a fast and convenient way to export a photo.

Now that you know how to share, print, and back up photos in Photoshop Elements, You can use this knowledge to your advantage in the rest of this book's lessons.

Self study

1 Create an online album of your favorite holiday photos and share it using *Photoshop.com*, allowing recipients to order prints for themselves.

2 Send a recent photo of yourself to family and friends using Photo Mail.

3 Order prints and have them shipped to your address without ever leaving your chair!

4 Experiment with the color management settings in the Print Space drop-down menu of the Print Photos dialog box.

5 Try to export photos by dragging them into your favorite graphics application, and build a layout that incorporates them.

Review

Questions

1 What is the difference between a contact sheet and a picture package?

2 What is the purpose of color management?

3 How many images can be on the title page of a photo book?

4 Can my cousins in London set up their own *Photoshop.com* account?

Answers

1 A contact sheet displays all your selected images in thumbnail view on a single page. A picture package enables you to place multiple copies of the same image on a single page.

2 Color management helps you to achieve consistent color among digital cameras, scanners, computer monitors, and printers.

3 Printed photo books have a cover that is designed to show a single centered photo on the title page.

4 No, at this time, *Photoshop.com* membership is only available in the United States.

What you'll learn in this lesson:

- How to place type inside your images

- How to make cartoon bubbles

- How to create a watermark for your photos

- How to use layer effects with type

Working with Type

With Photoshop Elements, you can quickly add text to your photos that can easily be modified. Whether you want to create your own postcards, greeting cards, or add silly captions, Photoshop Elements has the tools you need.

Starting up

Within the Photoshop Elements Organizer: You will work with several files from the Lessons folder in this lesson. Make sure that you have copied the Lessons folder from the supplied DVD to your hard drive. In order to access these files in the Organizer, you need to import them. See "Adding files and folders to the Organizer" on page 11.

Within the Photoshop Elements Editor: The Photoshop Elements Editor defaults to the last panel layout that you used. Before starting, make sure your tools and panels are consistent with the examples presented in these lessons by resetting the panels. Do this by choosing Window > Reset Panels or by pressing the Reset panels button (↻) in the Options bar.

See Lesson 7 in action!

Use the accompanying video to gain a better understanding of how to use some of the features shown in this lesson. The video tutorial for this lesson can be found on the included DVD.

Welcome screen

If you're currently viewing the welcome screen, press the Edit button (✎) to enter the Editor workspace.

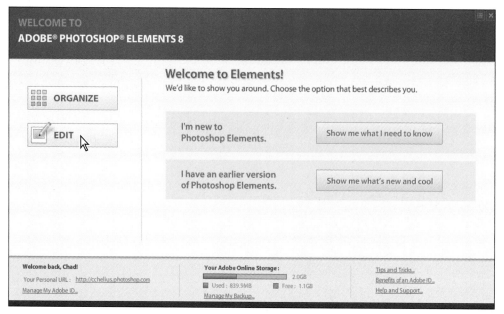

The Photoshop Elements welcome screen.

Placing text on a layer

In this lesson, you will discover how to add text to your images inside of Photoshop Elements by using the Type tool. This first exercise will show you how to insert text at the bottom of an image, to label a photo. Later on, you will change the font, size, and location of this text.

1   Press the Organizer button (▦) in the Menu bar of the Edit workspace. This reveals the Organizer.

2   Locate the file named *soccer.psd* and select it.

3   Press the arrow to the right of the Fix tab in the menu bar and choose Full Photo Edit from the drop-down menu or use the keyboard shortcut, Ctrl+I (Windows) Command+I (Mac OS).

    Now that you've opened an image, you will explore how to add a type layer. You don't actually have to build a new layer to insert type. When you click on an image with the Type tool, Photoshop Elements automatically creates a new type layer.

4   Choose the Horizontal Type tool (I) from the Toolbox. You can right-click the tool to expose the hidden tools underneath the Type tool to make sure you have the correct tool.

5   Click anywhere at the bottom center of this image. In your Layers panel, you should see a new layer named Layer 1 and you should also see a blinking cursor in the bottom middle of your screen.

This is what a new text layer looks like.

6   Type **Fall 2009 Youth Soccer**. Dont worry about the size or font. In the next section, you will learn how to format the text.

Formatting a text layer

Now that you know how to place text in an image, you will learn how to change its size and font.

1   Using the Horizontal Type tool (I), click and drag from the *r* in Soccer to the left, all the way to the *F* in Fall to select the text. If you have difficulty selecting with the click and drag method, you can simply double-click the thumbnail icon of the Type layer to select all the text.

2   Now that the text is selected, look at the Options bar at the top of the screen. The first option on the left is for changing the font. Use the drop-down menu to the right of the font name by clicking on the downward-facing arrow. You can choose any font you'd like, or if you'd like to follow along, choose Hobo Std.

Choosing a new font from the drop-down-menu.

3   Make sure your text is still selected, and use the drop-down menu to choose a size for your text. You can choose any size you'd like, or if you'd like to follow along, choose 72.

Choosing a size from the drop-down menu.

4   Even though the drop-down menu only goes up to 72, you are not limited to that size.
Highlight 72 in the Options bar and type **80**. You should automatically see the change on
your screen. If you need to reposition your type, choose the Move tool ( ) and move the
text so it is centered in the image.

Manually changing a font size.

Use your arrow keys!

Another way to change any number value in any field inside of Photoshop Elements is to just
click inside the field, either to the right or left, or even in the middle of a number, and then use
your up and down arrow keys on your keyboard to change the value. This way, you can visually
pick what size you want. Try it with your font name as well; you can preview how your text will
look in all the fonts you have loaded in your machine!

Editing a text layer

You should understand that since text is on its own layer, it is completely editable, even after
you have deselected the text and closed the document, as long as it is saved in the .psd format.
In this exercise, you will save the document, close it, and make some more changes to the text.

1   Save the file *soccer.psd* to your computer by choosing File > Save As. In the Save As
dialog box, type **soccer_work** in the Name text field and make sure the format is set to
Photoshop, and save it to the Lessons folder.

Now, you will reselect the text, change the color, and change its position.

2   Select the Horizontal Type tool ( ) from the Toolbox. Click on the type; you should now
see a blinking cursor in the type. Click three times in a row to select the sentence. Now
that the type is selected, you can change the color of the type.

3   In the Options bar at the top of the workspace, click on the drop-down menu next to the color block. You can choose any color you'd like, or if you'd like to follow along, choose black.

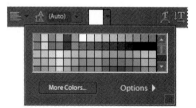

Choosing a different color.

Now that the text is a different color, you will change its position.

4   Select the Move tool (⊹). You may have to click it twice—once to deselect the text, and again to select the Move tool. Click and drag the text to the top of the screen and keep it centered.

5   Choose File > Save, then File > Close to close the file.

The finished file.

Making cartoon bubbles

If you ever wanted to add cartoon bubbles to your photos to show what people might be thinking at the time of a photo, or to add what you think would be a funny caption to a photo, you're about to learn how.

In Photoshop Elements, you can make any number of shapes, from rectangles to circles and lines. You can also use some of the pre-built custom shape tools inside of Photoshop Elements.

1   Press the Organizer button (⊞) at the top of the Edit workspace. This reveals the Organizer.

2   Locate the file named *fun.psd* and select it.

3   Press the arrow to the right of the Fix tab at the top of the workspace and choose Full Photo Edit from the drop-down menu or use the keyboard shortcut, Ctrl+I (Windows) Command+I (Mac OS).

    Next you will draw a cartoon bubble coming out of the little girl's mouth. Later, you'll add some text.

4   Press and hold the Rectangle Shape tool (▬) in the Toolbox to expose the hidden tools. Choose the Custom Shape tool (♥).

Navigating to the Custom Shape tool.

5 From the Shape drop-down menu in the Options bar, double-click the second shape, Talk1, from the default set of custom shapes.

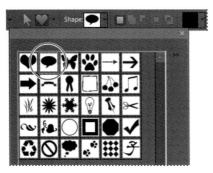

Navigating to the Talk1 icon.

If you would like to choose another bubble shape, press the menu options button (▶▶) in the Shape drop-down menu. The menu options list shows more shape categories to choose from.

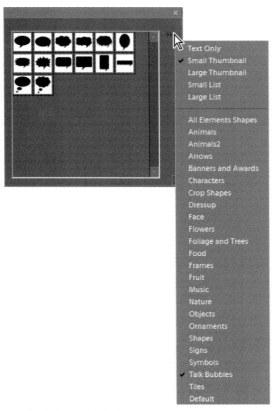

Showing all the Talk Bubbles shapes.

6 With the talk bubble shape selected, click-and-drag with the Shape tool to make a talk bubble to the right of the girl's face. Don't worry if it's not perfect; you can move it later. Notice that a new layer named Shape 1 is added to your Layers panel. Because this shape exists on its own layer, you can edit this bubble at any time, just like text.

Drawing the cartoon bubble.

7 Now that the bubble is drawn, you can change its color. Changing the color of shapes is just like changing the color of type. In the color block in the Options bar, choose white, or whatever color you think would look good. Remember that you have to also put type over this box, so make sure you pick a lighter color.

You can also change the color of a shape layer by double-clicking on the layer in the Layers panel.

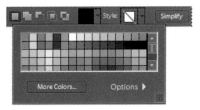

Changing the color of the talk bubble.

8 Now that the color is changed, you can change its size and position on the screen by selecting the Move tool. Select the Move tool (⊹) in the Toolbox, then reposition it where you want. To change the size, you can drag from a side, the top or bottom, or a corner point. In order to do this, make sure that *Show Bounding Box* is checked in the Options bar at the top of the workspace. If you resized the shape, you will need to click the green check mark below the bounding box to commit the change.

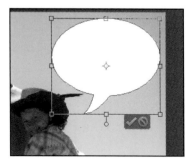

Changing the shape of the talk bubble.

Adding text over the cartoon bubble

In order to add text over the talk bubble, you will need to make a new text layer. This time, instead of just clicking on a layer, you will click-and-drag to make a text frame that you will type in.

1 Choose the Horizontal Type tool (I) from the Toolbox. Click-and-drag with the tool to define the text area.

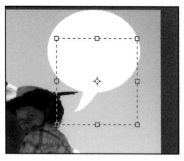

Defining a type frame.

2   Notice that Photoshop Elements remembers all the settings you had picked in the last exercise. The first thing you should do before you start typing is to make sure your text color is set to black inside the Options bar. This way, you can ensure that you will see the text as you are typing.

3   Type **This is Fun!**

4   Click four times with the Horizontal Type tool or press Ctrl+A (Windows) or Command+A (Mac OS), to make sure the type is selected, then change the font. If you'd like to follow along, choose Giddyup Std.

5   Now change the size so that it fits within the frame. You can pick 59 for the point size. (Depending on how big of a text frame you originally drew, you may have to pick a smaller size.)

6   Choose Center Text from the text alignment drop-down menu.

7   For the finishing touches, you should select the Move tool and position the text wherever you think it looks best over the bubble.

8   Choose File > Save. In the Save As dialog box, type **fun_working** and choose Photoshop from the Format drop-down menu. Press Save. Choose File > Close to close the file.

The finished cartoon bubble.

Adding effects to type

In this exercise, you will add the word *copyright* and use the Emboss effect to give it a watermark look. This is the same thing that professional photographic studios do to protect their images from illegal copying. Then you will drag that text layer over another image to apply the same text to that image.

There are many effects that you can apply to type inside the Effects panel, including filters, layer styles, and photo effects. Filters can be applied to type, but the type must be simplified first. This means that the type is no longer editable. Layer styles can be applied to type without simplifying the type first. Photo effects are applied to all the layers inside an Elements document. In this exercise, you will use a filter, then later on, you will use a layer style.

1   Choose File > Open. In the Open dialog box, navigate to the Lessons folder and double-click the *saddle1.psd* file. Imagine you worked for a production company and you needed to put that information over both this photo and another photo that were taken by that production company.

    You can also open the file using the Organizer, if you prefer.

2   Select the Horizontal Type tool ( ) from the Toolbox, and click in the middle bottom area of the image.

3   Type **Underwood Productions Copyright 2009**.

4   Click-and-drag to highlight all the text or press Ctrl+A (Windows) Command+A (Mac OS). Change the font to Myriad Pro by typing its name in the Font Name text field in the Options bar.

5   Change the type size to 28, by typing **28** in the Size text field.

6   Change the color of the type to white.

7   Select the Move tool ( ) to move the type to the bottom-right corner of the photo.

The text added to the image.

Now you will add a filter to make the type appear embossed into the photo.

8 Make sure the Filter button (🔵) is pressed in the Effects panel. By default, the only filters that appear are the artistic filters. Use the drop-down menu next to Artistic to reveal all the other filters that can be applied. Choose Show All to see all the filters you can use.

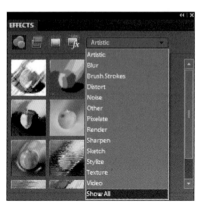

Showing all the filters.

9 Scroll down the list of filters to find Emboss. If you hover your cursor over a filter for a second, a tool-tip appears with the name of the filter. You can also select Show Names from the Effects panel menu to make identifying the filters easier.

10 Double-click Emboss to apply it.

11 A dialog box opens, warning you that the Type layer must be simplified in order to proceed. Press OK. This means that the type attributes will no longer be editable, but the filter will be applied to the Type layer.

A warning dialog box appears when you simplify the type.

12 The Emboss dialog box opens with the emboss settings. Leave the settings at their defaults and press OK. The text now has an embossed look.

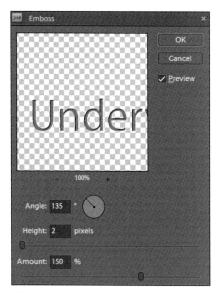

The Emboss dialog box. *The finished layer with the Emboss filter applied.*

Adding text to multiple images

Now that this image has the correct copyright information on a layer by itself, you can apply this to other images that you also want to contain this layer. In this exercise, you will apply this simplified type layer to another image.

1 Choose File > Open. In the Open dialog box, navigate to the Lessons folder and double-click the *saddle2.psd* file. You can also open the file using the Organizer, if you prefer.

2 Press the Arrange button (⊞) at the top of the workspace and choose Tile All in Grid. You should now be able to see both images inside the center work area of Photoshop Elements.

In order to get the layer from one image to the other, you only need to drag and drop the layer from the Layers panel over the other image.

3 Using the Move tool, click the *saddle1.psd* image and select the *Underwood Productions* layer. Click-and-drag this layer over the *saddle2.psd* file and release.

As long as the images are the same size and resolution, you can hold the Shift key as you drag from one image into another so that the layer appears in the same spot in the second image.

Dragging the text layer over another image.

4 Press the Arrange button and choose Consolidate all to show all images in their own window. Choose the Move tool (   ), select the image *saddle2.psd*, then visually move the type wherever you'd like.

Moving the embossed type into place.

5 Choose File > Save, save the file to your desktop, then choose File > Close. Do this for both *saddle1.psd* and *saddle2.psd*.

Warping type

In this exercise, you will learn how to warp type to a shape. In Photoshop Elements, you can warp type to arch, flag, wave, or even look like a fish, then change those settings any time you like, because warping type is a non-destructive edit. In this exercise, you will create the front cover of a book using a type warp and also a layer style.

1 Choose File > Open. In the Open dialog box, navigate to the Lessons folder and double-click the *mountain.psd* file. This will be the background image for a book cover. You can also open the file using the Organizer, if you prefer.

2 You now have to enter the title of the book. With the Horizontal Type Tool (ᴛ) selected, click above the mountain man's head and type **The Mountain Called Life**.

3 Change the text color to white.

4 Change the text alignment to

6 Center Text in the Options bar.

5 Change the font to Poplar Std. Change the size to 77 points.

7 Now it's time to warp the text. In the Options bar, press the Create warped text button (ᴛ).

Choosing the Create warped text button.

8 Choose Arch as the style, and change the bend to +45. Press OK.

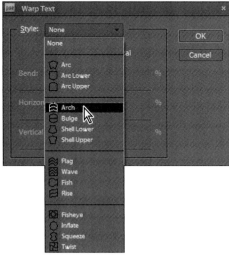

Changing the warp style.

9 Use the Move tool (⤢) to move it where it looks best.

10 Choose File > Save. In the Save As dialog box, make sure that the format is set to Photoshop and press Save.

Adding a layer style to type

Now that the text is placed on the book cover, you can apply a Layer Style effect to the text. The first thing you will notice is that when you apply a layer style, the text does not need to be simplified. This means that you can still edit the text after you apply a layer style.

1 Make sure the layer called *The Mountain Called Life* is still selected. In the Effects panel, press the Layer Styles button (▇), the second button from the left.

2 From the drop-down menu in the upper-right of the Effects panel, choose Drop Shadows.

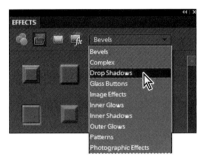

Choosing the correct effect.

3 Double-click the Soft Edge Drop Shadow effect to apply that effect to the selected type layer. Remember, hover your cursor over the icons, and text balloons will pop up with the name of the Layer Style. Notice that you didn't have to simplify the layer to apply this kind of effect.

4   Choose File > Save, then File > Close to close the document.

If you want the names of the different effects to appear in the Effects panel with the icons, press the Effects panel menu button (⋅≡) in the upper-right corner of the Effects panel. In the resulting menu, choose the option Show Names.

This is what the final book cover should look like.

Creating an animation with text

In this exercise, you will learn how to save an animated gif that you could send someone as an e-card. You will create a file with two layers that you will then animate inside the Save for Web feature.

1   Press the Organizer button (▦) at the top of the workspace. In the Organizer, locate and select the *halloween.psd* file. Press the arrow to the right of the Fix tab and choose Full Photo Edit from the drop-down menu to return to the Editor.

2   In order to save this file as an animated gif, you will need to change the file size, as it is far too big to use for the Web. Choose Image > Resize > Image Size. Make sure *Resample Image* and *Constrain Proportions* are checked at the bottom of the dialog box. Change the resolution to 72 and the width to 4 inches. Seventy-two pixels per inch is the proper resolution for the Web, and when you change the width, the height will automatically update because *Constrain Proportions* is checked. Press OK. Choose View >Actual Pixels to zoom in on the image. You may need to maximize the window to see the entire image by choosing Window > Images > Consolidate all to tabs.

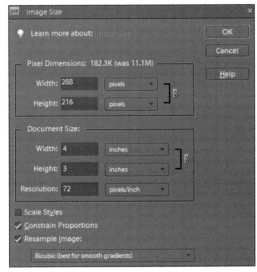

Changing the image size.

3   Select the Horizontal Type tool (I), and click in the top left area of the image. Type **Happy**.

4   Highlight the type and change the font to Snap ITC or any other font of your choice if you do not have this font available on your computer.

5   Change the size to 31.

6   Align the text to the left.

7   Click the color box in the Options bar to make your own color. Choose R:193, G:111, B:14. Press OK.

8   Use the Move tool (⊹) to position the text in the top left corner of the image.

With the Type tool still active, you can move type by either holding down the Control key and dragging, or by positioning the cursor just outside the text frame and dragging.

9   Choose the Horizontal Type tool again, click in the lower-right of the image, and type **Halloween**.

10 Position the text in the lower-right corner of the frame.

The image with two different text layers.

Adding a stroke

Now that you have the two text layers created, you will apply an effect to the text's stroke.

1 Select the *Happy* layer in the Layers panel.

2 In the Effects panel, make sure Layer Styles are active, and choose Strokes from the drop-down menu.

3 Double-click on the Gradient Stroke Black & Gray effect.

4 Now choose the *Halloween* layer, and double-click on the Gradient Stroke Black & Gray effect.

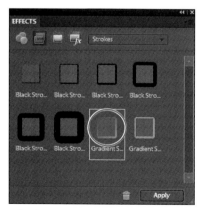

Select the Gradient Stroke Black & Gray effect.

Getting the layers ready for animating

When you save a gif using the Save For Web feature in Photoshop Elements, you can animate the layers. In the e-card animation you are making, you want one frame to say *Happy* and the next frame to say *Halloween*. In order to accomplish this task, you will need to have two layers with the appropriate text on each one.

1   Click the *Background* layer in the Layers panel to select it. From the Layers panel menu, choose Duplicate Layer. When the Duplicate Layer dialog box appears, press OK to name the layer Background Copy.

You now have all the pieces you'll need to make the animation. The next step is to merge the layers together.

2   Press the visibility icon (👁) next to the Happy and Background layer to hide them. Background Copy and Halloween are the only layers that are visible.

3   Press the Layers panel menu button (◦≡) and choose Merge Visible. Both layers merge into the Background Copy layer.

4   Press the visibility icon next to the Background Copy layer to hide it and next to the Background and Happy layers to make them visible.

5   Select the Happy layer and choose Merge Visible from the Layers panel menu.

This is what the layers should look like.

Time to animate

You can animate layers in the Save for Web dialog box when you choose GIF as the format.

1 Choose File > Save For Web.

2 In the Preset section, choose GIF 128 Dithered from the drop-down menu.

3 Check *Animate* at the bottom of the Presets section.

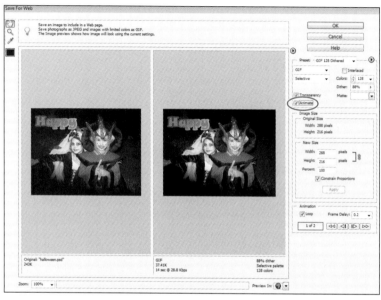

Make sure to check the Animate *option.*

4 In the Animation section, make sure *Loop* is checked.

5 To preview the animation, Click the arrow to the right of the Preview In icon at the bottom of the Save for Web dialog box. Choose Other, then navigate to a browser application on your computer and press Open. That browser now appears as the Preview In icon. Click the icon to preview the animation in your browser of choice.

Setting a browser to preview your animation.

6 Press OK to save the image. For Save As Type, make sure Images Only (.gif) is chosen. Press Save.

7   Open the image in your favorite browser to preview the image. If you would rather have a longer wait between frames, go back to the Save For Web dialog box and change the frame delay. Choose File > Save to save the file.

Self study

1   Open the file *snow.psd* and create warped text above the image that reads *Snow*. Add a layer style of a pattern to the *Bumpy* text to give the text a feeling of actual snow.

2   Open another instance of *snow.psd* and make two different text layers that read *Happy*, then *Holidays*. Follow the same steps you did in this lesson to make two different layers. Then animate those layers by saving the file as an animated gif.

3   Open the file *mountain2.psd* and make another book cover using whatever effects and warp you would like. Try to be creative with your titles.

4   Open the files *saddle1.psd* and *jump.psd* and copy the copyright text layer from *saddle1* to the *jump* file. Type **Jump** on the page and apply a warp effect.

Review

Questions

1   Is 72 points the largest size you can use for text?

2   If you would like to see your current text in all the different fonts you have on your machine, what should you do?

3   What are four ways to select text?

4   If you'd like to see all the different kinds of layer styles there are in the Effects panel, what should you do?

5   What file format can be animated in Save for Web?

6   What is the difference between applying a filter and a layer style to text?

Answers

1   No, you can manually enter any value into the Font size text field.

2   Select the text with the Type tool, click in the Font Name text field, and use your up and down arrow keys to preview the different fonts.

3   By clicking and dragging, double-clicking for a word, triple-clicking for a sentence, quadruple-clicking for a paragraph, clicking five times for all type or by using the keyboard command, Ctrl+A, or double-click the Type layer thumbnail to select all

4   You should choose Show All at the bottom of the Effects panel drop-down menu.

5   A gif file.

6   A filter makes you simplify the text, which leaves the text uneditable, while a layer style does not.

What you'll learn in this lesson:

- Understanding the histogram
- Improving an image with an adjustment layer
- Making selective changes
- Retouching with the Healing tools
- Using the Clone Stamp tool

Photo Retouching: Secrets of the Pros

In this lesson, you'll discover how to fix images using the photo retouching tools in Photoshop Elements. Some of the retouching you will do involves overall corrections, much like the ones you learned about in Lesson 5 "Adjusting Color." You will also find out how to make selective changes to affect only portions of an image. You will see how fixing blemishes is a breeze when working with the editing tools.

Starting up

Within the Photoshop Elements Organizer: You will work with several files from the Lessons folder in this lesson. Make sure that you have copied the Lessons folder from the supplied DVD to your hard drive. In order to access these files in the Organizer, you need to import them. See "Adding files and folders to the Organizer" on page 11.

Within the Photoshop Elements Editor: The Photoshop Elements Editor defaults to the last panel layout that you used. Before starting, make sure your tools and panels are consistent with the examples presented in these lessons by resetting the panels. Do this by choosing Window > Reset Panels, or by pressing the Reset panels button (🔾) in the Options bar.

See Lesson 8 in action!

Use the accompanying video to gain a better understanding of how to use some of the features shown in this lesson. The video tutorial for this lesson can be found on the included DVD.

Working with what you have

There is an old saying in the photo-retouching world: *Garbage in, garbage out.* There is only so much you can do to fix an image. If your image is flawed but has enough pixel information, you are way ahead of the game, and can probably fix the image with no serious issues. On the other hand, if you are provided with a low-resolution image, perhaps from a cell phone, your chances of making an improved image are much slimmer. This is mostly due to three reasons:

- The resolution may be too low, so the image may appear pixelated.

- There is a limitation in the dynamic range of tonal values that are recognized. The better the camera, the more tonal values it can recognize. The result of a higher dynamic range is a smoother transition from one shade of color to another.

- The image has already been edited. You will see, later in this lesson, how even minor edits can affect the quality of your image, giving more reasons for being cautious when editing your images.

Fortunately, there is a feature in Photoshop Elements that will help you determine whether images are lacking the information you need, before, and even while you are working on your image. This feature is the histogram. In this next section, you will open an image and make changes to the image. This will offer you the opportunity to make a comparison between an image with and without the information that is needed for retouching.

Using the histogram

The Histogram panel displays the overall distribution of information about tonal values, in the highlight, midtone, and shadow areas of an image. In this exercise, you will open an image and watch how your changes affect the histogram for that image. Keep in mind that you may open images whose histogram indicates a lack of information. These are the images that you can expect to have the most problems retouching and correcting.

1   If you have not yet launched Photoshop Elements, do so now. When the welcome screen appears, press the Edit button (🖉) to enter the Photoshop Elements Editor.

2   Choose File > Open and navigate to the Lessons folder. Locate and double-click the *Smiles.jpg* file. An image of a man and his son opens in the Full editing mode in Photoshop Elements.

If you are not sure if you are in the Full editing mode, look at the Edit tab in the upper right corner of your workspace. Make sure that Edit Full is the selected item.

Make sure you are in the Full editing mode.

3   Choose Window > Histogram to open the Histogram panel. Choose RGB from the Channel drop-down menu at the top of the panel. You may see an alert icon (▲) in the upper-right corner of the Histogram panel. If you do, click on it once to refresh the data in the Histogram panel.

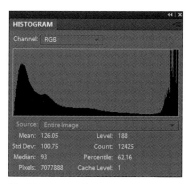

The Histogram panel.

Notice that the histogram shows a lot of information, as represented by the mountain-shaped looking data spanning the panel. To give you an idea of how a good histogram looks as compared to a bad histogram, look at the examples below.

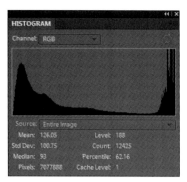 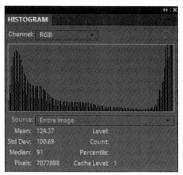

A histogram displaying a lot of data. *A histogram showing that data has been removed.*

Working over the image

Now you will have the opportunity to intentionally destroy an image. By running through the steps in this lesson, you will see how common steps that you might take can inadvertently destroy valuable information in your image, and how you can prevent this from happening.

1   With the *Smiles.jpg* image open, and the Histogram panel visible, choose Enhance > Auto Levels. The histogram's alert icon appears, indicating that you have made a change and the display needs to be refreshed. Click the alert icon (ᐃ).

Note that when you refresh the histogram display, there are now gaps in the data, indicating that some of the tonal values are missing.

2   Choose Enhance > Auto Contrast, then choose Enhance > Auto Smart Fix.

3 Click the alert icon in the histogram to refresh the display. Notice that the more corrections you make to an image, the more gaps appear in the histogram, indicating that data is missing. As you can see in the image below, the more data that is missing, the more *choppy* the image appears. The tonal values jump from one value to another, without a smooth transition. This is also known as *banding*.

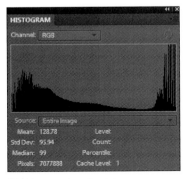

The histogram shows less data.   *The image, as it appears after having data deleted through editing.*

So how can you avoid this? First, become aware that as you make drastic changes to your images, they can be negatively impacted. Just keep an eye on the Histogram panel; when those big gaps start to appear, you are probably doing a little too much to your image.

Use adjustment layers, as discussed in Lesson 5, "Adjusting Color," Adjustment layers can be changed and deleted without destroying your original image data.

4 Choose File > Close to close the *Smiles.jpg* file. When the alert message appears asking if you want to save the changes, choose No.

Improving your image

Now that you know how to track the quality of your images, you will find out how to retouch an image using the editing tools that are available to you. In this part of the lesson, you will open an image with a mother and three daughters. The exercises will take you through a series of steps to eliminate flaws, such as food on the face, then proceed to more difficult selective changes to the skin tone.

1   In the Full editing mode in Photoshop Elements, choose File > Open. Navigate to the Lessons folder and double-click the *Family.jpg* file. An image of a mother and her three daughters appears. You can also open the file using the Organizer, if you prefer.

You will first perform an overall correction to the image to lighten it up a bit. You will do this using a non–destructive Levels adjustment layer. Note that you will be making a simple adjustment that will lighten the midtones (middle values) of this image. See Lesson 5, "Adjusting Color," for more in-depth details on using the Levels dialog box.

2   If you do not see the Layers panel, choose Window > Layers. The Layers panel appears.

3   Press the Create adjustment layer button (⬮) and choose Levels from the drop-down menu. The Levels dialog box appears inside of the Adjustment panel.

Select Levels from the Create adjustment layer drop-down menu.

4   Click and drag the midtone slider (middle marker) to the left until you see an approximate value of 1.28 appear in the Adjust midtone input level text field. This action makes the image lighter. To see the effect of the adjustment, press the Toggle layer visibility button (👁) off and then back on.

5 Increase the contrast slightly by clicking and dragging the shadow slider to the right until a value of 10 appears in the shadow input level text field. A Levels adjustment layer is created.

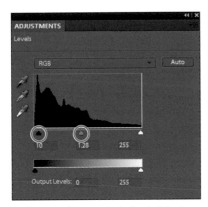

Make minor adjustments in the Levels dialog box to lighten the image.

Making a selective change using the adjustment layer's mask

Now that you have lightened the image, you will make a selective adjustment to just one section of the image, using the selection tools. In this example, you will select and darken the face of the girl in the front right of the photo.

1 Click and hold down the Rectangular Marquee tool (☐) and select the hidden Elliptical Marquee tool (◯).

Choose the Elliptical Marquee tool.

2 Click and drag from the upper left area of the girl's face to the lower-right area to make a selection that surrounds her face. You can reposition the selection by clicking and dragging it. Note that you need to have a selection tool active in order to reposition the selection without moving the pixel information.

3 Choose Select > Refine Edge. The Refine Edge dialog box appears.

Press the Custom Overlay Color button (▣) in the bottom-left corner of the Refine Edge dialog box. This reveals your selection, as the clear area in the red (default mask color) mask. You can view the changes in your selection by keeping an eye on the mask.

4   Click and drag the Feather slider to the right to about the 50-pixel position. This softens, or vignettes, the selection so that any corrections you make (within that selection) blend into the rest of the image more smoothly. Press OK.

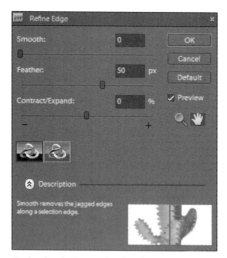

Feather the selection to soften the adjustments you will make.

You will now take advantage of the Adjustment Layer mask (the white rectangle) that sits to the right of the adjustment you made, in the Layers panel. If you remember, you lightened the entire image when you created the initial layer mask. You will now use your selection to block that adjustment from occurring around the girl's face.

5   To make sure that the adjustment layer's mask is selected, click once on the mask of the Levels 1 layer in the Layers panel.

Select the mask.

6   Press D on your keyboard to set the foreground and background color swatches to the default colors. Press X once. By pressing X, you switch the foreground and background colors. Look at the bottom of the Toolbox to verify that the black (foreground) color is in front of the white (background) color.

7   Choose Edit > Fill Selection; the Fill Layer dialog box appears. Leave it at the defaults, as shown below, and press OK. The layer mask now has a black feathered area. Where the black is on the mask, the image is no longer adjusted. Essentially, you are blocking the lightening adjustment that you made on the initial adjustment from occurring in the girl's face, and so her face is darkened. Because you feathered your adjustment, it is faded into the rest of the image.

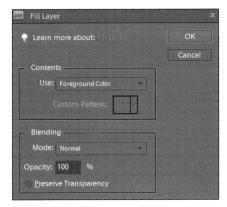

Choose to fill your selection with black.

The adjustment layer effects are blocked where the black appears.

8   Press Ctrl+D to deselect your selection, or choose Select > Deselect.

Brushing on corrections

Now that you have corrected the tonal values, you will use some of the retouching tools to clean up the faces of the girls.

1   In the Layers panel, select the *Background* layer to make it active.

Be sure to activate the Background layer before using the retouching tools.

2   Using the Zoom tool (🔍), click and drag over the lower section of the girl's face, in the lower-right area of the image. You want to make sure you catch the small tooth and the area to the right of her mouth, as well as the chin.

Click and drag around the girl's lower jaw to zoom into that region.

3   From the Toolbox, select the Spot Healing Brush tool (🖌). In the next step, you will choose a brush size to retouch with. Make sure that your Caps Lock key is NOT depressed. Having the Caps Lock key activated puts your cursor into precision mode, thereby preventing you from visually setting your brush size.

4   Press the] (right bracket) or [(left bracket) key to make your brush size larger or smaller. Resize the brush so that it is slightly larger than the freckle on the chin of the girl.

5   Click and drag to paint over the freckle on her chin. Notice that the Spot Healing Brush tool retouches in such a way that it quickly removes the freckle. When retouching blemishes, or other imperfections, you can either click once, or click and drag to smooth away imperfections in an area.

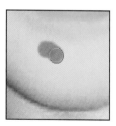 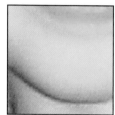

Click and drag with the   The result.
Spot Healing Brush tool.

You will now manually retouch the image.

Using the Healing Brush tool

When you use the Healing Brush tool, you can define the area of an image that you want to clone. Depending upon what you are retouching, this added control can be helpful. In this example, you will clean up the girl's face to the right of her mouth.

1   Click and hold the Spot Healing Brush tool (⌖) and select the hidden Healing Brush tool (✐).

2   Resize your brush to about 20 pixels. You can resize your brush by pressing the left and right bracket keys, [or], or by clicking and holding down on the Brush Picker arrow in the upper-left corner of the workspace. The size of the brush can be seen as you adjust it in the upper-left corner of your workspace as well.

Select a brush size.

3   Now hold down the Alt key (Windows) or Option (Mac OS) and click a patch of clear skin near the location of the girl's mouth. Release the Alt/Option key.

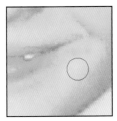

By holding down the Alt (Wndows) or Option (Mac OS) key and clicking, you define the area that you want to clone.

4   Click and drag over the food-stained area to the right of the girl's mouth. Use small strokes, almost like you are blotting the food away to clear the skin. Not only do you have to pay attention to the area you are brushing, but you also need to watch the cross-hairs. You don't want to clone unwanted information. Sometimes it is necessary to Alt+click (Wndows) or Option+click (Mac OS) in multiple places to achieve the desired tonality. If you make a mistake, press Ctl+Z (Windows) or Command+Z (Mac OS) to undo the last step. You can press Ctrl/Command+Z continuously to continue undoing, or press Ctrl/Command+Y to redo your steps.

The mouth, after it has been retouched.

5   Choose File > Save As. In the Save as dialog box, navigate to the Lessons folder and type **Family_working** in the Name text field. Make sure the format is set to Photoshop, then press Save. Keep it open for the next part of this lesson.

Using the Clone Stamp tool

The healing tools are very good when you need the soft retouching effect that they provide. The main difference between the Healing Brush and Clone Stamp tools is that when cloning with the Healing Brush, the tool attempts to match the tonality of the underlying area with what you are cloning, so you may see the cloned area's tonality adjust. The Clone Stamp clones exact information. In other words, what you see is what you get. Sometimes you need a little more precision, like when removing the girl's tooth from her lip. In this exercise, you will use the Clone Stamp tool to replace the girl's tooth with the surrounding lip.

1 Select the Clone Stamp tool (🔖) from the Toolbox. Look at the settings in the Options bar at the top to make sure the Mode is set to Normal and the Opacity is at 100 percent.

2 From the Show selected brush presets drop-down menu in the upper-left corner of the Options bar, choose the brush named Soft Round 9 pixels.

You can also soften or harden the edges of your brush by repeatedly pressing Shift+[(left bracket) or Shift+] (right bracket).

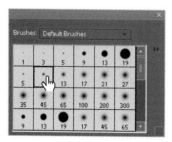

Choose a soft, small brush.

3 Position the cursor over a portion of the lip that is relatively close to the tooth. You are going to clone this section of lip, so you want the color to be approximately the same. Hold down the Alt (Windows) or Option (Mac OS) key and click to set this as your clone source.

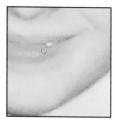

Alt/Option+click to set a clone source close to the area you will retouch.

4   Start clicking and releasing over the area of the tooth. If the clone source does not match, immediately press Ctrl+Z (Windows) or Command+Z (Mac OS) to undo the retouch, and Alt+click (Windows) or Command+click (Mac OS) on a source that will work better. With the Clone Stamp tool, you can get the best results from choosing a clone source, then dabbing on the area you want to retouch, then clicking to define a source (again), perhaps closer to the next area you plan to retouch. A good Clone Stamp user is frequently clicking away. Keep in mind that you can reduce the opacity of the Clone Stamp tool using the Opacity text field in the Options bar.

5   Press Ctrl+S, or choose File > Save, to save this file. Keep it open for the next part of this lesson.

Cloning an area with the Clone Stamp tool

In the last exercise, you retouched using the Clone Stamp tool. In this next part of the lesson, you will replace a tooth that is missing with another, existing tooth. You will also find out how to clone from one layer to another.

1   Press Ctrl+0 (Windows) or Command+0 (Mac OS) to fit the image into the window.

2   Select the Zoom tool (🔍), and click and drag over the mouth of the girl who is next to the mother. You are now zoomed in and can see that she is missing a tooth on the right side of her mouth.

Click and drag to zoom into the mouth.

3   Select the Clone Stamp tool (🔲), keep the brush size at 9 px, and make sure you are back to 100 percent opacity in the Options bar, if you changed that in the last part of this lesson. Click the checkbox next to Sample All Layers in the Options bar. This will allow you to sample pixel information from one layer and apply it to another if you need to.

4   Alt+click (Windows) or Command+click (Mac OS) the canine tooth on the left side of the girl's mouth.

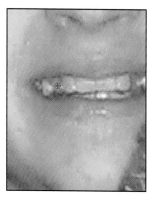

Alt+click to set the left canine tooth as a clone source.

5   If you do not see the Layers panel, choose Window > Layers.

6   In the Layers panel, Alt+click (Windows) or Command+click (Mac OS) the Create a new layer button (▣). By Alt/Option+clicking the Create a new layer button, you cause Photoshop Elements to open a New Layer dialog box, thereby allowing you to name the layer.

7   Type **new tooth** in the Name text field in the New Layer dialog box, and press OK.

8   Position the cursor over the right side of the mouth where the tooth is missing. You will be cloning the existing canine tooth into the empty area on the right side. Do not worry if it is not placed exactly in the right position, as you will be flipping the tooth and repositioning it in Step 9. Click and drag to start cloning the left canine tooth into the position where the right canine tooth would exist.

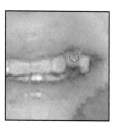

The tooth has been cloned, but is not yet flipped or positioned correctly.

9   When you are finished re-creating the tooth, choose the Move tool (⊕), make sure the options *Auto Select Layer* and *Show Bounding Box* are unchecked in the Options bar, then press Ctrl+T (Windows) or Command+T (Mac OS), or choose Image > Transform > Free Transform. The transform handles appear.

10 Flip the tooth horizontally by clicking the left-middle anchor point and dragging it over and past the right-middle anchor point. Adjust the points visually so that the tooth looks like it is scaled correctly, then press the Enter key to confirm the transformation.

11 Make sure that the Move tool is activated and, using the arrow keys on your keyboard, reposition the tooth.

If you have a hard time clicking and dragging the tooth, you may have Auto-select on in the Options bar. Click the checkbox to the left of Auto-select, *and then reselect the tooth layer in the Layers panel and click and drag it into position.*

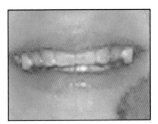

The replacement tooth after it has been flipped and repositioned.

Self study

As you get more practice using the retouching tools, you will become much better at making radical improvements to images, without it looking obvious.

Practice your retouching skills by using the Clone Stamp tool to gently dab out the braces in the mother's mouth.

For an easy fix, you can even eliminate the cord of the air conditioner with the Clone Stamp tool.

Review

Questions

1 Which tools requires you to define a clone source before you are able to use them.

2 Why should you frequently Alt+click (Windows) or Option+click (Mac OS) to pick new clone sources when using the Clone source tool and retouching large areas, such as skin.

3 When is it best to use the Spot Healing Brush tool?

Answers

1 The two tools that require you to select a clone source are the Healing Brush tool and the Clone Stamp tool.

2 You should frequently reselect a clone source when using the Clone Stamp tool, to make your retouch area blend more naturally with the original image.

3 It is best to use the Spot Healing Brush tool when you have small flaws that can be painted over quickly, such as blemishes, moles, dust, or scratches.

What you'll learn in this lesson:

- Use layers to separate and combine images
- Use Layer opacity and blending modes to create visually appealing compositions.
- Quickly silhouette images using the Magic Extractor
- Apply layer styles to create special effects

The Art of Illusion: Photo Composites

The ability to combine multiple photos into a single image is one of the hallmarks of Photoshop Elements. With extensive layer editing, masking, and styling tools, you can easily create stunning composites from different photos and text. Effects once reserved for professional studios are now at your fingertips.

Starting up

Within the Photoshop Elements Organizer: You will work with several files from the Image Library folder in this lesson. Make sure that you have copied the Image Library folder from the supplied DVD to your hard drive. In order to access these files in the Organizer, you need to import them. See "Adding files and folders to the Organizer" on page 11.

Within the Photoshop Elements Editor: The Photoshop Elements Editor defaults to the last panel layout that you used. Before starting, make sure your tools and panels are consistent with the examples presented in these lessons by resetting the panels. Do this by choosing Window > Reset Panels or by pressing the Reset panels button (⟳) in the Options bar.

See Lesson 9 in action!

Use the accompanying video to gain a better understanding of how to use some of the features shown in this lesson. The video tutorial for this lesson can be found on the included DVD.

Welcome screen

If you're currently viewing the welcome screen, press the Edit button (🖉) to enter the Editor workspace.

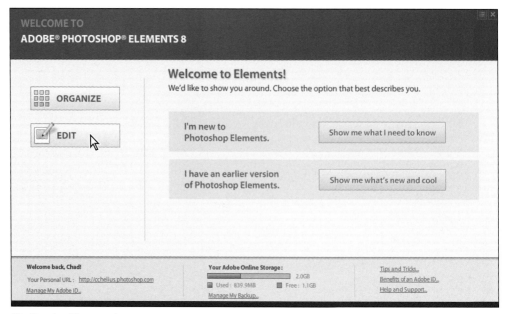

The Photoshop Elements welcome screen.

What is a photo composite?

A photo composite is an image that contains two or more photos compiled together. In Photoshop Elements, you create composite images by using layers.

Understanding layers

Think of layers as similar to stacked, transparent sheets of acetate that you can paint on. You can see through the transparent areas of each layer to the layers below. Each layer can be edited independently, allowing you to create the effect you want. Each layer remains independent of the others until you combine (flatten) the layers.

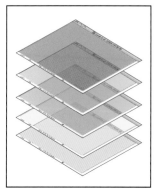

Layers can have transparent areas that let you see through to the layers below.

Layers are managed in the Layers panel. It's a good idea to keep this panel open and available whenever you're working in Photoshop Elements. The Layers panel is an important source of information as you edit photos. Because multiple layers in an image increase the file size, you can reduce the file size by merging layers that you're done editing. You can also use the Layer menu to work with layers.

Traditional layers are pixel-based (image) layers. There are various other layer types that you can use to simplify or enhance your workflow:

- **Fill layers** contain a color gradient, solid color, or pattern.

- **Adjustment layers** allow you to fine-tune color, brightness, and saturation without making permanent changes to your image (until you flatten, or collapse, the adjustment layer).

- **Type layers** and **shape layers** let you create vector-based text and shapes.

Working with layers

You'll now create a new file and work with layers inside it.

Creating a new blank file

Although the majority of the editing work you'll do in Photoshop Elements will use existing photos, in this exercise, you'll start by creating a new blank file.

1   Choose File > New > Blank File. The New dialog box appears.

2   In Name text field, type **America** as the name of your new file.

3   If it's not already selected, choose Default Photoshop Elements Size from the Preset drop-down menu. The Preset drop-down menu gives you the ability to choose from predefined file templates for different output such as Web, printing, and video content.

4   Change the value in the Height field to 4.5 inches. Note that the preset you chose in the previous step changes to Custom.

5   Leave the Resolution and Color Mode settings at their defaults, but from the Background Contents drop-down menu, choose Transparent.

6   Press OK. This file will serve as the base for your photo composite.

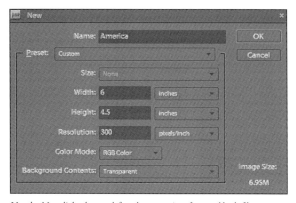

Use the New dialog box to define the properties of a new blank file.

Creating a type layer

1   Select the Horizontal Type tool (T), and click once on your transparent background. A blinking insertion cursor appears.

2   In the Options bar at the top of the workspace, set the following type options:

   •   From the Font drop-down menu, choose Arial.

   •   In the Size text field, type **100 pt**.

   •   Make sure that the text color is black.

3   Type the word **America**.

4   Press the Create warped text button (T) in the Options bar. This opens the Warp Text dialog box.

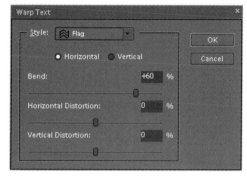

Customize type in the Warp Text dialog box.

5   Choose Flag from the Style drop-down menu, and drag the slider to set the Bend value to +60.

6   Press OK to warp your text to create a flag-like appearance. If you need to reposition your type, choose the Move tool (⊕) from the Toolbox and move the type into the top center of the file.

7   Choose File > Save and save your base file as **pse09_work.psd** in the Image Library folder. Leave this file open for later use.

Now you'll prepare the other parts of your photo composite.

Combining images

1   In the Editor, choose File > Open, and navigate to the Image Library folder. Select the *Marine.jpg* file and press Open. You can also open the file using the Organizer, if you prefer.

2   Choose File > Open again. In the Open dialog box, double-click the *Flag.jpg* file. You should now see three images in your Photo Bin, and you'll work to combine these images into one. You can also open the file using the Organizer, if you prefer.

3   Choose Window > Images > Consolidate All to tabs to display each image with its own separate tab.

4   Select the *Flag.jpg* tab to make the flag image active. Select the Move tool (⊹) and click directly on the flag image and drag on top of the *Marine.jpg* tab. Hold your cursor on the tab for a second until the *Marine.jpg* image is displayed, then move your mouse down on top of the Marine image and release. The flag image is placed on a layer above the Marine layer. If necessary, use the Move tool to center the image of the flag.

5   Click the *x* in the *Flag.jpg* tab to close the image.

Moving the Flag.jpg image onto the Marine.jpg as a new layer.

To successfully composite these images, you'll need to get acquainted with the Layers panel.

About the Layers panel

You access the Layers panel in the Editor by choosing Window > Layers. It lists all layers in an image, from the top layer to the *Background* layer at the bottom.

The layer that you are currently working on is called the *active layer*, and is highlighted for easy identification. As you work on an image, you should always keep track of which layer is active to confirm that the edits you're performing are affecting the correct layer. If you choose a command and nothing seems to happen, check to make sure that you have the correct layer selected.

Using the icons in the panel, you can accomplish many tasks, such as creating, hiding, linking, locking, and deleting layers. With some exceptions, your changes affect only the selected (active) layer, which is highlighted.

Information about each layer is displayed in the Layers panel.

Each layer in the panel displays a thumbnail, a title, and one or more icons that provide information about the layer:

The visibility icon (👁). The layer is visible. Press the visibility icon to show or hide a layer.

The Link Layers button (🔗). The layer is linked to the active layer.

The layer style icon (*fx*). The layer has a style applied to it. Click the icon to edit the layer style in the Style Settings dialog box.

The locked layer icon (🔒). The layer is locked.

The set icon (▣). The image contains layer groups and was imported from Adobe Photoshop. Photoshop Elements doesn't support layer groups and displays them in their collapsed state.

You'll use the buttons at the bottom of the panel to perform actions.

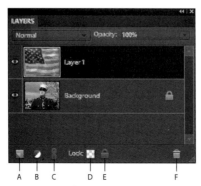

A   B   C   D   E   F

A. Create a new layer. *B*. Create a new fill or adjustment layer. *C*. Link layers.
D. Lock transparent pixels. *E*. Lock all layers. *F*. Delete a layer.

Also at the top of the panel, you'll find the Blending Mode drop-down menu, an Opacity text box, and panel menu button (·≣) displaying a menu of layer commands and panel options. (All these features are discussed later in this lesson.)

Editing layers

Now that you understand how layers work, you'll start editing them in your file.

Converting the Background layer into a regular layer

The *Background* layer is always the bottom layer in an image. Other layers stack on top of the *Background* layer, which often contains the actual image data of a photo.

The *Background* layer is always locked by default to protect that image. In order to rename (and later re-stack) the *Background* layer, you'll need to convert it to a regular layer.

1   In the Editor, double-click the *Background* layer in the Layers panel. The New Layer dialog box opens.

Double-click on the Background *layer to convert it.*

In the New Layer dialog box, you can set the Name, Blending mode, and Opacity of the converted layer.

2 Type **Marine** in the Name text field and leave the other options at their defaults. Press OK.

3 To avoid confusion, double-click the flag layer (currently Layer 1) and name it **Flag**. Press OK.

You also can double-click the name of a layer to change its name without using a dialog box.

Selecting a layer

Changes you make to an image only affect the layer that is active when the change is performed. As mentioned earlier, if you don't see the desired results when you edit an image, make sure that the correct layer is selected.

1 In the Layers panel, select the *Marine* layer. Note that only that layer is currently highlighted, or active.

2 Now select the *Flag* layer in the Layers panel.

To select layers interactively as you click in the image with the Move tool, select Auto Select Layer in the Options bar. To see which layer will be highlighted, select Show Highlight On Rollover.

Showing or hiding a layer

In the Layers panel, the visibility icon (👁) to the left of the layer name allows you to toggle the layer's visibility. To hide a layer, you simply click the visibility icon. Click in the visibility column again to show the layer.

1 In the Layers panel, click the visibility icon to the left of the *Flag* layer. You should now be able to see the *Marine* layer, as the layer that obscured it is now hidden.

2 Press the visibility icon to the left of the *Flag* layer to make it visible, obscuring the *Marine* layer underneath.

Drag through the visibility column to show or hide more than one layer. To display just one layer, Alt+click (Windows) or Option+click (Mac OS) the visibility icon for that layer. Alt/ Option+click in the visibility column again to show all the layers.

Changing the stacking order of layers

The term *stacking order* refers to which layers appear in front of or behind other layers.

By default, the *Background* layer must remain at the bottom of the stack. Since you've already converted it into a regular layer, however, you can rearrange the stacking order.

1   In the Layers panel, select the *Marine* layer.

To select more than one layer, hold down the Ctrl (Windows) or Command key (Mac OS) key and click each layer.

2   To change the stacking order, drag the *Marine* layer up so that it's positioned above the *Flag* layer. The flag is now obscured by the layer you just dragged on top of it.

You can also choose Layer > Arrange or press the Arrange button (▦) in the Options bar, and then choose Bring to Front, Bring Forward, Send Backward, or Send to Back to change a file's stacking order.

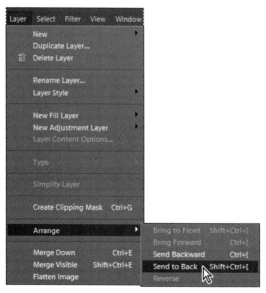

Rearrange the stacking order of layers using the Layer > Arrange command.

Locking or unlocking a layer

Layers can be fully or partially locked to protect their contents. When a layer is locked, a lock icon appears to the right of the layer name, and the layer cannot be deleted, have content added to it, or be edited.

 With the exception of the Background *layer, you can move locked layers to different positions in their stacking order inside the Layers panel.*

Since it will ultimately serve as the background for your first composite file, you'll now lock the *Flag* layer.

1   In the Layers panel, select the Flag layer, then press the lock icon (🔒) at the bottom of the panel.

2   Note that you can move this layer in the stacking order, but it cannot be edited in other ways. Make sure the *Flag* layer is returned to the bottom of your layers before proceeding.

Deleting a layer

Deleting layers that you no longer need reduces the size of your image file.

1   Select the *Flag* layer in the Layers panel.

2   Try to delete the *Flag* layer by pressing the Delete icon (🗑). You cannot delete this layer, because you locked it in the previous steps.

Since you'll be needing both these layers for this exercise, do not delete either one.

Using opacity and blending modes

Next you'll set the opacity and blending mode for the *Marine* layer.

About opacity and blending options in layers

Opacity in a layer is the degree to which it obscures or shows the layers beneath it. For example, a layer with 1 percent opacity is nearly transparent, while a layer with 100 percent opacity is completely opaque. Transparent areas maintain their transparency, regardless of the opacity setting.

Blending modes are used to define how a layer blends with the pixels in layers below it. You can create a variety of special effects using blending modes.

Specifying the opacity of a layer

1 Select the *Marine* layer in the Layers panel.

2 In the Layers panel, type **70** in the Opacity text field, or click the arrow at the right of the Opacity box and drag the Opacity slider that appears to 70 percent.

The Marine image is now semi-transparent, and the flag image is partially showing through.

Reducing the opacity allows underlying layers to show through.

Specifying a blending mode for a layer

1 Select the *Marine* layer in the Layers panel.

2 Choose the Luminosity option from the Blending Mode drop-down menu.

3   Experiment by pressing the up or down arrows on your keyboard to try other blending mode options in the menu.

Experiment with different blending modes in the Layers panel.

4   Set the blending mode of the Marine layer to Normal before proceeding to the next exercise.

Now you'll remove the distracting background from the *Marine* layer.

Using the Magic Extractor

The Magic Extractor makes it easy to select people or objects so that you can superimpose them on other backgrounds. You'll use it as a way to silhouette the marine image in this exercise.

Use the Magic Extractor to make accurate selections based on the appearance of foreground and background areas that you specify. You define these areas by placing colored marks in the areas you want to select. After you mark the areas and choose to extract the unmarked areas, only the foreground area appears in the photo in the Editor.

1   In the Layers panel, click to select the *Marine* layer.

2   Choose Image > Magic Extractor.

The Magic Extractor dialog box opens with the Foreground Brush tool ( ) selected by default.

3 Click and drag multiple times to mark the area you want to extract. In this case, click the Marine's hat, face, and uniform.

4 Choose the Background Brush tool (✐) and click and drag multiple times to mark the area that you do not want included in your selection. In this case, click on the sky, the cars in the background, and the tree.

Use the Magic Extractor to remove an unwanted background from an image.

When selecting objects with varied colors and textures, you can drag across all the colors and textures to ensure a more accurate selection.

5 To help with your selection, try using the Zoom tool (🔍) or the Hand tool (✋) to magnify and navigate around the photo.

6   To specify a different brush size, choose a new size from the Brush Size menu. You can also use the keyboard to increase or decrease the brush size. Pressing] increases the size of the brush while pressing [decreases the brush size.

7   Click Preview to see the current selection.

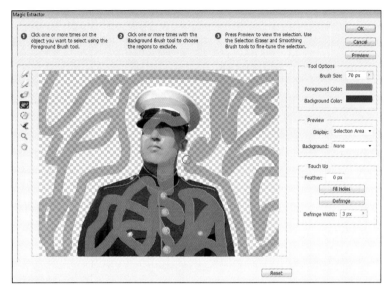

Press the Preview button to preview your selection.

8   To add to or subtract from the selection, place more marks in the image using either the Foreground or Background Brush tool. You can press the Preview button again to see the effects of your new extraction.

9   Press OK to extract the selected areas. If you want to start over and remove all marks, press Reset.

You should now see the image of the Marine, silhouetted from its background.

10 Use the Move tool ( ) to reposition the *Marine* layer to the lower right side of the image, as shown.

You can see through the background of a silhouetted image to the layer or layers below.

If you haven't been successful in removing the entire background, try some of the methods listed in the sidebar below.

Editing a Magic Extractor selection

In addition to placing marks in an image, you can fine-tune a Magic Extractor selection in the following ways:

- To erase foreground or background dots, select the Point Eraser tool (⊘) and click or drag over the marks you want to remove.

- To add areas to a selection, select the Add to Selection tool (⁂) and click or drag over the area you want to add.

- To remove areas from the selection, select the Remove From Selection tool (⊗) and drag over the areas you want to remove.

- To smooth the edges of your foreground selection, select the Smoothing Brush tool (◀) and drag over the areas you want to smooth.

- To soften the edges of your selection, specify a higher value in the Feather box.

- To fill remaining holes in the main selection, click Fill Holes.

- To separate and remove an area from the main selection, select the Remove From Selection tool and drag a line between the main selection and the area you want to remove. Then click Fill Holes.

- To remove fringe colors left between the foreground and background, click Defringe. To increase or decrease the amount of fringe removed, specify a value from the Defringe Width menu.

Flattening an image

Next you'll flatten your composite image into one layer to prepare it for further compositing.

When you flatten an image, Photoshop Elements merges all visible layers into the background, greatly reducing the file size. In most cases, you won't want to flatten a file until you've finished editing individual layers.

1 Make sure that both layers in your file are visible.

2 Choose Flatten Image from the Layers panel menu (◄≣).

You can see the difference between your image's layered file size and its flattened file size by choosing Document Sizes from the status bar drop-down menu at the bottom of the document window.

Completing the composite

Now you'll combine this composite image with the type layer you created earlier.

1   Choose Select > All to select all the content in your composited file.

2   Choose Edit > Copy to copy this content to the Clipboard.

3   Open the base file, with the *America* text layer, that you created earlier.

4   Choose Edit > Paste to paste the composite into the base file.

5   In the Layers panel of your new composite file, drag the type layer above the flattened image layer, and position it at the top.

The layered look of this file is characteristic of most composite images. Now you'll use clipping groups and layer styles to make the type layer more interesting.

Copy and paste from one image to another for further compositing.

Working with clipping groups

To improve the look of the type layer in your new composite file, you'll create a clipping group.

About layer clipping groups

A clipping group is a group of layers to which a mask is applied. The bottommost layer, or base layer, defines the visible boundaries of the entire group. In this exercise, the base layer contains some text, and the layer above it contains a photograph. If the photograph appears only through the type outline in the base layer, it also takes on the opacity of the base layer.

You can group only contiguous layers. The name of the base layer in the group is underlined, and the thumbnails for the layer above is indented. In addition, the layer above displays the clipping group icon.

Creating a clipping group

1   In the Layers panel, create a duplicate of the image layer by dragging it over the New Layer button ( ). Name the new layer **base**, and position it at the bottom of the layer stack.

2   Click and drag the original image layer (layer 1) to a position directly above the type layer.

3   Hold down Alt (Windows) or Option (Mac OS), position the pointer over the line dividing the top two layers in the Layers panel (the pointer changes to two overlapping circles), and then click.

Alternatively, in the Layers panel, select the top layer of a pair of layers you want to group, and choose Layer > Group With Previous.

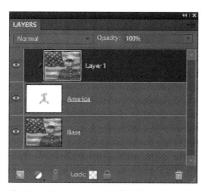

Create a unique transparent effect for your type with a clipping group.

It may now be difficult to see the clipping group layer, because the layers in the clipping group have the same opacity and mode attributes of the bottommost layer in the group.

Using Layer styles

You'll now make your clipping group layer stand out by adding layer styles to it.

About layer styles

Layer styles let you quickly apply effects to an entire layer. In the Effects panel, you can view a variety of predefined layer styles and apply a style with a click of your mouse.

Use the Effects panel to apply layer styles.

The layer style's effects are automatically updated whenever you edit that layer. Layer styles are also cumulative, which means that you can create a complex effect by applying multiple styles to a layer. You can also change a layer's style settings to adjust the final result.

When a layer style is applied to a layer, an effects icon (*fx*) appears to the right of the layer's name in the Layers panel. Layer styles are linked to the layer contents. In other words, when you move or edit the contents of the layer, the effects move with them.

Choose Layer > Layer Style > Style Settings to edit the settings of a layer's style.

Edit the properties of layer styles in the Style Settings dialog box.

Working with layer styles

Not only can you apply special effects to a layer, but you can also hide or show the styles in a layer, and even change the scale of a layer style.

Apply a layer style

1   Select the *America* layer in the Layers panel.

2   In the Effects panel, choose Layer Styles from the category menu and in the drop-down menu, choose Bevels to start with.

3 Do any of the following, experimenting until you find a style you like:

- Select a style, and click Apply.

- Double-click a style.

- Drag a style onto a layer.

You can also drag the style to the image; it is applied to the selected layer.

Apply a layer style to the type layer for a special effect.

Hiding or showing all layer styles in an image

1 Select the *America* layer in the Layers panel.

2 In the Effects panel, choose Layer Styles from the category menu.

3 Choose Layer > Layer Style > Hide All Effects to hide the style.

4 Choose Layer > Layer Style > Show All Effects to show the style.

Change the scale of a layer style

1 In the Layers panel, select the layer containing style effects you want to scale. In this case it would be the America layer.

2 Choose Layer > Layer Style > Scale Effect.

3 Select Preview to see the changes in your image and drag the Scale slider to the left and right to see the changes that the Scale has on the Effect.

4 Identify how much you want to scale the effects. For example, if you are increasing the size of an outer glow, 100 percent is the current scale, and so 200 percent doubles the glow size. Press OK.

Copying style settings between layers

1 In the Layers panel, select the *America* layer.

2 Choose Layer > Layer Style > Copy Layer Style.

3 Select the bottom layer in the Layers panel, and choose Layer > Layer Style > Paste Layer Style. Note the changes to the edges of the silhouetted *Marine* layer.

4 Choose Edit > Undo or use the keyboard shortcut, Ctrl-Z.

Removing a layer style

1 In the Layers panel, select the layer containing the style you want to remove.

2 Choose Layer > Layer Style > Clear Layer Style or drag the layer style icon (*fx*) to the right of the layer onto the trash can at the bottom of the Layers panel.

3 Choose Edit > Undo or use the keyboard shortcut, Ctrl-Z (Windows) or Command+Z (Mac OS). Choose File > Save. Close any open documents.

Congratulations, you've completed the lesson! With your newly acquired knowledge of photo compositing, you've uncovered a whole new world of capability within Photoshop Elements.

Self study

1 Create another new type layer and composite it with the other layers, re-stacking as you feel necessary.

2 Use the Magic Extractor to include more of the background in the Marine image before compositing.

3 Try adding a new layer containing shapes, and apply different layer styles to the shapes on that layer.

4 Scale the layer style you've applied to this new shape layer to create a more dramatic effect.

Review

Questions

1 What is the fastest way to convert the *Background* layer to an editable layer?

2 What are two properties of the background layer?

3 How do you define selections using the Magic Extractor?

4 Can multiple layer styles be applied to a single layer?

Answers

1 Double-click the *Background* layer in the Layers panel.

2 It is always on the bottom of the other layers and it is always locked to prevent you from moving or editing it.

3 You define selection areas by placing colored marks in the areas that you want to extract.

4 Yes. Layer styles are cumulative, which means that you can create a complex effect by applying multiple styles to a layer.

What you'll learn in this lesson:

- Creating a photo panorama
- Creating a photo slide show
- Adding text, audio, and graphics to a slide show
- Applying transitions to your slide show

Making Photoshop Elements Creations

Photoshop Elements offers a variety of ways to enhance and share your photos with others. Slide shows, photo books, calendars, and collages can easily be created.

Starting up

Within the Photoshop Elements Organizer: You will work with several files from the Lessons folder in this lesson. Make sure that you have copied the Lessons folder from the supplied DVD to your hard drive. In order to access these files in the Organizer, you need to import them. See "Adding files and folders to the Organizer" on page 11.

Within the Photoshop Elements Editor: The Photoshop Elements Editor defaults to the last panel layout that you used. Before starting, make sure your tools and panels are consistent with the examples presented in these lessons by resetting the panels. Do this by choosing Window > Reset Panels or by pressing the Reset panels button (↻) in the Options bar.

See Lesson 10 in action!

Use the accompanying video to gain a better understanding of how to use some of the features shown in this lesson. The video tutorial for this lesson can be found on the included DVD.

Creating a panorama

If you have photos of a wide scene, like a landscape, you can join them together into a single image. In the next exercise, you'll use a series of four incremental photos of a river running through farmland. The strong, distinctive lines that are running through the pictures make this a good candidate for creating a panorama.

1   If you are still in the Organizer, press the arrow to the right of the Fix tab at the top of the workspace and choose Full Photo Edit, then select File > New > Photomerge Panorama. If you are using the free trial version of the software, this option is not available; skip to the next exercise.

2   In the Photomerge dialog box, click the Browse button, navigate to the Lessons folder, then select files *Farmland_01* to *Farmland_04*. Press Open.

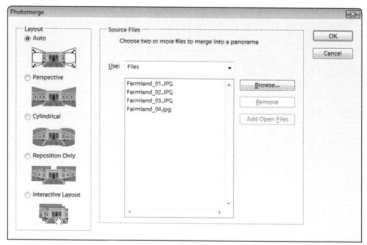

The Photomerge dialog box.

3   Choose *Auto* from the Layout section of the Photomerge dialog box.

The *Auto* setting allows the program to choose the best layout method based on the analysis it performs of the images during the Photomerge process. If you are looking for the quickest option, then choose *Automatic*.

4 Press OK and wait while Photoshop Elements opens and closes windows to create your panorama. The panorama is a new document with four layers arranged to line up the different images. The number of layers depends on the number of individual images you used in the Photomerge process. Each image is converted into its own layer, and any areas that are extraneous—the ones that aren't needed to produce a completed panorama—are masked out and hidden by the program.

5 Select the Crop tool (✄) from the Toolbox and draw a marquee around the image to crop out the excess background area.

The Photomerge process always creates an excess background area that must be cropped.

6 Click the checkmark at the bottom of the crop window to finalize the crop.

7 Select File > Save. Name the file **My Panorama**, and confirm that Photoshop is set as the file type, and that the Lessons folder is the location. Press Save.

8 Close the file.

Creating a slide show

A slide show is fun to build. It allows you to combine images, music, narration, and text to create a unique multimedia display. Like most photo creations in Photoshop Elements, slide shows can be created from the Organizer, the Editor, or the welcome screen. The easiest place to create them is the Organizer, as you will discover in the following steps.

1   If it isn't already open, launch the Photoshop Elements Organizer.

2   In the Organizer, type **img** in the search box. All the images that you will use in the slide show have the word *img* in the title. This is a great way to isolate them in the Organizer window.

The search field is a good way to filter images.

If you adjust the thumbnail size slider at the top of the Organizer workspace to make each image thumbnail smaller, you can display all 18 images on the screen at once. Note that if you've performed some of the previous lessons in this book, you may have more than 18 images.

3 Click the first file in the window, which should be *IMG_0840.JPG*. Hold down the Shift key and click on the last picture in the window, which should be *IMG_1113.JPG*. This selects all 18 images at once. You can also select all the images currently displayed in the Photo Browser by using the keyboard shortcut, Ctrl+A (Windows) or Command+A (Mac OS).

4 Select the Create tab on the right, and press Slide Show. Because images were selected when you created the slide show, they are automatically included.

Press the Slide Show button in the Create tab.

5   Press OK in the Slide Show Preferences dialog box that appears, accepting the default settings. The default settings allow you to create a slide show where each image is held for five seconds, and a two-second fade transition is applied between each picture. You may have to wait a couple seconds for the Slide Show Editor to open.

You can use the Slide Show Preferences dialog box to define the parameters of the overall slide show—for example, how long each slide is visible, what type of transition you would like between the slides, and how the soundtrack behaves. All these settings are also editable individually from inside the Slide Show Editor.

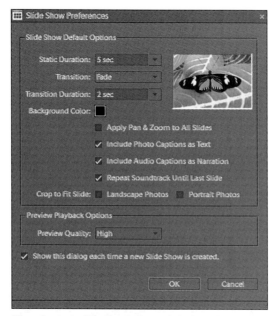

The settings in the Slide Show Preferences dialog box control the overall behavior of the slide show.

Understanding slide show preferences

When you create a slide show, you can set the default behavior of the show. Each of these settings can be adjusted on an individual level in the Slide Show Editor after the slide show has been created.

Static Duration: This drop-down menu determines how long each individual slide displays. You can choose a value from the menu or type in the duration you want for each slide. Individual slide durations can be adjusted later.

Transition: Sets the default transition to apply between each slide. You can pick any transition you like from the menu. Apply no transition by setting the drop-down menu to none, or set the slide show to use a random transition.

Transition Duration: Sets the duration of each transition in your slide show.

Background Color: Sets the background color for each slide.

Apply Pan & Zoom to All Slides: Applies an automatic pan and zoom to every slide. The start and end points for the pan and zoom can be manually adjusted later. See the "Panning and zooming" section later in this lesson for more details.

Include Photo Captions as Text: Captions can be added to each image in the Organizer; this checkbox automatically converts those captions into slide text.

Include Audio Captions as Narration: If you have a microphone attached to your computer, then you can add audio captions to images in the Organizer.

Repeat Soundtrack Until Last Slide: Has little effect when the slide show is created, but once a sound track is added, it is automatically set to repeat.

Crop to Fit Slide: Crops the image so that it fits into the available slide area. You can choose to crop landscape images, portrait images, both, or neither. With this option disabled, images are scaled proportionally to fit inside the slide.

Preview Quality: Sets the quality that the slide show previews at in the Slide Show Editor.

6   Once the Slide Show Editor opens, press the Play button to preview the slide show. Each slide displays for a few seconds and then gradually fades into the next slide in the storyboard. This is because you left the preferences set to the defaults of a five-second hold with a two-second fade transition. You will edit these settings later in this lesson.

7   Stop the slide show from playing by pressing the pause button, then press the Save Project button from the upper-left corner of the Slide Show Editor. Name your project **air show** and press Save. The project is automatically saved to the Organizer. The Save dialog box informs you that the project will be saved to the Organizer with the current day's date.

Adding text to your slide show

Your slide show is not limited to images. You can use the Photoshop Elements text tools to add both titles and captions to your work. The Text tool is accessible from the "Extras" menu on the Palette Bin.

1   Click the first slide in the storyboard to make it visible in your work area. You may have to scroll to the left to see it, depending on where you stopped the slide show.

2   From the top of the Editor, press the Add Text button. A text box with some generic text is added to the selected slide.

The Add Text button creates a text box and fills it with generic place holder text.

3 In the Edit Text dialog box, type **Off we go into the wild blue yonder**, inserting a
return after the word go to split the text into two lines. Press OK.

The Edit Text dialog box allows you to change the text you have created.

4 Place your cursor over the text box; the cursor becomes a hand. Reposition the text by clicking and dragging while the cursor is over the text box. Move it to the bottom of the slide so it sits over the clouds.

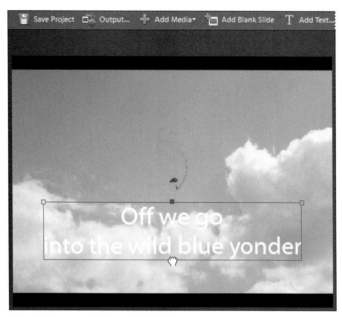

Reposition the text to the bottom of the slide.

5 With the text frame highlighted, click the Click to add formatted text to your slide show button (T) in the Extras panel. Right-click on the thin, black text in the second-to-last row and choose Apply to Selected Text Item.

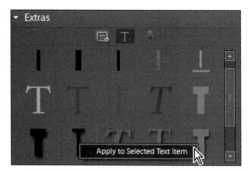

Apply to Selected Text Item *is the only option that appears when you right-click on a text style.*

From the Text Properties panel, located below the Extras panel, you can change the font, size, color, opacity, alignment, and style of the text. The panel is contextual, which means that it changes, depending on the type of object you have selected. When text is selected, you have access to the properties that control the text frame. When an image is selected, you see the properties for editing it.

Adding graphics

Adobe Photoshop Elements includes many ready-made graphics that you can use to add flair to your projects. Like the Text tool, graphics are located in the Extras tab of your Palette bin.

1   Click slide 2 in the storyboard to load it into the work area.

2   From the Extras section of the Palette Bin, press the Graphics button (▣) to reveal the available graphics. The graphics are broken up into various categories; Animals, Costumes, and Flowers to name a few. Select a Graphic that you like and drag it onto your slide.

Photoshop Elements ships with a wide range of graphics for use in your projects.

 Now that you have a graphic selected, the Properties panel changes to give you the parameters that are available for editing graphics. From here, you can alter the size of a graphic and apply graphic styles to it.

Applying transitions

Transitions are displayed as you move from one slide to the next; they are denoted on the storyboard by the small boxes between the slides. When you created the slide show, a fade transition was automatically added between each slide. Photoshop Elements offers a wide variety of transitions that you can use to make your slide shows more interesting. The number and types of properties that you can edit depend on the individual transitions.

1   Click Transition 1, which is located between the first and second slides in your storyboard.

2   In the Properties panel, click the Transition drop-down menu and select Wipe from the list. This pops up a secondary property, Direction. Click the Direction drop-down menu and set it to the second option, top to bottom.

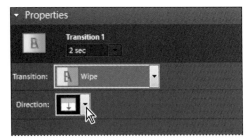

Each transition has its own unique set of options that you can edit.

 The random *setting allows the slide show to play any one of the available transitions. There are more than 20 from which it selects at random.*

3   Click the Duration drop-down menu and select 3 seconds to create a slower transition.

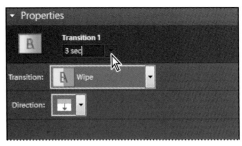

Select the transition's duration from the menu or type in the desired value.

You can set transitions to one of the default duration settings, or to customize the length by selecting the custom *option from the drop-down menu.*

4 Change at least three other transitions in the slide show.

You can hold down the Ctrl (Windows) or Command key (Mac OS) key to select multiple transitions at once and edit them as a group.

5 Click the first slide in the slide show, then press the Play button to preview it.

6 Press Ctrl+S (Windows) or Command+S (Mac OS) on your keyboard to save the changes to your slide show.

Panning and zooming

The phrase *pan and zoom* refers to the movement of a camera with the subject. In Photoshop Elements, the Pan & Zoom effect allows you to simulate the appearance of camera movement over a still image. This technique, which you often see in documentary filmmaking, can be used to add emphasis and liven up an otherwise static image.

The Pan & Zoom effect is not supported by some output file types, most notably PDF.

1 Select slide 3 in your storyboard to load it into the project window.

2 Press the *Enable Pan & Zoom* checkbox in the Properties panel.

3   A green bounding box named *Start* appears in the work area; this indicates the start position of the Pan & Zoom effect. Scale this bounding box by dragging with your cursor at one of its corner points. Move the bounding box by positioning the cursor inside of it and dragging. Position it over the skydivers so that it matches the following figure.

The Start bounding box determines the focus when the slide is first displayed.

4   Click on the End point thumbnail in the Properties panel, and position the new bounding box to enclose the entire frame.

The End bounding box determines the final appearance of the image.

5   Preview the slide show by clicking the Play button at the base of the work area. Press the pause button to stop the slideshow from playing.

Reordering slides

When you first added the slides to the project, you did not have the opportunity to set the order sequence. It is often necessary to change the order of the slides to fit the story you are telling. There are three ways to do this: using the drop-down menu, dragging and dropping on the storyboard, and using the Quick Reorder menu. You can also reset any changes you have made to the slide order from here.

Setting the slide order

Click the Slide Order drop-down menu in the upper-right corner of the storyboard to choose one of the auto-sorting methods for the slides: from organizer, date based, random, or folder location.

Drag and drop on the storyboard

1   On the storyboard, click slide 5, then drag it past slide 6.

2   When a vertical blue bar appears, drop the slide; this changes the slide order.

Quick Reorder menu

The Quick Reorder menu is the best way for changing the order of multiple slides. It allows you to view your entire slide show at one time.

1   Press the Quick Reorder button (≜) located in the upper-left corner of the storyboard.

2   In the menu that appears, drag and drop slides to change their positions. Press the Back button (◆) when you have finished editing to return to the main Slide Show Editor.

 You can press the Shift or Ctrl (Windows) or Command (Mac OS) keys on your keyboard to select multiple slides.

Working with audio

The photos you choose are the most important part of any slide show. However, they aren't the only part: text and graphics are often added to a slide show to enhance the effect of certain slides or to add emphasis to important parts of your images. Another important factor for creating a good slide show is your audio. While you don't have to use audio when creating one, good audio can help to establish the mood of your project. Audio can be added to a slide show, either as background music, commentary track, or as a voiceover to match specific slides.

Adding audio

To add an audio file that plays in the background of your slide show, you can do so very easily using the Add Media button (✚). Audio plays as your slide show progresses, and automatically stops at the end of the show.

1   Press the Click Here to Add Audio to your Slide Show button at the bottom of the storyboard.

2   Navigate to the airshow folder in the Lessons folder and select *airshow soundtrack.mp3*. Press Open and the audio file will appear at the bottom of the storyboard on the audio track. Preview the slideshow by pressing the Play button at the bottom of the viewer. Press the pause button to stop the slideshow.

3   The audio is a little too loud, but you can adjust this. Click the audio track and lower the audio slider in the Properties field in the Palette bin by dragging the slider to the left. Press the Play button above the audio slider to hear the music play as you are adjusting it. Press the pause button above the audio slider to stop the music playback.

If you want to auto adjust the duration of each slide to play for the entire duration of your audio track, press the Fit Slides To Audio button (▣) at the top of the Storyboard.

Adding narration

If you have a microphone attached to your computer, you can use it to add narration to one or more slides in your project. Unlike background audio, the narration track is attached to each slide and automatically changes the slide's duration. The narration interface looks very similar to a standard tape recorder, with controls to record, stop, and play. It also includes controls for inserting saved audio tracks as narrations and deleting saved narration tracks.

The recorder is just like a physical tape recorder.

1   From your Palette bin, click the Narration tool (🎤) to activate it.

2   Select the slide you would like to add the narration to, and press the Record button.

3 When you are finished with your narration, press the Stop button.

Adding narration can increase the duration of the slide. If your narration is longer than the slide's display duration, Photoshop Elements automatically increases the slide's display length.

4 Press the Play button to listen to the narration you have just created. If you are happy with it, move on to the next slide. If you are not happy with the narrative track, press the Delete button (🗑) to delete it.

If you are using a soundtrack with your slide show, it can interfere with the viewer's ability to hear the narration, if the soundtrack is too loud.

Choosing an output option

Once you have created your slide show, you need to decide how to distribute it to your audience. Photoshop Elements supports a variety of distribution methods.

Once you have chosen your file type and decided on the specific settings you want, press OK to build your file. Once the file has been created, you can do whatever you like with it; you can e-mail it to your family and friends, burn it to disk, or save it on a flash drive.

Save as a file

This option saves the slide show as either a Windows Media Video (.wmv) or a Portable Document Format (.pdf) file. For the WMV format, you must specify a file size (larger sizes equate to larger but better-quality files). The PDF option does not support certain slide show features, most notably Pan & Zoom, and some transitions will appear different, such as the clock wipe, which becomes a fade when converted to PDF.

1 Press the Output button (🐾) in the Options bar at the top of the Slide Show Editor.

2 In the Slide Show Output dialog box, choose Save As a File from the list on the left. Choose Movie File (.wmv) as the type and High (800x600) from the Slide size pull-down menu. Press OK.

3 In the Save Slide Show dialog box, navigate to the Lessons folder and press Save. When Photoshop Elements has finished created the Windows Media file, you will be given the choice to import it into your Catalog. Press Yes.

4 Choose Save Project from the Options bar, then close the Slide Show Editor to return to the Organizer.

Burn to disk

This option allows you to burn the slide show to either a VCD (video CD) or DVD for display on a standard console DVD player, depending on your hardware configuration. To create a VCD, which can play on most modern DVD players, you need a drive capable of burning CD-ROMs, whereas for the DVD, you need a DVD burner.

Send to TV

As the name implies, this export feature lets you watch your slide show on your television directly from your computer. You need to have Windows Media Center Edition for this option to work.

Creating a photo calendar

You can use your photos to create a wide variety of different projects, including a photographic calendar. Photo calendars can be ordered directly through Photoshop Elements 8 using two services, Shutterfly and Kodak. Shutterfly calendars are created on the Shutterfly web site after Photoshop Elements uploads the pictures. Kodak calendars uses the Adobe Photoshop Services web site. You must register with this service to order bound calendars. You need a valid e-mail address to register for the service and receive notifications. Signing up for Photoshop Services is free, but you will need a valid credit card to place an order.

A photo of the calendar showing a mom and her little girl.

You need the latest version of the Flash Player plug-in to use the Web features of the calendar creation process.

1 Make sure the Slide Show window is closed, and in the Organizer, type **California** into the search text field. This isolates only the images with the word *California* in the title.

2 Click on the first image in the Photo Browser, then press Ctrl+A on the keyboard to select all the images.

You can also select the first image, hold down the Shift key on the keyboard, and select the last image in the group to select them all.

3 From the Create tab on the right of the workspace, press the Photo Calendar button and choose the service (ShutterFly or Kodak) that you would like to use. In this example the Kodak web service is selected. This launches the web-based calendar creator, then press the Create a Calendar button.

The Create tab offers a wide variety of project options.

4 The Photo Calendar dialog box takes you through four quick steps to create your calendar. The first step you have already completed by selecting your images and opening the dialog box; the second step signs you in to your Photoshop Services (*Photoshop.com*) account; the third step uploads your images; and the final step creates the calendar.

Because there were photos highlighted when you opened the dialog box and Photoshop Elements keeps you signed in to *Photoshop.com* services, you can press the Next button and the dialog box automatically displays the progress uploading your images.

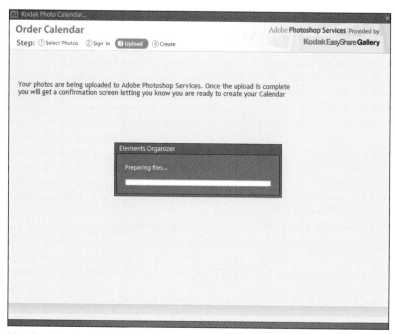

The Photo Calendar dialog box is a wizard that begins the process of creating a calendar.

5 After your photos are uploaded, press the Next button. The dialog box closes, and the Adobe Photo Services web site opens in your default web browser. Adobe Photo Services is powered by Kodak Gallery and provides a web-based tool for creating projects.

Set the starting month and the date from the drop-down menus located above the styles. In this example, January is used for the starting month and 2010 for the year.

The Adobe Photo Services web site is used to complete the layout and order your calendar.

Select the theme you prefer from the list on the right side of the page. In this example, *Remarkably Retro* is used. Press Next when you are done.

6   A dialog box appears, asking if you would like to autofill your calendar. Autofill can automatically create a calendar using all the images that you uploaded. This is a tool for quickly creating the calendar; you can always edit the specific images and layout after you have used autofill. The alternative would be to lay out each page manually using the Page by Page button. Press the Autofill button to continue.

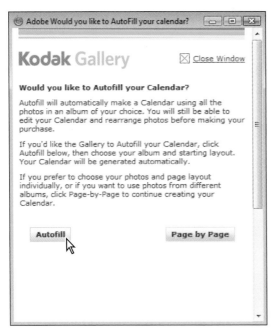

Autofill can be a very useful tool for quickly creating calendars.

7   Click the drop-down menu to the right, and choose the album you would like to use for your calendar. Because you have just uploaded the files for your calendar, it should be selected by default. If this is your first time using Adobe Photo Services, then you won't have any other albums from which to choose.

The default name for the galleries in Photo Services is the date and time that the files were uploaded.

8   Choose a layout from the choices below. For this example, the 1-up layout is used. This places one image on each page of the calendar.

Press Next. If you don't have the Flash Player installed, a dialog box appears, stating that you need the latest Flash Player plug-in to continue. If you are certain your current version of the Flash Player is up-to-date, then press the *I have the latest version of the plug-in* button. This takes you to the editing area of the calendar.

9   On the Create your Calendar page, you can choose to edit the images in your calendar page by page. On the cover page, type **Southern California** into the Title text field and your name in the Author text field.

10 At this point, you can also edit the layout and order of the images in your calendar project. Locate the image of the wooden stair taken from the bottom of the stairs. Click and drag this image onto the one on your cover. A blue control panel pops up that allows you to move, rotate, and zoom in on the image that you just placed. Press the black arrow on the panel to close it.

The cover can have information about the name of the calendar and author added to it.

11 Press the First Month button to advance until you see a copy of the stair image. In the example, it is located on the page for the month of November. Locate the image of the deserted beach, then drag and drop it onto the image of the stairs.

Images on pages can be swapped with those in the bay at the bottom of the screen.

12 Press the Order button to preview your completed calendar and select your desired quantities.

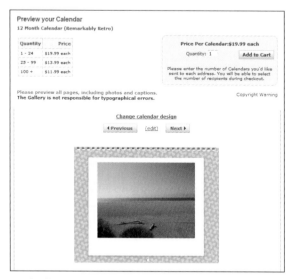

You should preview the entire calendar one last time before you add it to your cart.

13 Press the Add to Cart button to add your calendar to your Adobe Photo Services shopping cart. After you press the button, you are taken to your shopping cart, and from here, you can either create another project or enter the Checkout phase to complete your transaction.

Self study

1 Take a few photos of a wide vista landscape, a tall building, or a row of houses, and practice making a panorama from them. Remember, when you take the photos, each image should overlap the previous one a bit so that the program can stitch them together. Using a tripod can significantly improve your results as well.

2 Take some photos of your own and build a more personal slide show.

Review

Questions

1 How do you begin the slide show creation process from the Photoshop Elements Organizer?

2 How would you change the duration or type of a transition?

3 What are the three output options available for your slide shows?

Answers

1 From the Organizer, click the Create button to open the New Creations dialog box. You can also open the New Creations dialog box from the File menu, by selecting File > Create > Slide Show.

2 Select the transition that you want to edit from the storyboard. The transition's properties visible in the lower section of your Palette bin, and you can change these properties.

3 Save as a File, Burn to Disk, and Send to TV.

What you'll learn in this lesson:

- Understanding the Camera Raw file format
- Using the Camera Raw dialog box
- Saving a DNG file as a backup
- Vignetting a photo

Photoshop Elements for Digital Photographers

Photoshop Elements can work with Camera Raw files and archive in the Adobe Digital Negative format.

Starting up

Within the Photoshop Elements Organizer: You will work with several files from the Lessons folder in this lesson. Make sure that you have copied the Lessons folder from the supplied DVD to your hard drive. In order to access these files in the Organizer, you need to import them. See "Adding files and folders to the Organizer" on page 11.

Within the Photoshop Elements Editor: The Photoshop Elements Editor defaults to the last panel layout that you used. Before starting, make sure your tools and panels are consistent with the examples presented in these lessons by resetting the panels. Do this by choosing Window > Reset Panels or by pressing the Reset panels button (↻) in the Options bar.

See Lesson 11 in action!

Use the accompanying video to gain a better understanding of how to use some of the features shown in this lesson. The video tutorial for this lesson can be found on the included DVD.

Working with Camera Raw files

A Camera Raw image file contains the unprocessed data from the image sensor (CCD) of a digital camera; essentially, it is a digital negative of your image. By working with a Raw file, you have greater control and flexibility, while still keeping the original image file. There is no standard Raw format in use today; each one is proprietary and differs from one camera to another.

Below is a partial list of the various Camera Raw formats and the companies that use them.

FILE FORMAT	BRAND
.raf	Fuji
.crw, .cr2	Canon
.tif, .k25, .kdc, .dcs, .dcr, .drf	Kodak
.mrw	Minolta
.nef	Nikon
.orf	Olympus
.dng	Adobe
.ptx, .pef	Pentax
.arw, .srf, .sr2	Sony
.x3f	Sigma
.erf	Epson
.mef, .mos	Mamiya
.raw	Panasonic
.cap, .tif, .iiq	Phase One
.r3d	Red
.fff	Imacon
.pxn	Logitech
.bay	Casio

Even if you have been a photographer for many years, understanding all the settings that are available in your digital camera can be difficult. Using incorrect settings can lead to poor quality images. Incorrect settings for white balance, sharpening, or color balance can lead to images that are too dark or have color tints. Because Raw files are taken directly from the camera's sensors prior to any image processing, Photoshop Elements can undo and recalculate tonal adjustment.

Understanding the Camera Raw dialog box

Because a Camera Raw file contains the completely uncompressed image data from your digital camera, you can access certain features that would be unavailable in other formats, such as JPEG. The Camera Raw dialog box allows you to manipulate features such as the white balance, tint, and exposure. At first glance, the Camera Raw dialog box can seem overwhelming, but when studied one component at a time, the features are quite manageable.

White Balance: White balance is necessary because the appearance of the color white will change, based on the lighting conditions of your scene. So when you white balance a camera or, in this case, set the white balance for the image, you are setting what color in an image is neutral white.

Temperature: You may often hear artists, designers, and photographers talking about warm and cool colors. They aren't just being metaphorical; colors actually do have temperatures. These color temperatures are measured using the Kelvin scale. So in this system, warm colors— oranges, yellows, and reds—usually have a color temperature of around 2500–3000K, while the cool colors are often measured at 5000K and above. When using the color temperature slider, if you move the slider to the left, you can correct a photo taken at a warmer color temperature and the image becomes bluer, or cooler. Conversely, move the slider to the right to correct a photo taken at a cooler color temperature, and the image becomes warmer.

Tint: Due to the impurities found in most lighting conditions, the color balance of images must often be fine-tuned. The tint slider is used to compensate for a red or green color cast. When using the slider, you move it to the left into the negative values to add green to your image, and to the right into the positive values to add red.

Exposure: The Exposure slider is used to adjust the brightness or darkness of an image. When the slider is moved to the left, it darkens the image, and when it is moved to the right, it brightens the image. The values used by the exposure control are equivalent to the f-stops that control a camera's aperture. Making an adjustment to the exposure setting of +1 is equivalent to widening the aperture one full f-stop, while an adjustment of -1 would be like reducing the aperture by 1.

Recovery: Sometimes the whitest areas of your image actually contain visual information that isn't visible, because it has been clipped to white. The Recovery slider attempts to recover the details from the highlight area of your image.

Fill Light: Sometimes the darker or shadow areas of your image still have visual information that can be recovered. The Fill Light slider attempts to recover details from shadow areas of your image, without over-brightening the black areas.

Blacks: In a digital image, the tonal value of pixels isn't a concrete value, and you can redefine them. This is the case with the Blacks slider, which allows you to specify which input levels are mapped to black in the final image. By increasing Blacks, you expand the areas that are mapped to black, increasing the amount of black pixels in the image. This creates the appearance of increased contrast in the image. The greatest change is in the shadow areas, with less change in the midtones and highlights.

Brightness: Creating a similar effect to the Exposure slider, the Brightness slider adjusts the brightness of the image. It functions a little differently: whereas the Exposure control tends to clip the image in the highlight areas (areas that are completely white) and shadow areas (areas that are completely black), the Brightness slider compresses or expands the highlight and shadow areas.

Contrast: The Contrast slider adjusts the midtones of an image to make the dark areas darker, while at the same time making the bright areas brighter. At higher values, the slider increases the midtone contrast, while lower values produce an image with less contrast.

Clarity: The effect of the Clarity slider is similar to using the Sharpen filters found in the main Photoshop Elements Editor. It is used to sharpen the edges in your image to enhance edge clarity.

Vibrance: The Vibrance slider is used to adjust the saturation of colors in your images so that clipping is minimized as the colors approach maximum saturation. The main advantage of Vibrance slider is that it can also be used to prevent skin tones from becoming oversaturated.

Saturation: As the name implies, the Saturation slider is used to adjust the color saturation of an image. The values used range from −100, which would give you a pure monochromatic value, all the way to +100, which would double the color saturation values in the image.

ICON	TOOL NAME	USE
🔍	Zoom tool	Increases or decreases the magnification level of a Camera Raw preview.
✋	Hand tool	Allows you to reposition a Raw image, when magnified, in the preview pane.
🖋	White Balance tool	Balances colors in a Raw image when you click on a neutral gray area in the image.
🔲	Crop tool	Crops a Raw image right in the preview pane.
📐	Straighten tool	Realigns an image.
🩹	Retouch tool	Heals or clones a Raw image in the preview pane.
👁	Red-Eye Removal tool	Removes red eye from a Raw image.
☰	Open preferences dialog box	Used to change preferences, such as where .xmp files are saved.
↺	Rotate image 90 degrees counterclockwise	Rotates an image 90 degrees counterclockwise.
↻	Rotate image 90 degrees clockwise	Rotates an image 90 degrees clockwise.

Using the Camera Raw dialog box

Camera Raw files cannot be directly edited in Photoshop Elements. When you open a Raw file, it opens in the Camera Raw dialog box. Because raw files are unprocessed, they can be easily manipulated to adjust the color and tonal balance of your images.

1   In the Organizer, type **Sophie** into the search text field; this isolates the file *Sophie. CR2*. This is a Camera Raw file taken from a Canon Digital Rebel XT camera. Right-click the image and choose Edit with Photoshop Elements from the contextual menu that appears.

2 The Camera Raw dialog box opens in the Editor. The Camera Raw dialog box actually automatically opens whenever you open a supported Raw file in Photoshop Elements.

A. Tools. B. Histogram. C. Adjustment controls.

The Camera Raw file is manipulated using the controls found on the right side of the dialog box interface. These controls allow you to set the color and tonal balance of your image and provide a visual representation, through the histogram values, of the various pixels in the image.

A: The Basic panel contains controls for adjusting the tonal balance of the image.

B: The Detail panel contains controls for image sharpening and noise reduction.

C: The Camera Calibration panel allows you to set a camera profile to use.

D: The Shadow Clipping Warning indicates the areas of the image that are underexposed, with large areas of shadow being clipped. Clipped shadows appear highlighted if they are not corrected using the exposure controls.

E: The Highlight Clipping Warning also indicates the areas of an image that are overexposed, with large highlight areas being clipped. Clipped areas appear highlighted if they are not corrected using the exposure controls.

F: The Histogram displays the tonal variation of the image as a graph.

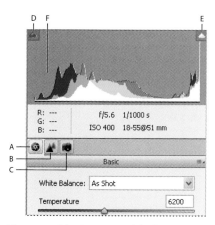

The options of the Camera Raw dialog box.

3   If you have been adjusting the image settings while reviewing this section, press and hold
    the Alt (Windows) or Option (Mac OS) key on your keyboard and press Reset. When
    you press the Alt/Option key, the Cancel button becomes the Reset button.

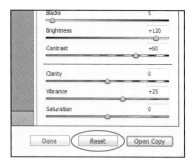

*When Alt/Option is pressed, the Cancel button changes
to the Reset button.*

4   The first thing you will do is balance the color of the image. Choose the White Balance
    tool (✐) from the tools at the top of the dialog box. A good neutral area to use as a
    reference for white in this image is the name tag on the girl's sweater. Click it with the
    White Balance tool. The tonal range of the image changes; the values shift using the
    white in the name tag as the reference point.

*With the White Balance tool selected,
click on the name tag.*

The image looks a bit underexposed, and the girl's face is somewhat dark. You'll bring
out more detail in the girl's face with the Brightness slider. By using a combination
of the Brightness and Recovery sliders, you can bring out additional details without
overexposing the image.

5   Click and drag the Exposure slider to the left until you reach the -0.35 mark, or type
    -.35 into the Exposure text field.

Set the exposure.

6   Click and drag the Brightness slider to the right to about the 120 mark, or type **120**
    into the Brightness text field. This causes the highlight areas to be blown out, or to lose
    their detail.

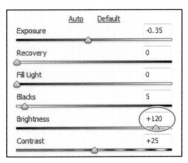

Set the brightness.

7   You will recover some of the lost highlight detail by clicking and dragging the Recovery
    slider to the 60 mark, or by typing **60** into the Recovery text field.

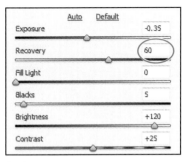

Set the recovery.

8   Increase the contrast of the image by clicking and dragging the Contrast slider to the 60 mark, or by typing **60** into the Contrast text box.

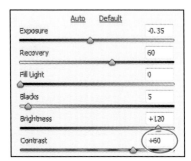

Set the contrast.

9   Click and drag the Vibrance slider to the 25 mark, or type **25** into the Vibrance text field. Use the Vibrance slider to adjust the richness of the color values in an image.

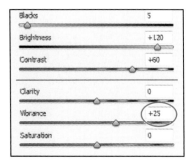

Set the vibrance.

10 Choose the Crop tool (⌗) from the tools at the top of the dialog box. Click and drag to draw a marquee and create an image that is tighter on the girl's head and shoulders, as shown in the following image. The crop area is used if you open the image in Photoshop Elements, but it doesn't affect the original Raw file.

You can crop an image in the Camera Raw dialog box.

11 From this point, there are two things you can do with the file: Open the file in Photoshop Elements by pressing Open File or save the file as a DNG file, which is what you will do in the next part of this lesson.

Keep the Camera Raw dialog box open for the next exercise.

Saving a DNG file

You will save your image as a DNG file. A DNG, or digital negative file maintains information on all the corrections you have made, and the original unprocessed Camera Raw data. Adobe created the DNG format as a standard for Camera Raw files; this is a standard that they hope all camera vendors will eventually support. For your purposes, it provides you with the opportunity to save your original Camera Raw files in a format that can be reopened repeatedly, edited, and saved again without any loss of quality or data and unlike native RAW formats, the DNG format can embed metadata directly into the DNG file instead of storing the data in a sidecar file as is the case with most RAW formats.

1   Press Save Image in the lower-left corner of the Camera Raw dialog box. The Save Options dialog box opens.

2   Leave the Destination set to *Save in Same Location*, and then click on the arrow to the right of the second drop-down menu in the File Naming section, and choose 2 Digit Serial Number. This automatically numbers your files, starting with the original document name followed by 01.

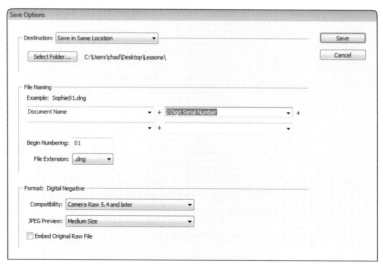

The Camera Raw Save Options dialog box.

3   Press Save. You are returned to the Camera Raw dialog box.

4   Press Open Image. The adjusted and cropped image is opened in Photoshop Elements, and you can continue working on it with Photoshop Elements' wide range of tools. If you save the file now, you see the standard Save As dialog box. The saved image will be a copy of the original. Close the file and don't save the changes.

To edit the DNG you created, open it using the Photoshop Elements Editor.

Processing multiple files

The Process Multiple Files dialog box.

The Process Multiple Files command applies settings to the images in a folder or a group of files. It allows you to apply identical adjustments to a group of images automatically When processing files, you have the option to leave all the files open in the Editor, close and save the changes to the original files, or save modified versions of the files to a new location, which leaves the originals unchanged.

1   From the Photoshop Elements Editor, choose File > Process Multiple Files. Choose the files you want to process from the Process Files From drop-down menu:

Folder: Processes files in a folder that you specify.

Import: Processes images from a digital camera or scanner that is currently attached to your computer.

Opened Files: Processes all open files from the Editor. If there are no files open, this option is grayed out.

2   For Destination, press Browse and select a folder location for the processed files. Note that if you choose Folder as the destination, you have to specify a file-naming convention and select file compatibility options.

3   Under Image Size, select Resize Images if you want each processed file to be resized to a uniform size.

To apply an automatic adjustment to the images, select an option from the menu in the top right corner of the dialog box.

To attach a label to the images, choose an option from the Labels menu, and then customize the text, position, font, size, opacity, and color.

4   Press OK to process and save the files.

Vignetting a photo

A vignette is a decorative process where an image is intentionally faded toward the corners or edges. It can be used to focus a viewer's attention toward the center of a photograph, or to cover unnecessary content at the edges.

1　From the Organizer, type **holiday** into the search text field to isolate the redeye image. Right-click on *holiday.jpg* and select Edit with Photoshop Elements from the contextual menu that appears.

2　In the Editor, choose File > Save As. The Save As dialog box opens. Change the filename to **vignette** and for the format, choose Photoshop. Press Save. If a dialog box appears stating that *Save in Version Set with Original* is checked, press OK.

To add an interesting effect to this image, you will convert it to black and white, increase the contrast, and then vignette it to place emphasis on the faces of the children.

3　Choose Enhance > Adjust Color > Remove Color to convert the color image to black and white.

Removing color from an image.

The color has been removed from the image, but the resulting image doesn't have much contrast.

4   Choose Enhance > Adjust Lighting > Levels. In the Input Levels section of the Levels dialog box, drag the black slider to the right until the number field below it reads 10. Drag the white slider to the left until the number field reads 215. Press OK.

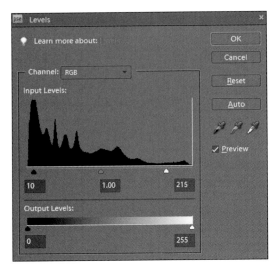

The Levels command is used to control the tonal values of an image.

The Levels dialog box is used to control the tonal range of an image. The Input sliders are used to set the minimum tonal value that you want to be black and white. As the sliders are dragged closer toward the center, more areas of your image are changed to black and white, thus increasing the contrast in the image.

5   Press D on your keyboard to set the foreground and background colors to the default black and white. Choose Filter > Distort > Diffuse Glow. In the Diffuse Glow Options dialog box, type **0** in the Graininess text field, **3** in the Glow Amount text field, and **14** in the Clear Amount text field. Press OK.

The Diffuse Glow filter is used to add a glow to the highlight areas of an image. The glow color is set by the currently active background color of your document.

6   Choose the Rectangular Marquee tool (▢) from the Toolbox, then click and drag to draw a selection marquee around the entire image or type Ctrl+A (Windows) or Command+A (Mac OS) on your keyboard.

The Rectangular Marquee tool makes rectangular selections.

7   For the vignette effect, you need to frame the image. With the Rectangular Marquee tool still selected, press and hold the Alt (Windows) or Option (Mac OS) key on the keyboard and draw a smaller selection inside the image. Holding down the Alt/Option key removes the new selection from the previous one.

Holding down the Alt/Option key causes your new selection to be removed from the current one, while holding down the Shift key adds to the current selection.

8   Press the Create a New Layer button in the Layers panel. Double-click the name of the new layer and rename it **Frame**.

9   With the new Frame layer selected, hold down the Alt (Windows) or Option (Mac OS) key on the keyboard and press the Backspace key. This fills the selection with your current background color, which should be black. Press Ctrl+D (Windows) or Command+D (Mac OS) to deselect.

To fill a layer or selection with the background color, the keyboard shortcut is Ctrl+backspace (Windows) or Command+Delete (Mac OS).

10   To create a vignette effect, you will soften the edge of the border. Make sure that the Frame layer is selected and choose Filter > Blur > Gaussian Blur. Type **40** in the Radius text field, then press OK. Because the frame is on its own layer, the blur filter is only affecting the black border.

11   Choose File > Save or press Ctrl+S (Windows) or Command+S (Mac OS) to save the file, then close the file.

The basics of filters

Most of the filters are accessible through the Filter menu. Certain filters are accessible all alone through their own dedicated control dialog boxes, while most automatically open the Filter Gallery. The Gallery allows you to apply a group of filters together simultaneously from a central location.

Filters permanently change the image, and aside from using the Undo command, they cannot be changed after being applied and saved.

Sharpening an image with Unsharp Mask

Some filters have very pronounced effects, while others, like the Sharpen filters, can be used for more subtle effects like correcting photos. It may sound strange that you sharpen an image with a filter called Unsharp Mask, but that is exactly what you will do in this exercise.

1   In the Organizer, type **little** in the search text field at the top of the workspace. This should reveal both the original *little girl.psd* file and the *little girl-done.psd* file created for this exercise. Right-click the *little girl-done.psd* file and choose Edit with Photoshop Elements from the contextual menu that appears.

This image has been retouched to correct the colors, but could still use a bit of sharpening to make it more clear.

The Photo Browser's Search text field can be used to quickly sort through images in your catalogs.

2   Choose View > Actual Pixels or press the Acutal pixels button in the Options bar with the Hand tool selected. This sets the document zoom to 100 percent and is a helpful way to look at your images if you are going to apply any correction or filters to them, such as Unsharp Mask.

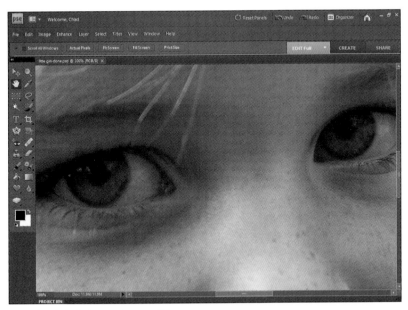

Using Actual Pixels shows an image at 100 percent zoom.

 You can choose Window > Panel Bin to hide the Panel Bin to maximize your screen space.

Select the Hand tool ( ) or press and hold down the Space bar on your keyboard. The cursor temporarily becomes the Hand tool. Click and drag to pan the document until you are looking at one or both of the girl's eyes in your window.

3   Choose Enhance > Unsharp Mask. The Unsharp Mask dialog box opens.

 You can click and drag inside of the Unsharp Masks preview window to change the viewing area.

What is Unsharp Mask?

Unsharp Mask is a traditional film compositing technique used to sharpen edges in an image. The Unsharp Mask filter corrects blurring in the image, and it compensates for the blurring that occurs during the resampling and printing process. Applying the Unsharp Mask filter is recommended whether your final destination is print or online.

The Unsharp Mask filter assesses the brightness levels of adjacent pixels and increases their relative contrast; it lightens the light pixels that are located next to darker pixels, as it darkens those darker pixels. You can set the extent and range of lightening and darkening that occurs, using the sliders in the Unsharp Mask dialog box. When sharpening an image, it's important to understand that the effects of the Unsharp Mask filter are far more pronounced on-screen than they appear in high-resolution output, such as in a printed piece.

The Unsharp Mask dialog box displays the following options:

Amount: Determines how much the contrast of pixels is to be increased. Typically an amount of 150 precent or more is applied, but this amount depends on the subject matter of the image being sharpened. Overdoing Unsharp Mask on a person's face can be rather harsh, and the value used in this case can be less than that used on an image of a piece of equipment, where the fine details are often very important.

Radius: Determines the number of pixels surrounding the edge pixels that are affected by the sharpening. For high-resolution, 300 ppi image, a radius of 1 and 2 is recommended. If you are creating oversized graphics for posters or billboards, for example, you might want to experiment with higher values.

Threshold: Determines how different the brightness values between two pixels must be before they are considered edge pixels and thus are sharpened by the filter. To avoid introducing unwanted noise into your image, a minimum Threshold setting of 10 is recommended.

4   In the Unsharp Mask dialog box, type **300** in the Amount text field. The texture of a child's skin is usually so soft that a higher Amount percentage can be used without bringing out unflattering detail.

5   Type **1** in the Radius text field and **5** in the Threshold text field. Press OK.

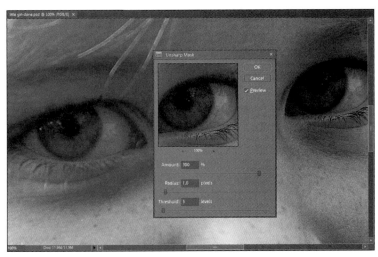

The Unsharp Mask filter works by increasing the contrast of the image.

6   Choose File > Save As or press Ctrl+Shift+S (Windows) or Command+Shift+S (Mac OS) to open the Save As dialog box. Change the filename to **little girl-done-unsharp. psd** and press Save. Keep the file open, as you will need it in the next exercise.

Using Undo History for comparisons

The Undo History panel in Adobe Photoshop Elements can be used for a wide variety of functions. In this exercise, you will use it to compare the image before the Unsharp Mask filter was applied to the finished file.

1   Open the Undo History panel by choosing Window > Undo History. This panel keeps track of the last 50 actions that you have performed while the current file was open.

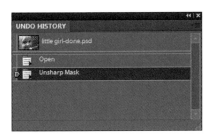

The Undo History panel records the last 50 actions performed by default.

The Undo History for a file is restarted every time the file is opened. The number of history states can be set in the Performance section of the Photoshop Elements preferences and is accessible by going to Edit > Preferences > Performance.

2   The thumbnail at the top of the Undo History panel is called a snap shot. Click the snap shot to see how your image looked when it was first opened.

3   Click the history state named *Unsharp Mask* to see the effects of the Unsharp Mask filter.

Make sure that when you finish comparing your images, you finish with Unsharp Mask highlighted.

4   Choose File > Save or press Ctrl+S (Windows) or Command+S (Mac OS) to save the file, then close the file.

Using the Blur filter to create depth of field

A depth-of-field effect is intended to help establish the illusion of depth in a flat photograph. Depth of field occurs when objects appear more (or less) blurry, based on their positioning from the camera lens. Depth of field is generally created by factors such as aperture, lens focal length, and distance from the subject being photographed. Due to other factors, you may not be able to capture the desired depth-of-field at the time the picture is taken. Because of this, depth-of-field effects are often achieved after the image has been transferred to the computer.

1   In the Organizer, type **flowers** into the search text field. This isolates every image that has *flowers* in the title. Right-click the *flowers.psd* image and choose Edit with Photoshop Elements from the contextual menu that appears. This file has been built with two saved selections that define the foreground and background of the image to make it easier to apply the filters that will create the depth-of-field effect.

2   In the Editor, the first thing you are going to do is remove the graininess that appears in the image. Choose View > Actual Pixels to view your image at 100 percent zoom, then choose Filter > Noise > Reduce Noise.

The Reduce Noise filter reduces both white and color noise in an image. Additionally, you can remove noise when a JPEG file is created. You can also select the *Remove JPEG Artifacts* option in the dialog box to remove the blocky artifacts and halos that are caused by saving an image at a low JPEG quality setting, but that is not needed here.

3   Type **8** in the Strength text field, **80** in the Preserve Details text field, and **80** in the Reduce Color Noise text field. Press OK.

The Remove Noise dialog box.

4   Choose Select > Load Selection. In the Load Selection dialog box, choose *background* from the Selection drop-down menu in the Source area. Confirm that Operation is set to *New Selection* and press OK.

While you could create the selection on your own using the selection tools, as you discovered in Lesson 5, "Adjusting Color," here the selection was saved for you so you can focus on creating the depth of field effect.

The Load Selection dialog box allows you to load a selection that was previously saved using Select > Save Selection.

5   Choose Select > Refine Edge to open the Refine Edge dialog box. Type **5** in the Smooth text field and **2** in the Feather text field, then press OK.

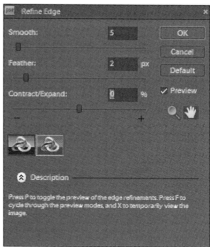

You can preview the Refine Edge command against a custom color to make it easier to see the effect of the feather setting.

Press Ctrl+H (Windows) or Command+H (Mac OS) on the keyboard to temporarily hide the selection edges but keep the area selected. This makes it easier to judge the effect of the filter you will apply next.

6   Choose Filter > Blur > Gaussian Blur. Drag the slider to see the effect of various radius settings before typing **1** in the Radius text field. Press OK.

Thanks to the selection, the background is blurry, and everything else is unaffected.

Press Ctrl+H (Windows) or Command+H (Mac OS) on the keyboard again to make the selection edges visible. It is important to remember to turn the selection edges back on whenever you do not need them to be invisible; otherwise, you may forget that you have something selected.

9   Choose File > Save or press Ctrl+S (Windows) or Command+S (Mac OS) on the keyboard to save the file.

Congratulations, you have finished this lesson.

Self study

1   Set your digital camera to capture a Camera Raw file. Use the Camera Raw dialog box to manipulate your photos.

2   Add a vignette effect to your own photos.

3   Practice improving your selections by selecting the people on your own rather than using the saved selections.

Review

Questions

1   What is a DNG file?

2   When processing multiple files, where are the three locations from which you can draw your files?

3   What does the Unsharp Mask filter do to an image?

Answers

1   The DNG (Digital Negative) format is Adobe's attempt to standardize the Camera Raw format. DNG is a non-proprietary universal file format.

2   **a. Folder:** This option processes files in a folder that you specify.

   b. Import: This option processes images from a digital camera or scanner that is currently attached to your computer.

   c. Opened Files: This option processes all open files from the Editor. If there are no files open, this option is grayed out.

3   The Unsharp Mask filter increases the contrast between pixels in an image. You can set the strength of the sharpening, along with how close the pixels need to be to each other and the amount of tonal variation of each pixel that needs to be present before they are affected by the Unsharp Mask filter.

Lesson 12

What you'll learn in this lesson:

- Creating a new blank document
- Using brushes
- Using gradients
- Working with vector shapes

Photoshop Elements for Artists

While Photoshop Elements is usually used for working with digital photographs. Artists and crafters use Photoshop Elements to create scrapbooking, custom birthday cards, or invitations.

Starting up

Within the Photoshop Elements Organizer: You will work with several files from the Lessons folder in this lesson. Make sure that you have copied the Lessons folder from the supplied DVD to your hard drive. In order to access these files in the Organizer, you need to import them. See "Adding files and folders to the Organizer" on page 11.

Within the Photoshop Elements Editor: The Photoshop Elements Editor defaults to the last panel layout that you used. Before starting, make sure your tools and panels are consistent with the examples presented in these lessons by resetting the panels. Do this by choosing Window > Reset Panels or by pressing the Reset panels button (↻) in the Options bar.

See Lesson 12 in action!

Use the accompanying video to gain a better understanding of how to use some of the features shown in this lesson. The video tutorial for this lesson can be found on the included DVD.

Creating a new document from scratch

In addition to opening and editing photos in Photoshop Elements, you can also create new documents from scratch. This is helpful when you want to create a photo collage, as you will do in this lesson. In the first set of exercises, you will create a collage using brushes, gradients, shapes, and patterns.

1   In the Photoshop Elements Editor, select File > New > Blank File to create a new document.

The New dialog box.

2   In the New dialog box, name the new file **Happy Birthday**.

3   Choose U.S. Paper from the Preset drop-down menu. This sets the size and resolution options to produce a high-quality printable image.

4   In the Size drop-down menu, select Letter. Letter is the standard printer paper size, with a width of 8.5 inches and a height of 11 inches.

5   In the Resolution field, change the default of 300 ppi to 150 ppi. While 300 is the default for all high-quality projects sent to a print shop, a resolution of 150 is usually more than satisfactory for home inkjet printers. Leave the other two options, Color Mode and Background Contents, as you find them, and press OK.

6   Choose Window > Images > Consolidate all to tabs to expand the document window to full size. Choose Window > Project Bin to collapse the Project Bin leaving more room for the document window.

7   Choose File > Save As. Navigate to the Lessons folder that you copied from the DVD, and press Save. Don't close the file.

Using brushes to add style to your work

The first thing you are going to do is to use brushes to add some texture to the background of your canvas. Brushes in Photoshop Elements are used to apply color to your artwork. They actually function a lot more like stamps than brushes in the traditional sense, as each is actually a tip shape that you can paint with. In this exercise, you will be using brushes and gradients to create a background.

Creating texture with brushes and gradients

1   Click on the Brush tool (✐) in the Toolbox to the left of the program interface. At the top of the interface in the Options bar, click the brush stroke drop-down menu to show the Selected Brush Preset; it lets you select the brush tip you want to use.

The Options bar across the top of your screen allows you to set options for your active tool.

2   From the Brushes drop-down menu at the top of the screen, select Special Effect Brushes and click on the Butterfly brush. Type **300px** into the Size text field to the right of the Brush preset menu. Change the opacity to 50 percent by clicking on the opacity controls and dragging the slider that pops up or type **50** into the opacity percent text field.

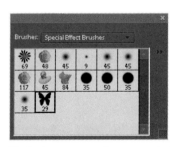

The brush presets menu allows you to select the brush tip you want to use.

3   Create a new layer by clicking on the Create a New Layer button (▣) at the bottom-left corner of the Layers panel. Double-click on the words *Layer 1*, and change the name of the layer to **Butterflies**.

The Create a New Layer button looks like a dog-eared piece of paper. The keyboard command for creating a new layer is Shift+Ctrl+N (Windows) or Shift+Command+N (Mac OS).

4 Make sure that your cursor is not flashing in any of the option fields at the top. If it is, press the Enter key to commit the value. Press **D** on the keyboard to reset the foreground and background colors to the default black and white. Click and drag across the canvas from the lower-left corner to the upper-right corner.

5 Type **150 px** in the Size text field and change the opacity value to 75 percent. Again, click and drag across the canvas, but this time, start in the upper left corner and drag to the lower right corner. You should end up with something that looks like the following figure.

Your results should be similar to this image.

6 Again, create a new layer by clicking on the Create a New Layer button at the bottom left corner of the Layers panel. Double-click on the words *Layer 1*, and change the name of the layer to **Gradient**.

7 Choose the Gradient tool (▭) in the Toolbox. A default black-to-white gradient loads into the gradient field. Click the gradient icon in the Options bar to open the Gradient Editor.

The active gradient displays on the left side of your tool options. Click on it to open the Gradient Editor.

8   The top of the Gradient Editor displays a library of gradients that ship with the program.
    The bottom of the panel allows you to edit an existing gradient or to create a new one.
    Click on the left color stop at the bottom of the gradient bar; its options load into the
    Stops section at the bottom. Click the Color swatch to open the Adobe Color Picker.

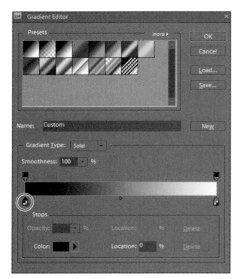

Change the settings in the Gradient Editor.

9   In the Color Picker, type the RGB values, R:**29**, G:**29**, B:**229**, to pick a bright-blue
    color. Press OK to exit the Color Picker.

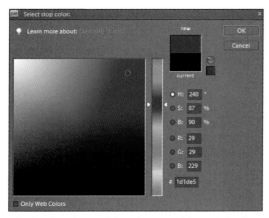

*The Photoshop Elements Color Picker is an Adobe standard and can
be found in most of their applications.*

10 Click on the color stop on the right, and then click the Color swatch picker to launch the Color Picker again. This time, set the RGB values to R:**229**, G:**29**, B:**29**, and press OK to exit the Select stop color box, and press OK to exit the Gradient Editor.

11 With the new Gradient layer highlighted, click in the upper left corner of the page and drag your cursor towards the lower right corner. This applies a gradient that covers the entire canvas.

12 In the Layers panel, click the Layer blending mode drop-down menu and select Color. This allows the Gradient layer to tint the Butterflies layer beneath it.

 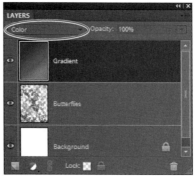

Change the blending mode to change the effect on the image.

13 Choose File > Save to save your work. If the Save As dialog box appears, click to deselect the option for *Save in Version Set with Original*, click the name of your previous file, Happy Birthday, then press Save to overwrite it. Do not close the file.

Fun with brushes

Brushes in Photoshop Elements have many options that allow you to create a variety of visual effects. You can set a brush's dynamic options by selecting the Brush tool, selecting the brush tip you want to work with, then opening the More Options menu ( ) in the Options bar.

Spacing: Controls the distance between each mark the brush tip makes as you drag it.

Fade: Sets the number of steps it takes the paint flow to fade out. The lower the value for Fade, the more quickly the fade-out effect is.

Hue Jitter: Sets the rate at which the brush color switches between the foreground and background colors.

Hardness: Controls the hard edge of the brush. Higher values give the brush a hard, solid edge, while lower values soften the edge. This setting isn't available for some brushes.

Scatter: Controls how close to the edge of a path brush marks are distributed. Low numbers keep the marks tightly together, while higher numbers allow for a wider distribution.

Angle: Sets the rotation value for the brush tip.

Roundness: Tilts the angle of the brush tip away from the viewer. This results in a brush that appears to flatten out at lower numbers.

Creating custom brushes

Brushes can be created from any selection.

1   Simply create a selection using any Selection tool. Select Edit > Create Brush from Selection.

2   In the Brush Name dialog box, name your new brush and press OK. It now becomes accessible from the brush menu in the Options bar.

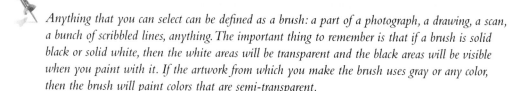

Anything that you can select can be defined as a brush: a part of a photograph, a drawing, a scan, a bunch of scribbled lines, anything. The important thing to remember is that if a brush is solid black or solid white, then the white areas will be transparent and the black areas will be visible when you paint with it. If the artwork from which you make the brush uses gray or any color, then the brush will paint colors that are semi-transparent.

The Impressionist brush

Impressionism was an artistic movement in the early nineteenth century. It was characterized by bold brush strokes and vibrant colors. The Impressionist brush in Photoshop Elements has the ability to simulate the appearance of this art style and can be used to spice up a design. It does this by warping the areas of an image to resemble the strokes of a paint brush. In this exercise you will merge a flower image into the Happy Birthday file and create an impressionist version of the flowers.

1   With the Happy Birthday file still open, choose File > Open. Navigate to the Lessons folder that you copied from the DVD and select the *Flowers.tif* file. Double-click the file to open it, then choose Window > Images > Consolidate all to tabs.

2   Open the Project Bin choosing Window > Project Bin. Activate the Magic Wand tool (✎) in the Toolbox, and click the white area of the image. A selection border should appear that completely encloses the white area of the image.

3   Choose Select > Inverse to reverse the selection so that the flowers become selected. Activate the Move tool (✤) by clicking on it in the Toolbox.

4   Click on the flowers with the Move tool and drag them into the thumbnail of the Happy Birthday image in the Project Bin. This copies the flowers into the image. If necessary, reposition the layer so the flowers appear in the lower right. If you hold down the Shift key on your keyboard while dragging the selection onto the thumbnail in the Project bin, it will center the image when it is copied to the new file.

You can drag from the document window to the Project Bin to move content between files.

5 In the Layers panel of the Happy Birthday image, the flowers show up as a new layer. If it is not already there, click and drag this new layer below the Butterflies layer. This places it right above the Background layer. Double-click on the name of the layer and rename it **flowers**.

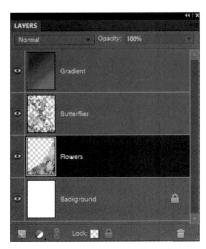

Layer positioning, called stacking order, can be changed by dragging and dropping layers.

6 Click and hold on the Brush tool (✐) and choose the Impressionist Brush tool (✐) from the list of options. In the Options bar, type **25** in the Size text field, just as you did when working with the regular brush. In the Layers panel, click the visibility icons (👁) for the Butterflies and Gradient layers to turn them off. This allows you to see the flowers layer all by itself.

7 Click on the flowers layer once again to make sure that it is the active layer. Click and drag with the Impressionist brush all over the flowers in the document window. You should notice that the photograph begins to look more like a painting. Continue to click and drag all over the flowers until you end up with an image that looks like a painting.

For an interesting effect, you can try holding the brush still in one location for a while instead of dragging it.

8 Click the visibility icons back on for the Butterflies and Gradient layers to see the effect. The flowers are now tinted by the gradient and create an interesting background texture for the design.

9 Choose File > Save to save your file.

Using shapes creatively

Shapes are vector-based objects that can be used like brushes to add emphasis and excitement to your work. The details of vector-based artwork aren't really important here, but the advantage of vector-based shapes is that, unlike photographs, they can be scaled to any size without a loss of quality. Photoshop Elements ships with many pre-created shapes that can cover a wide range of different needs. Everything from animal silhouettes to comic-style thought balloons are represented here. In this exercise, you will use a shape to create a picture frame for an imported graphic.

1 In the Layers panel, click the top layer, Gradient, to activate it. Choose File > Place to import a photo into this document. Navigate to the Lessons folder that you copied from the DVD and double-click the *Family in the Park.jpg* file to open it.

2 Click the checkmark at the bottom of the image to approve the placement of the file.

All placed items must be approved before you can work with them in Photoshop Elements.

3 Click and hold the Rectangle tool (■) in the Toolbox, and select the Custom Shape tool (♥) from the menu that pops up.

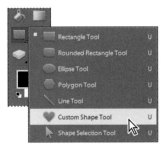

There are several shape options, from simple circles and rectangles to more complex custom shapes.

4 In the Options bar at the top of the workspace, choose frame 19 from the Shape drop-down menu and double-click it. Click and drag from the upper-left corner of the photo to the lower-right corner.

Additional shapes can be loaded by shape icon in the Options bar and choosing them from a list.

 If the frame doesn't fit exactly, press Ctrl+T (Windows) or Command+T (Mac OS) on your keyboard and select the Move tool, position the cursor over one of the squares of the bounding box on any side, then click and drag to enlarge or contract it. You have to click the check mark to approve your transformation.

5 Double-click on the new Shape layer's name in the Layers panel and rename it **Frame**. Hold down the Shift key and click the Family in the Park layer to select it as well. Press the Link Layers button (⅋) at the bottom of the Layers panel to link the two layers together.

6 With the Move tool active, press Ctrl+T (Windows) or Command+T (Mac OS) on your keyboard or choose Image > Transform > Free Transform and position the cursor outside one of the corner points of the bounding box that surrounds the layer, and wait for it to become a curved arrowhead. Click and drag to rotate the layer. Click the checkmark to approve the change.

7 Choose File > Save.

 The keyboard command for Save is Ctrl+S (Windows) or Command+S (Mac OS), while the keyboard command for Save As is Ctrl+Shift+S (Windows) or Command+Shift+S (Mac OS).

Fun with the other drawing tools

Although you haven't used them in this lesson, there are other drawing tools in the program that can be used either individually or in combination with other tools to produce some very creative results.

Pencil tool: The Pencil tool creates hard-edged, freehand lines. In addition to the most obvious use—sketching in Photoshop Elements—the Pencil tool functions much like a brush with a consistently hard edge.

Dodge, Burn, and Sponge tools: Taken from two traditional tools used in photography, the Dodge tool is used to lighten areas of an image, while the Burn tool darkens them. These tools are used to bring out details in the shadow and highlight areas of an image. A third tool associated with them, the Sponge tool, is used to saturate or desaturate the color areas of an image.

Blur, Sharpen, and Smudge tools: The Blur and Sharpen tools are used to soften hard edges in an image and increase the contrast between pixels, respectively. The Smudge tool simulates the effect of rubbing against wet paint, picking up the color where the drag begins and moving through the image as the drag continues.

The Eraser tool: The Eraser tool is used to change pixels in an image. When used on the background layer, the tool erases to the current background color, and when used on any other layer, it erases to transparency.

The Cookie Cutter tool: The Cookie Cutter tool uses a series of custom shapes to mask out an image. Anything inside of the shape remains, while what is outside is removed. You can think of it as a kind of custom crop tool.

Working with patterns

In addition to brushes and shapes, another useful and fun feature that Photoshop Elements has is patterns. Patterns are repeatable images or parts of images that can be applied similar like how color is applied. In this exercise, you will define and apply a pattern to the Happy Birthday image.

Creating patterns

Patterns can be created from the content of any square or rectangular selection. Any type of artwork—including photographs, drawings, and scanned art—can be used to create a pattern. If you can draw a rectangular selection around it, you can define it as a pattern.

1   In the Editor, choose File > Open and navigate to the Lessons folder that you copied from the DVD that came with this book. Open the file named *flower pattern.psd*.

2   Select the Rectangular Marquee tool (□) from the Toolbox on the left. Click and drag with the tool to select the entire canvas.

You can use the keyboard command Ctrl+A (Windows) or Command+A (Mac OS) to select all the contents of a document.

3   Choose Edit > Define Pattern from Selection to create the pattern.

Patterns saved with the program are always accessible in any file.

4   In the Pattern Name dialog box, type **flower pattern** and press OK.

5   Close the file.

Applying patterns

1   Open the *Happy Birthday.psd* file from the Editor.

Choosing File > Open Recently Edited File is a quick way to locate and open a file that you have recently been working on.

2   In the Layers panel, click the Flowers layer to select it, and then click on the Create a New Layer button. Double-click on the name of the new layer, and rename it **pattern**.

3   Choose Edit > Fill Layer. Choose Pattern from the Use drop-down menu of the Contents section. From the Custom Pattern menu, choose the pattern you created in the previous step; it is the last one in the menu. Leave all other options as you find them, and press OK.

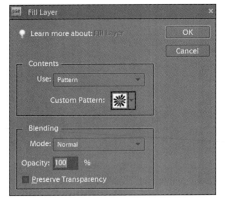

The Fill Layer dialog box can fill a layer with a color or pattern.

4 In the Layers panel, change the blending mode for this layer to Soft Light. The addition of the pattern creates an even more textured background.

5 Choose File > Save to save your work. Close the file.

Scrapbooking made easier

Creating scrapbooks and photo albums to record memorable events has been a tradition in many families for a long time. However, over the last decade or so, scrapbooking has become more widespread than ever before. This exercise will take you through the process of creating a scrapbook page using Photoshop Elements. You will use the various tools and effects in the program to create the impression of both texture and dimensionality in your work.

Creating a texture

This part of the lesson will take you through the creation of the initial document you will use to construct the scrapbook page. You will also create a background wood texture using a combination of several different filters available in the program.

1 In the Photoshop Elements Editor, select File > New > Blank File to create a new document.

2 In the New dialog box, type **Scrap Book Page** in the Name text field.

3 Choose U.S. Paper from the Preset drop-down menu. This sets the size and resolution options to produce a high-quality printable image.

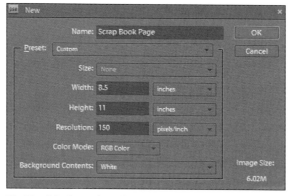

The New dialog box can be used to create original artwork for a variety of applications.

4 In the Size drop-down menu, make sure Letter is selected. Letter is the standard paper size, with a width of 8.5 inches and a height of 11 inches.

5 In the Resolution text field, change the default of 300 ppi by typing **150**. Leave the other two options, Color Mode and Background Contents, at their defaults and press OK.

6 In the Layers panel, double-click the background layer and type **Wood** in the Name text field.

Double-clicking a background layer launches the New Layer dialog box to convert it into a layer.

7 Double-click the foreground color swatch located at the bottom of the Toolbox to open the Color Picker. Type **d19011** in the hex code (#) text field at the bottom of the dialog box and press OK. Hex, or hexadecimal, colors are used on the Web to define color values. Here you use it as a quick way of referencing the color values for the brown. Any RGB color can be referenced using hex code.

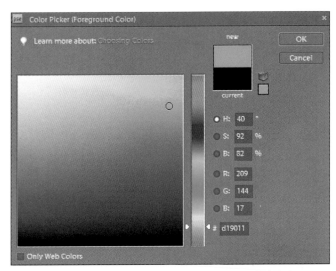

The Photoshop Elements Color Picker supports HSB, RGB, and Hexadecimal color values.

8 In the Toolbox, choose the Paint Bucket tool (✦), then click the document to fill the current layer with the brown color you chose in the last step. Later, on your own, you can experiment with different variations on the brown color used here to create the appearance of different types of wood.

9   Choose Filter > Noise > Add Noise to open the Add Noise dialog box. From here you can control the amount and type of noise created. Type **15** in the Amount text field and choose Gaussian from the Distribution section. Click the *Monochromatic* checkbox at the bottom of the dialog box and press OK. The noise will be used in the next few steps to create the wood grain appearance.

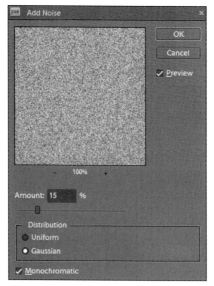

The Add Noise filter uses a mathematical algorithm to add speckling to the image.

You see the term Gaussian *quite often in Photoshop Elements. It is a specific type of function that creates a normal distribution of values and describes the way each pixel is transformed. A Gaussian blur reduces image noise, so it is useful for old photos with excessive grains when applied at smaller values.*

10 Choose Filter > Blur > Motion Blur. The Motion Blur filter simulates the effects of motion on a layer. Type **90** in the Angle text field and **100** in the Distance text field and press OK.

The Motion Blue filter modifies the noise to have a top-to-bottom look.

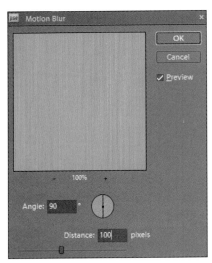

The Motion Blur dialog box can give a layer the illusion of movement.

11 Duplicate the *wood* layer by right-clicking on it in the Layers panel and choosing Duplicate Layer. Type **grain** in the As text field to name the new layer, then press OK.

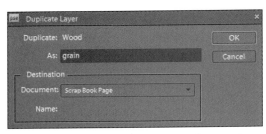

From the Duplicate Layer dialog box, you can use the Destination section to create a new document.

12 With the *grain* layer selected, choose Enhance > Adjust Color > Remove Color. This will remove all color from this layer, so that you can use it to create the appearance of the wood grain.

13 With the *grain* layer still selected, choose Filter > Artistic > Poster Edges. Leave the settings in the Poster Edges dialog box at their defaults and press OK.

The image resembles a rough black-and-white wood texture.

14 In the Layers panel, choose Soft Light from the Blending mode drop-down menu, and type **70** in the Opacity text field.

The image resembles a stylized, perfect wood texture.

The image now resembles stylized wood. Real wood has imperfections, such as knots in the grain that twist and misshapen it. You will add these imperfections in the next step.

15 Choose Filter > Distort > Liquify to open the Liquify dialog box. You are going to use the Bloat and Twirl tools to simulate knots in the wood grain.

16 Select the Bloat tool (⬙) from tools on the left side of the Liquify dialog box. In the Tool Options section on the right side of the dialog box, type **300** in the Brush Size text field. Click in the upper left corner of the artwork to make that area appear to bulge outward. The longer you hold the mouse down using the Bloat tool, the greater the effect will be. Click and release the mouse a couple of times to create a slight bulge in the grain.

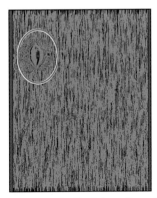

The Bloat tool adds a bulging effect to the image.

17 Select the Twirl Clockwise tool (◉) and click the area to which you just applied the Bloat tool. Begin by holding the Twirl Clockwise tool in place for a few seconds while you click with the mouse, then begin to move the tool slightly up and down over the bulging area to deform the grain around the knot.

Experiment with the tools to get different effects. You many want to use a different-sized brush or drag the tools diagonally instead of up and down. If you feel you have made a mistake, you can always hold down the Alt (Windows) or Option (Mac OS) key on your keyboard until the Cancel button becomes a Reset button to return to the original state of your artwork.

18 Type **200** in the Size text field to reduce the brush size, and repeat steps 16 and 17 on another area of the image. Type **100** in the Size text field to further reduce the brush size and repeat steps 16 and 17 again on another area of the image.

This allows you to create the appearance of different-sized knots within the wood. Place the knots at random while trying to be as asymmetrical as possible.

Press OK to close the Liquify dialog box and apply the changes to your document.

The completed wood texture.

19 Choose Layer > Merge Down to combine the two layers into one.

20 Choose File > Save As to save your document. Navigate to the Lessons folder that you copied from the DVD. Press Save to add your file to this folder. Because you named the file upon creation, the name field is already occupied.

Creating a text effect

Text doesn't only have to be just functional; it can also be a lot of fun. So far, you have mostly used the filters in Photoshop Elements to alter and correct images, but you can also use them to apply some very interesting special effects to both text and images.

When completed, the text should appear to be zooming toward you.

In this exercise, you will create a fun text effect that you sometimes see where the text seems to be zooming toward the viewer.

1   Choose File > New > Blank File. Type **Kids** in the Name text field. Choose U.S.
    Paper from the Preset drop-down menu and make sure the Size is set to Letter. Choose
    RGB Color from the Color Mode drop-down menu and press OK to create the new
    document.

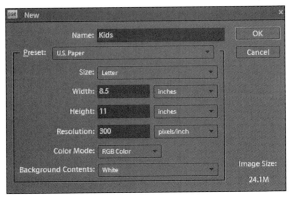

The New dialog box includes presets for a variety of different projects.

2   Choose Edit > Fill Layer. In the Contents section, choose Black from the Use drop-
    down menu. Leave all other settings at their defaults and press OK. This fills the
    document background with black.

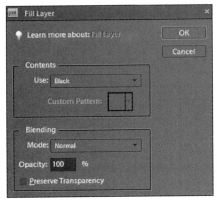

*The Fill Layer dialog box allows you to fill a layer with
a solid color or a pattern of your choosing.*

3   Choose the Type tool (⊥) from the Toolbox. In the Options bar at the top of the workspace, choose Arial Black from the Font Family drop-down menu and type **100** in the Font Size text field. Change the text color to white (R: 255, G: 255, B:255) by clicking on the Set the text color option in the options bar

Click in the middle of your document with the Text tool and type **KIDS** in all caps. Click the green checkmark at the top of the workspace to commit the change and deselect the active text. Because filters really can't be used on live text, after a few adjustments to the position of the text, the next step will be to convert the text into a graphic by combining it with the background layer.

4   Choose the Move tool (⊹) from the Toolbox and select the KIDS text layer from the Layers pane to activate it. Hold down the Shift key on your keyboard and click the Background layer so that they both become selected.

5   In the Options bar, press the Align button (⊡) and select Vertical Centers from the drop-down menu that appears. Press the Align button again and choose Horizontal Centers.

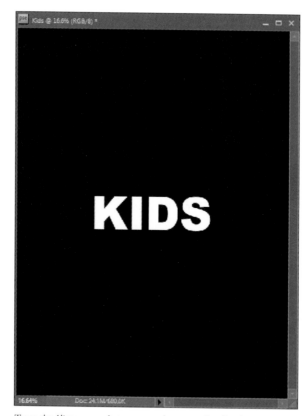

To use the Align commands, two or more layers must be selected.

6   Select the KIDS text layer from the Layers panel, and press Ctrl+E (Windows) or Command+E (Mac OS) on the keyboard to merge the KIDS text layer with the background layer.

Alternately, you can use the menu command Layer > Merge Layers. This works as long as the text layer is selected, and above the layer you want to merge it with.

7   Select the new merged Background layer and choose Filters > Blur > Gaussian Blur. Type **1.5** in the Radius text field. This blurs the text shape to produce a soft edge. Press OK.

You can experiment with values that are slightly lower or higher based upon your preference and taste.

The Gaussian Blur filter creates a hazy effect around the edges of the text.

8   Choose Filter > Stylize > Solarize. The Solarize filter doesn't have any options to set but instead automatically converts the black letters into an outline of the text and blends the positive and negative areas of an image. This is why blurring was necessary. Blurring pushed some of the white outside the edges of the text, resulting in more of an outline around the text after using the Solarize filter. Without the blur, there would not have been enough of a text outline when the Solarize filter was used.

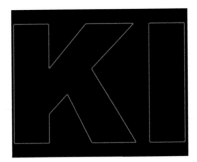

The Solarize filter reverses the positive and negative areas of an image.

9 Choose Enhance > Adjust Color > Adjust Hue/Saturation. In the Hue/Saturation dialog box, click the *Colorize* checkbox. Type **75** in the Saturation text field or move the slider to 75, and make sure the Hue and Lightness text fields are set to 0, then press OK. This results in changing the white outline to red around the text. If you have a hard time seeing it, it is probably due to your zoom level.

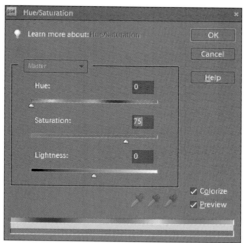

The Hue/Saturation effect allows you to control the color in your image.

10 Choose Filter > Distort > Polar Coordinates and select the *Polar to Rectangular* radio button. Press OK.

The Polar Coordinates filter creates a distortion in which a selected layer's contents are converted from a rectangular coordinate system to a polar system, or vice versa. While there are some interesting uses of this filter, it is most commonly seen as an intermediary step in tutorials.

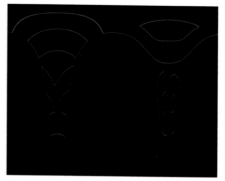

The distortion caused by the Polar Coordinates filter is used as an intermediary step in this lesson.

11 Choose Image > Rotate > 90° Right.

The Rotate command rotates an image 90 degrees left or right, 180 degrees, and arbitrary values.

12 Choose Filter > Stylize > Wind. In the Wind dialog box, choose Wind from the Method section and choose From the Left in the Direction section. Press OK. Press Ctrl+F (Windows) or Command+F (Mac OS) twice to run the filter two more times. The next few steps will return the image to a viewable state.

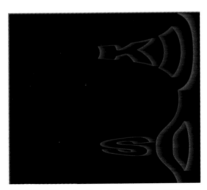

The Wind filter simulates the effect of wind blowing against a surface and pieces being blown off.

13 Choose Image > Rotate > 90° Left.

14 Choose Filter > Distort > Polar Coordinates, and choose the *Rectangular to Polar* radio button.

15 Choose the Crop tool (⬚) from the Toolbox. Click and drag to draw a marquee around the text. Click the green checkmark at the top of the workspace to commit the change.

When completed, the text should appear to be zooming toward you.

16 Choose File > Save As. Navigate to the Lessons folder you copied to your hard drive. Confirm that the format is set to Photoshop and that the file is named **Kids.psd**, then press Save.

Reversing the text effect

The text appears to have a motion trail behind it. This creates the impression that it is zooming toward the viewer. With a few simple changes, the results of this effect can be completely reversed along with the direction of the motion trail.

This variation on the tutorial follows the exact same steps right up to step 11.

- Choose Image > Rotate > 90° Left.

- Choose Filter > Stylize > Wind. In the Wind dialog box, choose Wind from the Method section, then choose From the Left in the Direction section. Press OK. Press Ctrl+F (Windows) or Command+F (Mac OS) twice to run the filter two more times.

- Choose Image > Rotate > 90° Right.

- Choose Filters > Distort > Polar Coordinates and choose *Rectangular to Polar* from the options at the bottom of the dialog box.

Reversing the effect.

Adding text to the background

When you have two images, you can combine them together using your selections and the Copy and Paste commands.

1 Double-click the *Kids.psd* file, located in the Project Bin, to make it active or choose Window > Kids.psd.

2 Choose Select > All to select the entire document.

The Select All command creates a marquee around the entire image area.

3 Choose Edit > Copy or use the keyboard shortcut, Ctrl+C (Windows) or Command+C (Mac OS). This copies the image to your computer's clipboard, so that it can be pasted in the next step.

4 Double-click the *Scrap Book Page.psd* file, located in the Project Bin or choose Window > Scrap Book Page.psd, to make it active. Choose Edit > Paste or use the keyboard shortcut, Ctrl+V (Windows) or Command+V (Mac OS), to paste the file into the new document. In the Layers panel, double-click the new layer named *Layer 1*. In the Layer properties dialog box, type **text** in the Name text field, and press OK.

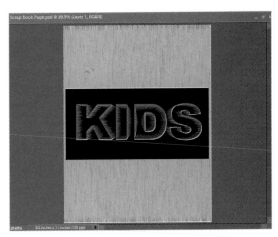

When using the Copy and Paste commands, new layers are created for the pasted artwork and are placed above the selected layer in the destination document.

The text file includes a black background that just doesn't fit with the wood texture of the page. You will remove the background color layer using blending modes.

5   Choose the Move tool (⬆) from the Toolbox, then click and drag the text to the top of the document.

6   In the Layers panel, make sure the text layer is selected and choose Screen from the Blending mode drop-down menu. This blending mode removes the darkest areas from a layer and leaves only the lightest, which in this case would be the lettering.

Blending modes are used to control how light from lower layers is visible through the layers above.

Now, the text is too light to easily be seen. A quick reversal should change this.

7   With the text layer selected, choose Filter > Adjustments > Invert, or use the keyboard shortcut, Ctrl+I (Windows) or Command+I (Mac OS), to reverse the color values of the targeted layer. Choose Multiply from the Blending mode drop-down menu in the Layers panel. This blending mode has the exact opposite effect of the Screen blending mode and makes the text easier to see.

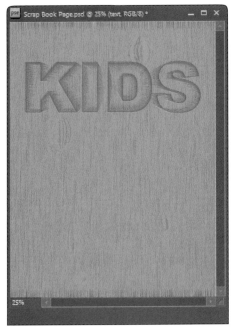

The finished project.

8   Choose File > Save or use the keyboard shortcut, Ctrl+S (Windows) or Command+S (Mac OS). Close the *Kids.psd* file by double-clicking it in the Project Bin and choosing File > Close. Leave the *Scrap Book Page.psd* file open, as you will need it in the next step.

Add images and create a border

Now that you have a background and title in place, you will proceed to edit and add images to fill in the rest of the page. Three images have been prepared for use in this exercise. You will import one of them into your scrapbook page document and add a few effects to it for emphasis. At the conclusion of the exercise, you will be given the opportunity to continue this project on your own so that you can add your own artistic flair.

1 With the *Scrap Book Page.psd* file open, select the *wood* layer in the Layers panel. Choose File > Place and, in the resulting Place dialog box, navigate to the Lessons folder. Select the *scrapbook_01.psd* file and press Place. This imports the file as a new layer.

   It is important to select the *wood* layer in this step because when you use the Place command, the file you are placing is inserted on a new layer right above the currently highlighted layer. When working on a project that uses both text and images, you usually want to keep the text on top of all other layers.

2 When a file is placed into Photoshop Elements, you are given the opportunity to resize, rotate, and move it into the position you like before finalizing it. In the Options bar at the top of the workspace, click the checkbox next to *Constrain Proportions*. Type **65** in the Width text field. Because you have the *Constrain Proportions* option checked, the image's height will automatically change.

In Photoshop Elements, the Options bar allows you to set the options for the tools you are currently working with.

   Click the green checkmark located on a tab attached to the bottom of the placed photo to commit the current changes to the layer.

3 In the Layers panel, double-click the scrapbook_01 layer. In the Layer Properties dialog box, type **museum** in the Name text field, and press OK. Choose the Move tool (⊕) from the Toolbox, then click and drag the layer to the upper right corner of the Scrap Book Page document, but below the text.

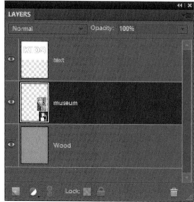

Drag the museum layer to the upper right of the document.

4   Hold down the Ctrl (Windows) or Command (Mac OS) key and click the *museum* layer thumbnail. This selects everything on the layer that isn't transparent. In this case, that would be the entire photo. This is referred to as loading the opacity mask of the layer.

5   Choose Select > Modify > Expand to open the Expand Selection dialog box. Type **15** into the Expand By text field and press OK to enlarge the selection by 15 pixels.

6   At the bottom of the Layers panel, press the Create a New Layer button ( ) to add a new layer above museum. Double-click the new layer, named *Layer 2*, and, in the Layer Properties dialog box, type **border** in the Name text field. Press OK. Click and drag the *border* layer below the *museum* layer in the Layers panel.

7   Choose Edit > Fill Selection. In the Fill Layer dialog box that appears, choose White from the Use drop-down menu in the Contents sections and leave all other settings at their default. Press OK.

The Fill Layer dialog box can be used to add color or a pattern to a layer or selection area.

8   Press the Create a New Layer button in the Layers panel to add a new layer above the border layer. Double-click the new layer, named layer 2 again, and, in the Layer Properties dialog box, type **border2** in the Name text field. Press OK. Click and drag the new *border2* layer below the *border* layer in the Layers panel.

9   Choose Select > Modify > Expand to open the Expand Selection dialog box. Type **10** in the Expand By text field, then press OK to enlarge the selection by 10 pixels.

10 Choose Edit > Fill Selection. In the Fill Layer dialog box that appears, choose Black from the Use drop-down menu in the Contents section and press OK.

11 In the Layers panel, the *border2* layer should still be highlighted. Hold down the Shift key on the keyboard and select the *border* and *museum* layers to highlight them as well.

12 Choose Layer > Merge Layers to combine all three layers together into one. The new layer is named museum.

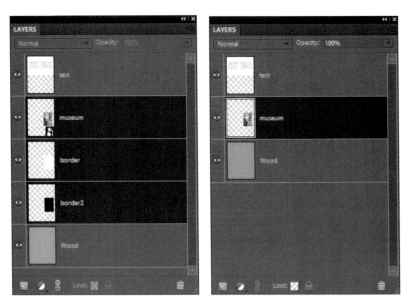

When selected layers are merged, they take on the name of the topmost layer.

13 Choose Select > Deselect or use the keyboard shortcut, Ctrl+D (Windows) or Command+D (Mac OS), to remove the selection border.

The double border on the photograph is used to add emphasis and separate it from the background.

14 Chose File > Save or press Crtl+S (Windows) or Command+S (Mac OS) on your keyboard to save your file. If the Save As dialog box appears, click the checkbox next to *Save in Version set with original* to uncheck it, and press Save. If a warning dialog box appears telling you that you are going to replace your file, press OK.

15 Now it's all up to you. Import the other two images and use your imagination to come up with your own creative results. Here are a few things you might try:

- When you place an image, rotate it slightly to give it a sense of movement.

- Instead of using black and white, try varying the color of the borders you use. Try using the same brown color that you used in the wood-textured background.

- Change the stacking order of the layers and overlap the photos to create a more interesting composition.

- Add drop shadows from the layer effects to the photos.

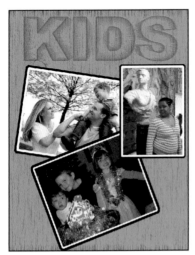 

The variations available on a project like this are unlimited.

Self study

1 Practice making brushes from your photos and by scribbling with the Brush tool on the canvas and selecting parts of it. See what happens when you make all or part of an image into a brush.

2 Open a few of your own images, and experiment with using the Impressionist brush at different sizes to transform different parts of the images.

Review

Questions

1 What happens if you define a brush from artwork that uses grays or colors?

2 What does the Impressionist brush do?

3 What do layer blending modes do?

Answers

1 The brush applies color that is semi-transparent when you use it.

2 It warps the areas of an image to resemble the visible brush strokes used in Impressionist painting.

3 Layer blending modes control the ways that a layer interacts with the color of layers below.

What you'll learn in this lesson:

- Gaining a better understanding of resolution

- Understanding the different formats used on the Web and in video

- Saving a selection for use as an alpha channel

Creating Web and Video Graphics

In this lesson, you will explore using Photoshop Elements to create graphics specifically for the Web and video projects.

Starting up

Within the Photoshop Elements Organizer: You will work with several files from the Lessons folder in this lesson. Make sure that you have copied the Lessons folder from the supplied DVD to your hard drive. In order to access these files in the Organizer, you need to import them. See "Adding files and folders to the Organizer" on page 11.

Within the Photoshop Elements Editor: The Photoshop Elements Editor defaults to the last panel layout that you used. Before starting, make sure your tools and panels are consistent with the examples presented in these lessons by resetting the panels. Do this by choosing Window > Reset Panels or by pressing the Reset panels button (⟳) in the Options bar.

See Lesson 13 in action!

Use the accompanying video to gain a better understanding of how to use some of the features shown in this lesson. The video tutorial for this lesson can be found on the included DVD.

The differences between print and the screen

Printing is only one of several places your work may be destined. Many people are now posting photos and artwork to their own blogs, web sites, and photo-sharing sites, such as Flickr. In addition, the affordability of video cameras and editing software, such as Premiere Elements and iMovie, has led to an explosion in the production of homemade video.

Resolution and color for the Web and video

Every digital image, whether it is created with a digital camera, a scanner, or from scratch in a program like Photoshop Elements, is composed of pixels. The word *pixel* is a conjunction of the words *picture* and *element*, and it is generally considered to be the smallest individual part, or unit, of a digital image. For additional information, please refer to Appendix C, "Understanding Digital Files." There are two main standards for image resolution: 300 ppi is the standard used in the printing of high-quality magazines and books, and 72 ppi is the standard used on the Web and in video. Because these types of graphics are intended to be displayed on screens of varying sizes, the document's print size is less relevant to understanding how it will appear than its pixel dimensions are. The pixel dimensions tell you exactly how many pixels of screen space your images will take up. For example, if your document's width is 800 pixels and the viewer's monitor or display resolution is set to 800 x 600, your graphic will take up the full width of the screen, but if the screen resolution had been set to 1600 pixels wide, it would only take up half of the screen width.

The greater the resolution of an image, the smaller each individual pixel in it is and the greater the detail the image can contain.

Of the images above, the image on the left is a grid of 72 pixels per inch while the one on the right contains 300 pixels per inch. The grid on the right contains more than four times as many pixels as the one on the left and can therefore hold more detail.

You can view a document's pixel dimensions from the Image Size window, by choosing Image > Resize > Image Size.

The other major area where documents built for print differ from those built for the Web and video is in the color mode. Print documents use the CMYK (Cyan, Magenta, Yellow, and Black) color mode, while those built for the Web and video always use the color mode for mixing colors of light, RGB (Red, Green, and Blue).

RGB is an additive color model in which absolute values (value = 255) of each of the primary colors are combined to create white. CMYK is what is called a subtractive color model. In this model, its colors are subtracted (reduced to 0 percent) or withheld to create the color white.

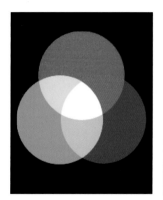
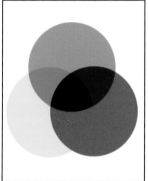

RGB model.   CMYK model.

Preparing images for the Web

The process of preparing images for the Web is called *optimizing*. In general, this process involves making sure the file uses the correct color mode and then compressing it to make it smaller so that it loads faster when viewed on the Web. The Photoshop Elements Save for Web dialog box allows you to preview your optimized file and test out various settings to achieve the best result.

Web image formats

GIF: An acronym for Graphic Interchange Format, this format is typically used on the Web to display logos, motifs, and other limited-tone imagery. The GIF format supports a maximum of 256 colors, as well as what is called 8-bit transparency, and it is the only one of the three formats mentioned here that supports built-in animation. Each individual frame of an animated GIF also supports a maximum of 256 different colors. The format uses what is known as LZW compression to compress an image without degrading its visual quality, except when it comes to the total number of colors in that image.

The two-color illustration seen here would be a good candidate for using the GIF format.

JPEG: An acronym for Joint Photographic Experts Group, the JPEG file format has found wide acceptance on the Web as the main format for displaying photographs and other continuous-tone imagery. The JPEG format supports a range of millions of colors, allowing for the accurate display of a wide range of artwork, but it lacks support for transparent pixels. An image with transparency must be matted against a solid color before it is converted to the JPEG format.

PNG: An acronym for Portable Network Graphic, the PNG file format was intended to blend the best aspects of both the GIF and JPEG formats while addressing the weaknesses inherent in each format. PNG files come in two different varieties: PNG-8 can support up to 256 colors like the GIF format, while PNG-24 can support millions of colors like the JPEG format. Both varieties of the PNG format use lossless compression to minimize an image's file size while maintaining the image quality. Both varieties of PNG also support transparency, and as an improvement on GIF transparency, a PNG-24 file supports varying degrees of transparency.

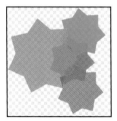

An image that has multiple degrees of transparency that you want to preserve would be a good candidate for the PNG-24 format.

There is one other image format that is supported for display in browsers without the use of a plug-in like Flash Player or Silverlight. WBMP was formerly the default image format for creating graphics to display on cell phones and other devices with limited color displays. It is rarely used.

Saving files for the Web

In this part of the lesson, you are going to open a Photoshop Elements document and use the program's Save for Web & Devices function to optimize it for display on the Internet. While you want to keep your working files in the native Photoshop format, you always have to optimize your images before they can be displayed on the Web.

Creating a JPEG

In this part of the lesson, you will save your file as a JPEG image. The JPEG format offers a good balance between image size and quality, and is the standard for the kind of continuous-tone imagery that you have in the practice file.

1   In the Organizer, type **Home** into the Search text field; this isolates the file *HomePage.psd*. Right-click the image and choose Edit with Photoshop Elements from the contextual menu that appears.

This document is 800 x 600 pixels. This is one of the standard sizes for full-page web graphics and is based on the screen size of the average 15-inch computer monitor.

2   Choose File > Save for Web.

3 The Save for Web dialog box is set up to display a side-by-side view of your original artwork next to your optimized artwork. On the right side of the dialog box, you can set the optimization settings for the file you will create. Choose JPEG medium from the Preset drop-down menu. This produces a medium-quality file that should be easily visible over the Web.

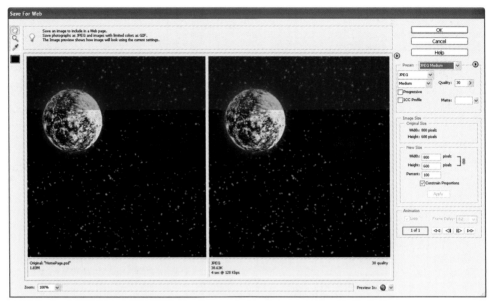

The Save for Web dialog box allows you to see the original image next to the optimized one that you will create.

The JPEG format uses what is called "lossy" compression. This means that it reduces the file size of your image by deleting any information that is not needed to display it at the specified quality settings. Once that information has been discarded, there is no way to get it back. This compression is what allows JPEG files to be small enough to be displayed on the Internet and over mobile devices.

JPEG options

In addition to your quality settings, the JPEG format has three other options that can affect the size and appearance of your optimized document.

Progressive: Click to select the check box in order to create a progressive JPEG file. A progressive JPEG downloads and displays in stages, from low quality to your final image.

ICC Profile: Click to select the check box to embed the ICC profile that you were using while you worked on this document. Color profiles are used to create color consistency across a range of display devices and applications.

Matte: This feature allows you to add a color matte or fringe to the edges of your image. Used with images that have transparent or soft, blurry edges, this effect allows you to avoid distinct, visible edges.

4   Press OK to open the Save Optimized As dialog box and navigate to the Lessons folder. Press Save to finish saving the file, then close the file. If a dialog box appears prompting you to save the changes to the original *HomePage.psd,* press No.

Creating a PNG

To create a web-ready PNG file, you follow the same steps that you used to create a JPEG. The differences arise once you open the Save for Web dialog box. There are actually two types of PNG files. The PNG-8 format is intended to replace the GIF format and can save an image with a maximum of 256 colors, while the PNG-24, like a JPEG, can save an image with millions of different color values. In this lesson, you will create a PNG-24 to take advantage of the variable transparency that it allows.

The PIXEL.psd file.

1   Using the Editor workspace, open the file *PIXEL.psd* from the Lessons folder.

2   Choose File > Save for Web; this opens the Save for Web dialog box.

3   Choose PNG-24 from the Preset drop-down menu on the right side of the Save for Web dialog box. This displays the options available for a PNG file.

The presets in the Save for Web dialog box are often the best place to start when optimizing a file.

4   The image is 453 pixels wide and 229 pixels high; you will now reduce these dimensions. In the Image Size section of the dialog box, change the width to 300. The height value automatically changes, as the Constrain Proportions option is enabled by default.

You can also change the image size by adjusting the percentage or height values; it depends on what your target size or use for the image will be.

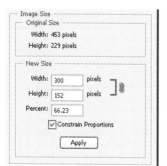

Width, Height, and Percent are all proportional to each other.

5   Press Apply to change the size of the image.

6   The original image was 178 kilobytes in size. The optimized image is 8.431 kilobytes in size. The third row of numbers is the expected time it would take to download the image.

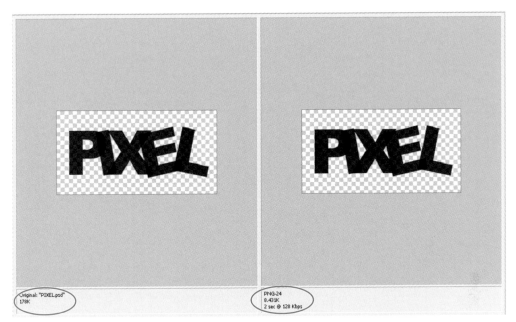

The side-by-side display of the dialog box allows you to compare your original to the optimized version.

 If you right-click on the expected download time, you can choose to see the time it would take to download the optimized file on different connections by choosing a different connection speed from the list that appears.

7   Press Cancel, and close the image in the Editor.

PNG options

In the Save for Web dialog box, the PNG-24 format doesn't offer as many options as the JPEG format. In fact, the PNG-24 format only offers three options: Transparency, Interlaced, and Matte.

Transparency: This checkbox simply controls whether transparent pixels in your image are rendered as transparent or not. It's the reason you can see the gray and white transparency grid behind your image. The fact that the *Transparency* option is enabled by default is the reason why the matte color option has been disabled. With a PNG-8 image, pixels are either fully transparent or fully opaque, but with a PNG-24 image, there is a range of transparency values that images can contain and so pixels can be transparent, opaque, or semi-transparent in the same image.

Interlacing: This is a process that allows for a PNG image to be displayed incrementally in the browser as it loads onto your viewer's computer. The visual effect is that the image at first appears blurry, and then becomes less and less blurry as more of it is downloaded, until finally it is the clear image that you optimized in Photoshop Elements. The advantage of interlacing is that it allows an image to download in stages; the disadvantage is that not all web browsers support this feature.

Matte Color: When the *Transparency* option is disabled, The Matte feature sets the color to which you want to convert all transparent or semi-transparent pixels.

The PNG-8 format has a few additional options to compensate for the fact that it allows you to save an image with a total of only 256 different colors. Most of these additional options control how the colors in the image are reduced, and try to correct the image for the display of limited colors.

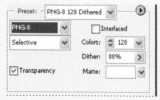

A PNG-8 file has more options than a PNG-24 file to allow you to control how colors are reduced and displayed.

Color Reduction Algorithm: This feature specifies the mathematical algorithm used to reduce the number of colors in your image. The four choices are: Perceptual, Selective, Adaptive, and Restrictive (web). The best choice for the color reduction algorithm is determined by the details of the specific image you are trying to reduce.

Maximum number of colors: This feature specifies the maximum number of colors allowed in the image. While the absolute maximum number of colors in a PNG-8 is 256, you can purposely use fewer colors to reduce the image size. Choosing the right number of colors is a compromise between visual quality and file size.

Amount of Dither: This is a technique used to reduce the color banding in images that can occur when colors are reduced. Dithering systematically places patterns of available colors to emulate colors that are removed by the selected color reduction algorithm. Dithering will increase the size of the image being optimized. The best dithering choice depends on the details of the image that is being optimized.

Preparing images for video

With the affordability in recent years of video camcorders and the growth of sharing sites like YouTube and Vimeo, more people than ever are creating and watching video online. Video standards vary by region, with the United States' NTSC settings and Europe's PAL settings being the two primary standards.

NTSC is an acronym for the National Television Standards Committee; it is the video standard used in the United States and Japan.

WIDTH	HEIGHT	FRAME RATE
720 pixels	480 pixels	30 fps

PAL is an acronym for Phase Alternating Line; it is the video standard used by most of Europe and Asia.

WIDTH	HEIGHT	FRAME RATE
720 pixels	576 pixels	25 fps

There are, of course, other video standards that are used in the world; for example, High Definition Video and film projects use their own set of standards for both frame size and rate. However, NTSC and PAL are the two most common formats used in the world today, and HDTV represents the future of video production.

In addition to the standards-based video mentioned previously, there is a wide variety of other video sizes and formats floating around the Web. Cellular phones, webcams, and mini-camcorders can all have different settings for frame rate and size. Whatever the video format you are going to work with, it is important to build your graphics in Photoshop Elements for the same size or larger.

Safe margins

Because of the nature of the television medium, if you were to create a graphic that took up the entire frame size, parts of it would not be displayed on all TVs. Two sets of margins have been created to ensure that you never have a title or image that vanishes off the side or bottom of the screen. Called *safe margins*, they define the area where it should be safe to place your content. The action safe area, which encompasses about 90 percent of the frame, is where you should be safe to have movement or animation. The title safe area, which encompasses approximately 80 percent of the frame size, defines the boundary of where text should be placed. The video presets that ship with Photoshop Elements include guides that define the safe margins of the image for you.

Safe margins are only applicable to video files that are going to be displayed on a television. If you are creating graphics for video projects that are only going to be displayed on a computer, then you can ignore them completely, as computers don't crop the visible area of video files.

The action safe area is the outer margin, and the title safe area is the inner margin created by the eight sets of overlapping guidelines. The safe margins are automatically a part of every new file created with the film and video presets in Photoshop Elements.

Imagery intended for video depends as much on what you plan to do with it after it leaves Photoshop Elements, as on the content of the actual imagery. Most video graphics are prepared in Photoshop Elements for import into either motion graphics programs like Adobe After Effects, or editing applications like Adobe Premiere Elements. The main thing you have to be concerned about is transparency. Each of the video applications on the market has its own set of importable formats. Here you will use the TIFF format to save an image with transparent areas. For this lesson you are going to open a pre-built file and save it as a TIFF with an alpha channel. The alpha channel is how video editing applications recognize transparency.

 If you plan on bringing your transparent file into one of the other Adobe applications, you can save it as a native Photoshop document. The TIFF format is necessary when you are using an application that does not support native PSD import.

Saving files for video

The program that you use for your video editing determines the type of optimizing you have to perform. If you are taking your image to a program like Adobe Premiere Elements or another Adobe program, you can just save it as a PSD file as you normally would. Other Adobe programs can usually read native Photoshop Elements PSD files without a problem. If, however, you are going to another video editing program, you usually have to save your file as a TIFF with an alpha channel. An alpha channel, called a saved selection in Photoshop Elements, lets video editing programs know which areas of an image are transparent and which are not.

1   In the Organizer, type **Video** into the Search text field; this isolates the file, *VideoFrame.psd*. Right-click on the image and choose Edit with Photoshop Elements from the contextual menu that appears. This image is intended to frame a video as it plays. If you receive a message asking if you'd like to correct the image, press No. You are receiving this error because the aspect ratio is intended for a TV screen not a computer screen. A secondary message box may appear informing you that this image would be best displayed on a television monitor. Just press OK to continue to the Editor.

2   Choose view > Show Guides if the guides are currently not displayed.

3   In the Toolbox, select the Magic Wand tool to activate it. In the Options bar across the top of the screen, click the checkbox for *Sample All Layers*. Then click in the empty center layer of the artwork to select it.

The Magic Wand tool selects colors that are similar to each other; when used on a transparent area, it selects the entire transparent area.

4   Choose Select > Inverse to reverse the selection, and now the artwork is selected.

The keyboard command for Inverse is Ctrl+Shift+I (Windows) or Command+Shift+I (Mac OS).

5   Choose Select > Save Selection. In the Save Selection dialog box, name the selection **artwork** and press OK.

Saved selections are saved as alpha channels. They store extra information about your file and can be used by other programs to determine transparency.

6   Select File > Save As. Choose a location to save your file and select TIFF as the format.

7   In the Save options field, make sure that layers is checked off. Press Save.

*Clicking off **layers** should automatically add the word "copy" to your filename; you will want to change it back.*

8   In the TIFF Options window, press OK. You have now saved a TIFF file that will have a transparent area in your video editing application. Close the file.

Self study

Take a couple of your own photos and optimize them for the Web. Experiment with using different settings for JPEG quality. If you have any illustrations or logos that contain mostly solid color areas, Save for Web using the GIF format. Explore how the different settings affect the colors of the artwork.

Review

Questions

1   What is the standard resolution for images created for the Web and video.

2   What are the four image formats used on the Web.

3   What is the color mode for all images created for the Web and video.

Answers

1   The standard resolution for images created for the Web and video is 72 ppi.

2   The four image formats used on the Web are JPEG, GIF, PNG-8, and PNG-24.

3   The color mode for all web and video graphics is RGB (Red, Green, and Blue).

What you'll learn in this lesson:

- Navigating Adobe Bridge
- Using folders in Bridge
- Making a Favorite
- Creating metadata
- Creating Collections

Using Adobe Bridge

Adobe Bridge is provided with Mac OS versions of Photoshop Elements 8 because the MacOS version does not include the Organizer capabilities. This chapter is only for MacOS users of Photoshop Elements.

Starting up

You will work with several files from the Lessons folder in this lesson. Make sure that you have loaded the Lessons folder onto your hard drive from the supplied DVD. See "Loading lesson files" on page XXI.

See Lesson 14 in action!

Use the accompanying video to gain a better understanding of how to use some of the features shown in this lesson. The video tutorial for this lesson can be found on the included DVD.

What is Adobe Bridge?

Whereas the Windows version of Photoshop Elements 8 uses the Organizer, the Mac OS version of Photoshop Elements 8 uses the Adobe Bridge to organize and manage media. The Adobe Bridge is an application included with Adobe Photoshop Elements 8 for the Mac OS and also with Adobe Creative Suite software. Adobe Bridge helps you locate, organize, and browse the documents you need to create print, web, video, and audio content. If you have Photoshop Elements running, or any one of the Creative Suite applications, you can start Adobe Bridge using the File menu, or you can press the Launch Bridge button (📷).

You can use Bridge to access documents such as images, text files, and even non-Adobe documents, such as Microsoft Word or Excel files. Using Adobe Bridge, you can also organize and manage images, videos, and audio files, as well as preview, search, and sort your files without opening them in their native applications.

Once you discover the capabilities of Adobe Bridge, you'll want to make it the control center for your Photoshop Elements projects. With Bridge, you can easily locate files using the Filters panel and import images from your digital camera right into a viewing area that allows you to quickly rename and preview your files. This is why the recommended workflow throughout this book includes opening and saving files in Adobe Bridge. Reading through this lesson will help you to feel more comfortable with Adobe Bridge, and will also make you aware of some of the more advanced features that are available to you for your own projects.

Navigating through Bridge

In order to utilize Adobe Bridge effectively, you'll want to know the available tools and how to access them. Let's start navigating!

1   Launch Adobe Photoshop Elements 8 on your computer by navigating to your Applications folder and double-clicking the Photoshop Elements icon. The Photoshop Elements Editor and the welcome screen are displayed.

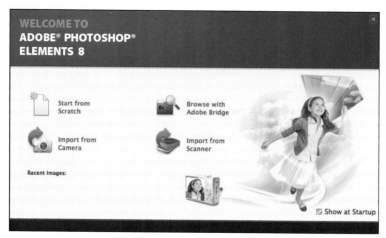

The Photoshop Elements 8 welcome screen.

2　Click the Browse with Adobe Bridge icon (⬛) in the welcome Screen to launch the Adobe Bridge application.

3　In the Adobe Bridge, click the Folders panel to make sure it is forward. Click Desktop (listed in the Folders panel). You see the Lessons folder that you downloaded to your hard drive. Click the Lessons folder and notice that the contents of that folder are displayed in the Content panel, in the center of the Adobe Bridge window. You can also navigate by clicking folders listed in the Path bar that is located in the upper left corner of the content window.

You can view folder contents by double-clicking on a folder, or by selecting the folder in the Path bar.

You can move through your navigation history by pressing the Go back and Go forward arrows in the upper left corner of the window. Use the handy Reveal recent file or go to Recent folder drop-down menu (🕙) to find folders and files that you recently opened.

3　Press the Go back arrow to return to the desktop view.

A. Go back. B. Go forward. C. Go to parent or Favorites.
D. Reveal recent file or go to recent folder. E. Path bar.

4　Press the Go forward arrow to return to the last view, which is the Lessons folder.

Using folders in Adobe Bridge

Adobe Bridge is used for more than just navigating your file system. Bridge is also used to manage and organize folders and files.

1 Click the tab of the Folders panel in the upper-left corner of the Bridge window to make sure it is still forward. Then click the arrow to the left of Desktop so that it turns downward and reveals its contents.

2 Double-click Computer to reveal its contents in the center pane of the Bridge window. Continue to double-click items, or click the arrows to the left of the folder names in the Folder panel, to reveal their contents.

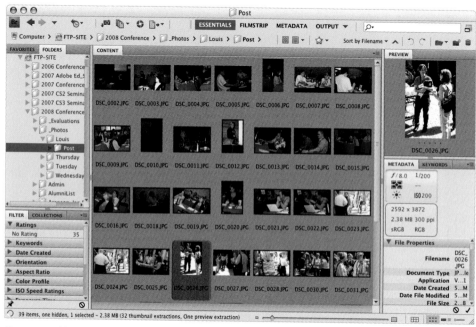

You can use Adobe Bridge to navigate your entire system, much like you would by using your computer's directory system.

Managing folders

Adobe Bridge is a great tool for organizing folders and files. It is a simple matter of dragging and dropping to reorder items on your computer. You can create folders, move folders, move files from one folder to another, and copy files and folders to other locations; any organizing task that can be performed on the computer can also be performed in Adobe Bridge. This is a great way to help keep volumes of images organized for easy accessibility, as well as easy searching. The advantage of using Adobe Bridge for these tasks is that you have bigger and better previews of images, PDF files, and movies, with much more information about those files at your fingertips.

3   Click Desktop in the Folder panel to reveal its contents again.

4   Click Lessons to view its contents. You'll now add a new folder into that lessons folder.

5   Click the Create a new folder icon (📁) in the upper-right corner of the Bridge window to create a new untitled folder inside the Lessons folder. Type the name **Music Extras**.

Creating a new folder in Bridge.

You can use Adobe Bridge to organize images. Because you can see a preview of each file, you can more easily rename them, as well as relocate them to more appropriate locations in your directory system. In the next step, you will move files from one folder to the new Music Extras folder you have just created.

6   Scroll through the content of the Lessons folder in Bridge until you locate a groups of images that begin with the letters IMG. Click once on the image named IMG_1381. JPG, then hold down the Command key and select image IMG_1426.JPG. By holding down the Command key, you can select non-consecutive items in Adobe Bridge. The two images appear simultaneously in the Preview panel, located in the upper-right corner of the Bridge window.

You can easily reduce and enlarge the size of your thumbnails by pressing Command+plus sign or Command+minus sign.

7 Click and drag the selected images to the Music Extras folder. When the folder becomes highlighted, release the mouse. The files have now been moved into that folder.

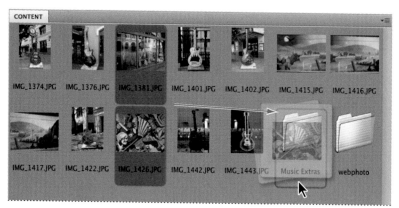

You can select multiple images and organize folders directly in Adobe Bridge.

8 Double-click the Music Extras folder to view its contents. You see the two images that you moved.

9 Click Lessons in the Path bar to return to the Lessons folder content.

Making a Favorite

As you work in Photoshop Elements, you will find that you frequently access the same folders. One of the many great features in Bridge is that you can designate a frequently used folder as a Favorite, allowing you to quickly and easily access it from the Favorites panel. This is extremely helpful, especially if the folders that you are frequently accessing are stored deep in your file hierarchy.

1 Select the Favorites panel in the upper-left corner of the Bridge window to bring it to the front. In the list of Favorites, click on Desktop. Because the Lessons folder is going to be frequently accessed in this lesson, you'll make it a Favorite. Unlike the Windows version of Photoshop Elements which uses a Catalog to organize images, the Bridge allows you to organize images by simply browsing to the folder on your computer that contains those images.

2   Place your cursor over the Lessons folder in the center pane (Content), then click and drag the Lessons folder until you see a horizontal line appear in the Favorites panel. When a cursor with a plus sign (🖢) appears, release the mouse. The folder is now listed as a Favorite.

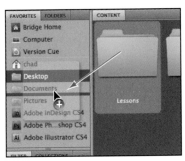

Drag a folder to the bottom of the Favorites panel to make it easier to locate.

3   Click the Lessons folder shown in the Favorites panel to view its contents. Note that creating a Favorite simply creates a shortcut for quick access to a folder; it does not copy the folder and its contents.

If your Favorite is created from a folder on an external hard drive or server, you will need to have the hard drive or server mounted in order to access it.

Creating and locating metadata

Metadata is information that can be stored with images. This information travels with the file, and makes it easy to search for and identify the file. In this section, you are going to find out how to locate and create metadata.

1   Make sure that you are viewing the contents of the Lessons folder in the center pane of Adobe Bridge. If not, navigate to that folder now, or click the Lessons folder in the Favorites panel.

2   Choose Window > Workspace >Reset Standard Workspaces. This ensures that you are in the Essentials view and that all the default panels for Adobe Bridge are visible. Alternatively, you can click and hold the Workspace drop-down menu, in the Application bar at the top of the Bridge workspace. You may need to maximize your Bridge window after you reset the workspace.

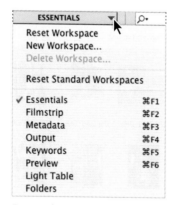

Resetting the workspace using the Workspace drop-down menu.

3   Locate IMG_1374.JPG in the content panel and click once to highlight it. Look for the Metadata and Keywords panels in the lower right area of the Adobe Bridge workspace.

4   If Metadata is not in front, click the Metadata panel now. In this panel, you see the image data that is stored with the file. Take a few moments to scroll through the data and view the information that was imported from the digital camera that was used to take the photo.

 Click and drag the bar to the left of the Metadata panel farther to the left if you need to open up the window.

5   Select the arrow to the left of IPTC Core to reveal its contents. IPTC Core provides a smooth transfer of metadata about images.

6   Here you see a series of pencils. The pencils indicate that you can enter information in these fields.

 If you are not able to edit or add metadata information to a file, it may be locked. Right-click on the file and choose Reveal in Finder. Right-click the file, choose Get Info, then change the Ownership and Permissions to Read and Write.

7 Scroll down until you can see Description Writer, and click the pencil next to it. All editable fields are highlighted, and a cursor appears in the Description Writer field.

8 Type your name, or type **student**.

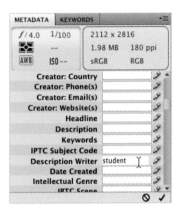

Reveal the IPTC contents and enter metadata information.

9 Scroll up to locate Creator: City. Click the pencil icon to the right of the Creator City text box, type the name of your city, and then press the Tab key. The cursor is now in the State text field. Enter your state information.

10 Check the Apply checkbox (✔), located in the bottom-right corner of the Metadata panel, to apply your changes. You have now edited metadata that is attached to the image, information that will appear whenever someone opens your image in Bridge or views the image information in Adobe Photoshop Elements Elements, using File > File Info.

Using keywords

Keywords can reduce the amount of time it takes to find an image on a computer, by using logical words to help users locate images more quickly.

1 Click the Keywords tab, which appears behind the Metadata panel. A list of commonly used keywords appears.

2 Press the New Keyword button (⊕) at the bottom of the Keywords panel. Type **guitar** into the active text box, and then Return.

3 Check the empty checkbox to the left of the guitar keyword. This adds the guitar keyword to the selected image.

4   With the guitar keyword still selected, press the New Sub Keyword button (🐾). Type **Gibson** into the active text box, then press Return.

5   Check the empty checkbox to the left of the Gibson keyword. You have now assigned a keyword and a subkeyword to the IMG_1374.JPG image.

Notice that the keywords you added appear at the top, under Assigned Keywords.

6   Press the New Keyword button (🞣) at the bottom of the Keywords panel; a blank text field appears. Type **Austin** and Return. Then check the checkbox next to Austin to assign the keyword to this image.

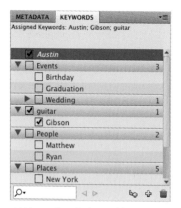

Add keywords to the keyword list, and then apply them to selected images.

7   Ctrl+click the Wedding keyword, and choose the option Rename. When the text field becomes highlighted, type **Conference** and press Return.

You can also enter information directly into the image by opening the image in Adobe Photoshop Elements. The categories that appear on the left include Description, Camera Data, IPTC Contact, and IPTC Content, among others. Once it is entered in the File Info dialog box, the information is visible in Adobe Bridge.

Opening a file from Adobe Bridge

Opening files from Adobe Bridge is how you'll begin the work process in Adobe Photoshop Elements. Not only is it very visual, but important data stored with the files also makes it easier to locate the correct file.

1   Make sure you are viewing the contents of the Lessons folder, then double-click the IMG_1402.JPG image to open the file in Adobe Photoshop Elements.

Sometimes you will find that double-clicking a file opens it in a different application than expected. This can happen if you are working in generic file formats such as JPEG and GIF or if you have several image editing applications installed on your computer. To avoid this problem, you can Ctrl+click the image, and choose Open With to select the appropriate application. You can set the default application that the Bridge should open when you double-click a file by choosing Adobe Bridge CS4 > Preferences and clicking the File Type Associations category on the left. Simply choose which application should open each file type and Bridge will do so from now on.

2   Choose File > Close to close the file in Photoshop Elements and choose File > Browse with Bridge to return to Adobe Bridge.

3   You can also click once to select an image and then choose File > Open, or use the keyboard shortcut, Command+O.

Searching for files using Adobe Bridge

Find the files that you want quickly and easily by using the Search tools built directly into Adobe Bridge, and taking advantage of the Filter panel. You'll start on the next page by using the ability to search by names and keywords to locate images.

Searching by name or keyword

Note that in the Default view of Adobe Bridge, you have a Search text box ready and waiting to use. To search for a file by keyword, simply type the name criteria into the text box and press Return.

1   Type **guitar** into the Search text box and Return. Because you are looking within the active folder only, you should get a result immediately. The image file, IMG_1374.JPG, to which you added the guitar keyword, appears.

The remaining steps show you how to broaden your search.

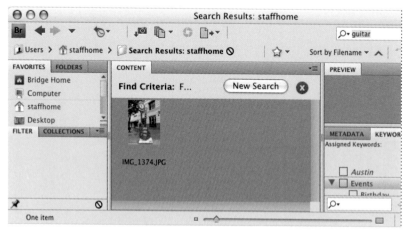

Search your folders using the tools built right into Adobe Bridge.

2   Click the Folders tab to make sure that this panel is forward, then click your computer name. This might be called Macintosh HD.

3   Make sure the guitar text is still in the Search text box and Return again. Now the entire hard drive is searched. In your case, maybe you are a musician, and you may find more guitar-related files. But in this example, the same image file is found.

4   Press the X to the right of the New Search button in the Content pane to cancel the search. You are returned to the Lessons folder.

Using the Filter panel

If you have ever been in the position where you knew you put a file into a folder, but just can't seem to find it, you will love the Filter panel.

Using the Filter panel, you can look at attributes such as file type, keywords, and date created or modified, in order to narrow down the files that appear in the content window of Adobe Bridge. Simply click any category in the Filter panel to display only images that meet the criteria that are selected.

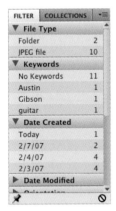

Find files quickly by selecting
different criteria in the Filters panel.

Collections

Collections allow you to organize images into a virtual Photo Album. With a Collection you can group related or unrelated photos together for easy viewing.

1 In the Search text box, type **IMG**, then press Return on your keyboard. This displays a list of all images in the Lessons folder that contain IMG in the file name or in any assigned keywords.

2 In the Filter panel to the right-click the triangle next to Keywords to expand this section. Hold down the Option key and double-click the Lesson 03 keyword. This hides all files with this keyword on it leaving only the files needed for this lesson. Press Command+A to select all the images in the Bridge window.

3 Click the Collections tab to bring it forward, then press the New Collection button (▦) at the bottom of the Collections panel. A dialog appears asking if you want to include the selected files in the new Collection. Press Yes.

4 A new Collection is created in the Collections panel with the default name of New Collection. Type **Austin Collection** and press Return to change the name of the collection. You now have a saved collection containing all the images of Austin.

Collections allow you to organize your images into virtual Photo albums.

5 In the Favorites panel, click Lessons to display all the images in the Lessons folder. Now click the Austin Collection that you just created to display all the Austin images.

Stacks

Stacks allow you to consolidate the view of images in the Adobe Bridge by grouping similar images together. One example might be if you have taken several pictures of the same subject or event, and the images are very similar in nature, a stack would allow you to group them into a consolidated view.

1 Make sure that the Austin Collection that you created in the previous section is still active by clicking the Austin Collection in the Collections panel.

2 Select the IMG_1415.jpg image, then hold down the Command key and select IMG_1416.jpg and IMG_1417.jpg to select all three images.

3 Choose Stacks > Group as Stack to consolidate all three images into a stack. A new icon is displayed with the number 3 in the upper left corner indicating that there are three images in the stack.

*Stacks allow you to consolidate several images together
so they occupy less space in the Bridge window.*

4 With the stack still selected, choose Stacks > Open stack or type Command + right arrow to view all images in the stack. To close the stack, choose Stacks > Close stack or type Command + left arrow.

If you decide at a later time that you don't want images grouped into a Stack, simply select the stack and choose Stacks > Ungroup from Stack.

Automation tools in Adobe Bridge

Adobe Bridge provides many tools to help you automate tasks. In this section, you will learn how to access and take advantage of some of these features.

Automated tools for Photoshop Elements: Web Photo Gallery

If you want to share images online, you can use the Web Photo Gallery, which creates a web site that features a home page with thumbnail images and gallery pages with full-size images. You select the images you want to include in the site and Adobe Bridge does the rest, from automatically creating navigation images, like arrows, links, and buttons, to creating Flash files. This is a fun feature that you can take advantage of quickly, even if you have no coding experience. If you have coding experience, or if you want to edit the pages further, you can open the pages in Adobe Dreamweaver or any other HTML editor to customize them.

1 Make sure that you are viewing the contents of the Lessons folder. If you do not see the contents of the Lessons folder in the content window in Bridge, choose the Favorites panel and click Desktop. Click the Lessons folder. If you stored the lesson files elsewhere, use the navigation tools in Bridge to locate your lesson files.

2   In the Content window, click once on image IMG_1374.JPG, and then use the scroll bar to locate the image named IMG_1443.JPG. Hold down the Shift key and click on the last image; this selects both images and all the images in between.

3   Click and hold down on the Output drop-down menu in the Application bar, and choose Output to Web or PDF; the workspace changes to reveal an Output panel on the right.

*Select multiple images and then select the Output
drop-down menu.*

*If you cannot see all the options in the Output panel, click and drag the vertical bar to the left of
the panel to increase its size.*

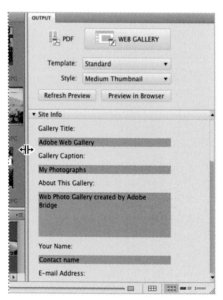

Click and drag to resize the Output panel.

4   Press the Web Gallery button at the top of the Output panel.

5   Click and hold the Templates drop-down menu, and choose HTML Gallery. As you can see, there are a lot of options to choose from, including Lightroom Flash Galleries. In this example, you will keep it simple.

6   From the Styles drop-down menu, choose Lightroom.

7   In the Site Info section of the Output panel, type a title in the Gallery Title text box; for this example, you can type **My First Web Gallery**.

8   You can also add photograph captions if you like, as well as text in the About This Gallery text box, to include more information. In this example, those are left at their defaults.

9   Using the scroll bar to the right of the Style Info section, click and drag to scroll down through the rest of the options. Note that you can add additional contact information, and define colors that you want to use for different objects on the page, including text.

10 Press the Preview in Browser button that is located in the upper half of the Output panel; your web site is automatically created.

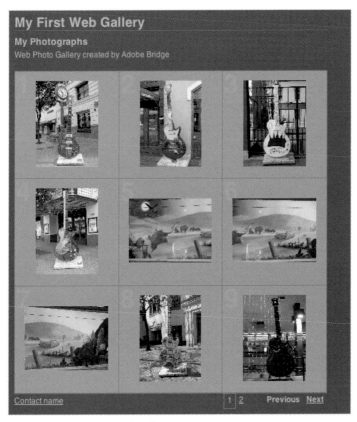

The completed web site, using Web Gallery.

Saving or uploading your Web Gallery

So now you have an incredible Web Gallery, but what do you do with it? The Web Photo Gallery feature creates an index page, individual gallery pages, and images, and so you need someplace to put them. You have a couple options available if you click the scroll bar to the right of Style information and drag down until you see the options for Gallery Name. Note that you can choose to save your Gallery to a location on your hard drive, or input the FTP login information directly in Adobe Bridge to upload your file directly to a server. In this example, you will save the Web Gallery to a folder named webphoto in your Lessons folder.

1   Scroll down to the bottom of the Output panel, where you see two options for output: Save to Disk, and Upload.

2   Click the radio button for *Save to Disk*, and then press the Browse button and navigate to the Lessons folder. Click the New Folder button to create a new folder and name it webphoto. Select the newly created webphoto folder and press Choose; then press the Save button in the Output panel of the Bridge.

A dialog box appears, indicating that you have successfully created a Web Gallery; press OK.

You have successfully saved your Web Gallery. Use Adobe Bridge to navigate and open the contents of this folder to see that a folder named Adobe Web Gallery is inside your webphoto folder. Open the contents to see that your components are neatly organized so that you can open them in your web editor and customize them, or send them to your web site administrator for uploading.

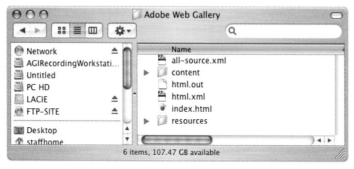

The completed web site, when saved to the hard drive.

Automated tools for Photoshop Elements: PDF contact sheet

By creating a PDF contact sheet, you can assemble a series of images into one file for such purposes as client approval and summaries of folders.

1   Make sure that you are viewing the contents of the Lessons folder. If you do not see the contents of the Lessons folder in the content window in Bridge, choose the Favorites panel and click on Desktop., then click the Lessons folder. If you stored the lesson files elsewhere, use the navigation tools in Bridge to locate your lesson files.

2   In the Content window, at the bottom of the workspace, click once on image IMG_1374.JPG then use the scroll bar to locate the image named IMG_1443.JPG. Hold down the Shift key and click on the last image; this selects both images and all the images in between.

3   If your Output panel is no longer visible, press the Output button and choose Output to Web or PDF. In the Output panel, click on the PDF button.

4   From the Template drop-down menu, choose 5 x 8 Contact Sheet.

Choose to create a PDF contact sheet from the Template drop-down menu.

5   In the Document section of the Output panel, choose U.S. Paper from the Page Preset drop-down menu.

Scroll down and notice that you have options for final size, document quality, and even security in the Output panel. You will leave these items at the default and scroll down to the Playback Options section of this panel.

6   Because this PDF is to be used as a contact sheet, and not a PDF slide show, scroll down to the Playback section of the Output panel and uncheck the three options that relate to a PDF presentation: *Open in Full Screen Mode*, *Advance Every 5 Seconds*, and *Loop After Last Page*.

7   Scroll down to the bottom of the Output panel and check the checkbox to *View PDF After Save*; then press the Save button. The Save As dialog box appears.

8   In the Save As dialog box, type **contact** and browse to save the file in your Lessons folder; press Save.

    A dialog box appears, indicating that you have successfully created a PDF contact sheet; press OK. The contact.pdf file is saved in your Lessons folder and your contact sheet is launched in Adobe Acrobat for you to view.

9   After examining your contact sheet in Adobe Acrobat, choose File > Close to close the contact.pdf file.

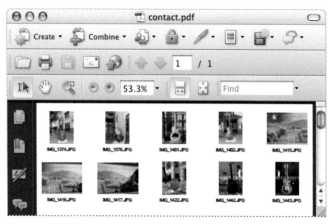

The completed PDF contact sheet.

Changing the view

You can work the way you like by adjusting the look and feel of Adobe Bridge. Changing the view can help you focus on what is important to see in the content section of the Bridge workspace. Whether you need to focus on content or thumbnails, there is a view that can help you.

1   Before experimenting with the views, make sure that you are in the default workspace by selecting Window > Workspace > Reset Standard Workspaces.

2   Press the Click to Lock to Thumbnail Grid button (⊞) in the lower right corner of the Bridge workspace. The images are organized into a grid.

3 Now press the View Content as Details button (▬▬) to see a thumbnail and details about creation date, last modified date, and file size.

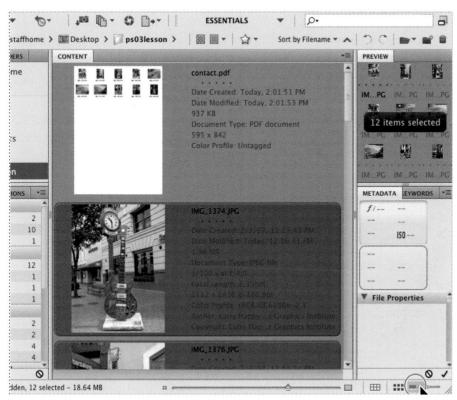

Changing the view of Adobe Bridge.

4 Choose the View as List button (▬▬) to see the contents consolidated into a neat list, which you can easily scroll through.

5 Press the View Content as Thumbnails button (⁞⁞⁞) to return to the default thumbnail view.

6 Experiment with changing the size of the thumbnails in the Content panel by using the slider to the left of the preview buttons. Don't forget, you can also change the thumbnail size by pressing Command+plus sign or Command+minus sign.

Integration with Photoshop Elements

The Adobe Bridge includes plug-ins that allow you to perform Photoshop Elements 8 related tasks directly from the Adobe Bridge Application. These features can be found by choosing Tools > Photoshop elements. As you read through this book, when you encounter a lesson that instructs you to perform a task with the Organizer which is Windows only, jump to the Bridge application and access many of these features from the Tools > Photoshop Elements menu.

Self study

As you work with Bridge, create some new Favorites of folders that you frequently use. You might also want to practice removing Favorites: highlight the Favorite and choose File > Remove from Favorites. Also, explore creating a PDF slide show when in the Adobe Media Gallery workspace. By turning on the Playback options in the Output panel, you can create a full-screen presentation of the images in the Content panel of Adobe Bridge.

Review

Questions

1   How do you access Photoshop Elements features from within Adobe Bridge?

2   Where do you find the metadata for an image, and how do you know if it can be edited?

3   Which panel in Adobe Bridge enables you to organize your files on your computer?

4   Which panel allows you to create Web Galleries, PDF presentations, and contact sheets?

Answers

1   Access automated tools by choosing Tools > Photoshop Elements.

2   You find metadata information in the Metadata and Keywords panels in the lower-right corner of the Bridge workspace. Metadata is editable if it has the pencil icon next to it.

3   You can use the Folders panel to organize your files.

4   You must be in the Output panel to create Web Galleries, PDF presentations, and contact sheets.

Appendix A - tools

ICON	NAME	KEYBOARD SHORTCUT	DESCRIPTION
	Move	V	The Move tool allows you to move either a part of your image that has a selection border around it or the currently active layer.
	Zoom	Z	The Zoom tool allows you to zoom in or out on an image. Clicking with the tool zooms in, pressing and holding the Alt key while the tool is active allows you to zoom out.
	Hand	H	While zoomed in on a part of the image, use the Hand tool to pan around to view a different area without having to zoom back out.
	Eyedropper	I	The Eyedropper tool is a color sampling tool. It allows you to sample the color value of whatever area it is currently hovering over.
	Rectangular Marquee	M	The Rectangular Marquee tool creates rectangular (square if you hold the Shift key while drawing) selection borders.
	Elliptical Marquee	M	The Elliptical Marquee tool creates oval (circular if you hold the Shift key down while drawing) selection edges.
	Lasso	L	The Lasso tool draws free form selection borders and is helpful when trying to selection organic shapes or areas without a set polygonal edge.
	Magnetic Lasso	L	The Magnetic Lasso tool can be used to draw precise selection borders because it will snap to the edge of the object you are drawing around. It works best for objects with clearly defined borders.
	Polygonal Lasso	L	The Polygonal Lasso tool draws straight line segments of a selection border.
	Magic Wand	W	The Magic Wand tool makes selection borders by selecting pixels that are similar to each other in color to the area you click. The tolerance setting in the tool options controls how selective the tool is.

ICON	NAME	KEYBOARD SHORTCUT	DESCRIPTION
	Quick Selection	A	The Quick Selection tool makes a selection border based on the similarity of the color and textures of the image when you click, or click & drag over an area of your image.
	Selection Brush	A	The Selection Brush tool is used to create selection borders in two different ways. In Selection mode, you paint over the area you want to select, while in Mask mode, you can paint over areas you don't want to select using a transparent overlay.
	Horizontal Type	T	The Horizontal Type tool creates standard left to right read text. Any font that you have installed on your computer can be used in Photoshop Elements.
	Vertical Type	T	The Vertical Type tool creates text that can be read from top to bottom. Any font that you have installed on your computer can be used in Photoshop Elements.
	Horizontal Type Mask, Vertical Type Mask	T	The Horizontal Type Mask and Vertical Type Mask tools create selection borders in the shape of either horizontal or vertical text.
	Crop	C	The Crop tool is used to make either rectangular or square crop areas. Anything outside of the crop border is discarded from the picture when the crop is approved.
	Recompose tool	C	The Recompose tool is used to scale an image without affecting the internal components of an image. This tool can actually adjust the relationship between objects without affecting the objects themselves.
	Cookie Cutter	Q	The Cookie Cutter tool crops a photo into a specific shape that you choose. After you add the shape to your photo, you can move and resize it until you have just the area you want.
	Straighten	P	The Straighten tool is used to realign an image either vertically or horizontally.
	Red Eye Removal	Y	The Red Eye Removal tool removes red eyes in flash photographs of people.

ICON	NAME	KEYBOARD SHORTCUT	DESCRIPTION
	Spot Healing Brush	J	The Spot Healing Brush tool removes blemishes, scratches, and other imperfections from an image by sampling from the pixels around the imperfection. The tool can either be used as a blotter by clicking, or as a brush by clicking and dragging.
	Healing Brush	J	The Healing Brush tool is very similar in function to the Spot Healing Brush. The difference is that an area to sample from must first be set to use the Healing Brush. The sample area is set by holding the Alt key and clicking with the tool.
	Clone Stamp	S	The Clone Stamp tool samples the pixels in an area of your image that you define and then applies it to a different location. Unlike the similar Healing Brush, the Clone Stamp doesn't perform tonal correction to match the clone target.
	Pattern Stamp	S	The Pattern Stamp tool applies a pattern from the Pattern Library. The program ships with pre-built patterns for you to use but you can also create your own.
	Eraser	E	The Eraser tool mimics the capabilities of a physical eraser by removing pixels. On layers, the tool erases to transparency, while on a background, it erases to the background color.
	Background Eraser	E	The Background Eraser tool turns color pixels transparent. The symbol for the tool is a crosshair inside of a circle. The cross-hair represents the hot spot, or sampling area, of the tool. When used, any pixels inside of the circular region that match the color of the pixels at the hotspot are erased, while pixels of other colors are unaffected.
	Magic Eraser	E	The Magic Eraser tool removes pixels from an image that are similar to each other in color value to the one you click on. You can think of it as a combination between the Magic Wand and Eraser tools.

ICON	NAME	KEYBOARD SHORTCUT	DESCRIPTION
	Brush	B	The Brush tool is used to apply color to areas of your image.
	Impressionist Brush	B	The Impressionist Brush tool changes the existing pixels in your image into a more stylized form. The result is that your photo looks like it was painted using stylized brush strokes.
	Color Replacement	B	The Color Replacement tool replaces the color in a targeted area by overlaying a tint of the active foreground color. The center crosshair of the tool defines the targeted area and the radius of the brush the affected area.
	Pencil	N	The Pencil tool is used to create hard-edged freehand lines.
	Smart Brush	F	The Smart Brush tool allows you to refine the colors and tonality of your image using a variety of preset effects. When you use the tool, it makes a selection based on color and texture similarly. The adjustment is then applied to the selected area.
	Detail Smart Brush	F	The Detail Smart Brush tool, like the Smart Brush, also refines the colors and tonality of your image. However, unlike the Smart Brush, which makes a selection this tool can be used to paint an adjustment layer right on top of an image.
	Paint Bucket	K	The Paint Bucket tool fills an area of pixels that are similar in color to the ones you click. You can use either the currently active foreground color or a pattern as your fill.
	Gradient	G	The Gradient tool is used to fill your currently selected layer with a gradient. A gradient is a type of fill that blends multiple colors together with either smooth or rough transitions. The gradient is controlled by two things; the type of gradient you choose from the Options bar and where you set the start and end points.

ICON	NAME	KEYBOARD SHORTCUT	DESCRIPTION
	Vector tools: Rectangle, Rounded Rectangle, Ellipse, Polygon, Line, Custom Shape, Shape Selection	U	The Vector Shape tools create vector graphics, which are graphics defined by lines and curves instead of pixels. Vector graphics can be scaled to any size and printed at any resolution without losing detail or clarity. You can move, resize, or change them without losing the quality of the graphic.
	Blur	R	The Blur tool is used to soften the edge of areas of your image by blurring pixels together.
	Sharpen	R	The Sharpen tool is used to increase the contrast between pixels in an image. During sharpening, the lighter pixels of an image are made lighter while the darker pixels in the image are made darker. As a result, slightly blurry areas are repaired.
	Smudge	R	The Smudge tool drags pixels from one area of an image to another. It is intended to simulate the effect of dragging your finger through wet paint.
	Sponge	U	The Sponge tool is used to saturate or desaturate the colors in an image.
	Dodge	U	The Dodge tool can be used to selectively lighten areas of an image. The tool options can be set to target either highlights, midtones, or shadows of an image.
	Burn	U	The Burn tool is used to selectively darken areas of an image. The tool options can be set to target either the highlights, midtones, or shadows of an image.
	Set Background & Foreground colors to default	D	Resets the background and foreground color swatches at the bottom of the tools palette to the default colors: Black & White
	Swap Background & Foreground colors	X	Swaps the currently active foreground and background colors

Appendix B - Keyboard Shortcuts

This is a partial list of the most commonly used keyboard shortcuts in the Photoshop Elements Editor application. For a complete list you should review the program's help files (click F1 from within Photoshop Elements). While there are keyboard shortcuts for working in both the Editor and Organizer workspaces, the keyboards shortcuts listed here are specifically for use in the Editor.

Shortcuts for viewing images

WINDOWS	MAC OS	RESULT
Ctrl+Tab	Command+Tab	Cycle forward through open documents
Ctrl+Shift+Tab	Command+Shift+Tab	Cycle backward through open documents
Ctrl+0 (or double-click Hand tool)	Command+0 (or double-click Hand tool)	Fit image in window
Ctrl+Alt+0 (or double-click Zoom tool)	Command+Option+0 (or double-click Zoom tool)	Magnify 100%
Spacebar		Switch to Hand tool (when not in text-edit mode)
Ctrl+Spacebar	Command+Spacebar	Switch to Zoom In tool
Spacebar+Alt	Spacebar+Option	Switch to Zoom Out tool
Spacebar+drag	Spacebar+drag	Reposition zoom marquee while dragging
Ctrl+drag over preview in Navigator palette	Command+drag over preview in Navigator palette	Zoom in on specified area of an image
Drag, or drag view area box in Navigator palette	Drag, or drag view area box in Navigator palette	Scroll image with Hand tool
Page Up or Page Down	Page Up or Page Down	Scroll up or down 1 screen
Shift+Page Up or Page Down	Shift+Page Up or Page Down	Scroll up or down 10 units
Ctrl+Page Up or Page Down	Command+Page Up or Page Down	Scroll left or right 1 screen
Ctrl+Shift+Page Up or Page Down	Command+Shift+Page Up or Page Down	Scroll left or right 10 units
Home or End	Home or End	Move view to upper left corner or lower right corner

Shortcuts for selecting tools

SHORTCUT	RESULT
Shift-press keyboard shortcut (preference setting, Use Shift Key for Tool Switch, must be enabled)	Cycle through tools that have the same keyboard shortcut
Alt-click (Windows) or Option-click (Mac OS) a tool	Cycle through nested tools
V	Move tool
Z	Zoom tool
H	Hand tool
I	Eyedropper tool
M	Rectangular Marquee tool, Elliptical Marquee tool
L	Lasso tool, Magnetic Lasso tool, Polygonal Lasso tool
W	Magic Wand tool
A	Selection Brush tool (or Quick Selection tool)
T	Horizontal Type tool, Vertical Type tool, Horizontal Type Mask tool, Vertical Type Mask tool
C	Crop tool
Q	Cookie Cutter tool
P	Straighten tool
Y	Red Eye Removal tool
J	Spot Healing Brush tool, Healing Brush tool
S	Clone Stamp tool, Pattern Stamp tool
N	Pencil tool
E	Eraser tool, Background Eraser tool, Magic Eraser tool
B	Brush tool, Impressionist Brush, Color Replacement tool
F	Smart Brush tool, Detail Smart Brush tool
K	Paint Bucket tool
G	Gradient tool
U	Rectangle tool, Rounded Rectangle tool, Ellipse tool, Polygon tool, Line tool, Custom Shape tool, Shape Selection tool
R	Blur tool, Sharpen tool, Smudge tool
O	Sponge tool, Dodge tool, Burn tool

SHORTCUT	RESULT
Tab	Show/Hide all palettes (not including Content and Layers palette)
D	Default foreground and background colors
X	Switch foreground and background colors

Shortcuts for working with selections

WINDOWS	MAC OS	RESULT
Ctrl+D	Command+D	Deselect a selection
Spacebar+drag		Reposition marquee while selecting
Any selection tool+Shift or Alt+drag	Any selection tool+Shift or Option+drag	Add to or subtract from a selection
Any selection tool+Shift+Alt+drag	Any selection tool+Shift+Option+drag	Intersect a selection
Shift+drag		Constrain marquee to square or circle (if no other selections are active)
Alt+drag	Option+drag	Draw marquee from center (if no other selections are active)
Shift+Alt+drag	Shift+Option+drag	Constrain shape and draw marquee from center
Ctrl (except when Hand or any Shape tool is selected)	Command (except when Hand or any Shape tool is selected)	Switch to Move tool
Alt-click and drag	Option-click and drag	Switch from Magnetic Lasso tool to Polygonal Lasso tool
Delete		Delete last anchor point for Magnetic or Polygonal Lasso tool
Enter/Esc	Return/Esc	Apply/cancel an operation of the Magnetic Lasso tool
Move tool+Alt+drag selection	Move tool+Option+drag selection	Move copy of selection
Any selection+Right Arrow, Left Arrow, Up Arrow, or Down Arrow		Move selection area 1 pixel
Move tool+Right Arrow, Left Arrow, Up Arrow, or Down Arrow		Move selection 1 pixel

WINDOWS	MAC OS	RESULT
Ctrl+Right Arrow, Left Arrow, Up Arrow, or Down Arrow	Command+Right Arrow, Left Arrow, Up Arrow, or Down Arrow	Move layer 1 pixel when nothing selected on layer
Magnetic Lasso tool+[or]		Increase/decrease detection width
Crop tool+Enter or Esc	Crop tool+Return or Esc	Accept cropping or exit cropping
/ (forward slash)		Toggle crop shield off and on

Shortcuts for working with text

WINDOWS	MAC OS	RESULT
Ctrl+drag type when Type layer is selected	Command+drag type when Type layer is selected	Move type in image
Shift+Left Arrow/Right Arrow or Down Arrow/Up Arrow, or Ctrl+Shift+Left Arrow/Right Arrow	Shift+Left Arrow/ Right Arrow or Down Arrow/Up Arrow, or Command+Shift+Left Arrow/Right Arrow	Select 1 character left/right or 1 line down/up, or 1 word left/right
Shift+click		Select characters from insertion point to mouse click point
Left Arrow/Right Arrow, Down Arrow/Up Arrow, or Ctrl+Left Arrow/Right Arrow	Left Arrow/Right Arrow, Down Arrow/Up Arrow, or Command+Left Arrow/ Right Arrow	Move 1 character left/right, 1 line down/up, or 1 word left/right
Double-click, triple-click, or quadruple-click		Select word, line, or paragraph
Ctrl-drag a bounding box handle	Command-drag a bounding box handle	Scale and skew text within a bounding box when resizing the bounding box
Horizontal Type tool or Horizontal Type Mask tool+Ctrl+Shift+L, C, or R	Horizontal Type tool or Horizontal Type Mask tool+Command+Shift+L, C, or R	Align left, center, or right
Vertical Type tool or Vertical Type Mask tool+Ctrl+Shift+L, C, or R	Vertical Type tool or Vertical Type Mask tool+Command+Shift+L, C, or R	Align top, center, or bottom
Ctrl+Shift+Y	Command+Shift+Y	Return to default font style
Ctrl+Shift+U	Command+Shift+U	Turn Underlining on/off

WINDOWS	MAC OS	RESULT
Ctrl+Shift+/ (forward slash)	Command+Shift+/ (forward slash)	Turn Strikethrough on/off
Ctrl+Shift+< or >	Command+Shift+< or >	Decrease or increase type size of selected text 2 pts/px

Shortcuts for working with the Layers palette

WINDOWS	MAC OS	RESULT
Alt+click New button	Option+click New button	Set layer options
Alt+click Trash button	Option+click Trash button	Delete without confirmation
Shift+Enter	Shift+Return	Apply value and keep text box active
Ctrl+click layer thumbnail	Command+click layer thumbnail	Load layer transparency as a selection
Ctrl+Shift+click layer	Command+Shift+click layer	Add to current selection
Ctrl+Alt+click layer thumbnail	Command+Option+click layer thumbnail	Subtract from current selection
Ctrl+Shift+Alt+click layer thumbnail	Command+Shift+Option +click layer thumbnail	Intersect with current selection
Ctrl+Shift+E	Command+Shift+E	Merge visible layers
Alt+click New Layer button	Option+click New Layer button	Create new empty layer with dialog
Ctrl+click New Layer button	Command+click New Layer button	Create new layer below target layer
Shift+Alt+[or]	Shift+Option+[or]	Activate bottom/top layer
Alt+[or]	Option+[or]	Select next layer down/up
Ctrl+[or]	Command+[or]	Move target layer down/up
Ctrl+Shift+Alt+E	Command+Shift+ Option+E	Merge a copy of all visible layers into target layer
Ctrl+E	Command+E	Merge down
Alt+Merge Down command from the palette pop-up menu	Option+Merge Down command from the palette pop-up menu	Copy current layer to layer below
Alt+Merge Visible command from the palette pop-up menu	Option+Merge Visible command from the palette pop-up menu	Copy all visible layers to active layer

WINDOWS	MAC OS	RESULT
Alt+click the visibility icon	Option+click the visibility icon	Show/hide all other currently visible layers
/ (forward slash)		Toggle lock transparency for target layer, or last applied lock
Double-click layer thumbnail		Edit layer properties
Double-click text layer thumbnail		Select all text; temporarily select Type tool
Alt+click the line dividing two layers	Option+click the line dividing two layers	Create a clipping mask
Double-click the layer name		Rename layer

Shortcuts for showing/hiding palettes

SHORTCUT	RESULT
F1	Open Help
F7	Show/Hide Content palette
F8	Show/Hide Info palette
F9	Show/Hide Histogram palette
F10	Show/Hide Undo History palette
F11	Show/Hide Layers palette
F12	Show/Hide Navigator palette

Appendix C - Understanding Digital Files

Understanding Resolution

Resolution is one of the most important concept in the world of computer graphics and is often misunderstood. Resolution is measured in units called pixels. A pixel, which is a conjunction of the words *picture* and *element*, is the smallest measurable area of a digital image. A single picture can be made up of millions of separate pixels, each pixel can be assigned its own color value and when viewed at their normal size (remember pixels are quite small) they appear as a seamless range of colors to form your pictures. The relationship of pixels to the overall picture is very similar to the relationship of individual puzzle pieces in a jigsaw puzzle. When viewed individually each piece just appears as a jumble of colors but once assembled and viewed from a distance, a seamless image emerges.

Images are often broken into two different categories high resolution (high res) or low resolution (low res). Though not set in stone, the term high resolution is usually used to describe images that are 300ppi or higher, while low resolution describes images that are below this standard. While technically a documents resolution can be any number, most software supports three standard settings:

Low resolution: 72ppi is the resolution commonly used for images that are going to be displayed on computer monitors and television screens. Web images, TV graphics, CD-ROM content is generally created at or converted to this standard.

Medium resolution: 150ppi is the resolution that many computer programs call medium resolution. This will normally produce a good quality image for printing on the average home inkjet printer. Some screen capture programs also use 96ppi as their default resolution.

High resolution: 300ppi is the resolution used by the printing industry for commercial printing, such as those used in books and magazines.

Understanding Color Modes & Bit Depth

Color Modes, or Models are mathematical formulas that are used to describe how color can be represented by numerical values. Each mode displays colors a little bit differently and each of them has a different range, or gamut, of colors, that it can create. Photoshop Elements will allow you to work with the following color modes:

Bitmap: Bitmap images do not have color or any tonal value beyond complete and pure black and white.

Grayscale: An image without color but that used the 256 different values of gray.

RGB Color: The three colors used in the RGB color model are Red, Green, and Blue. All digital cameras and scanners work using the RGB model, as do many video cameras.

Understanding File Formats

While Photoshop can be used to create files for nearly any imaginable use, the three most common applications of it are to produce graphics for Print, Web, and Video production.

Print Production Formats

The professional print production field uses a wide variety of image formats. The two most common are listed here. The two main considerations in print production are high resolution and good uncompressed image quality. While traditional offset printing uses the CMYK color model, some more modern digital printing techniques work better with RGB documents.

FORMAT	DESCRIPTION
PSD (Photoshop document)	The native Photoshop file format, used primarily when working within an Adobe Production workflow.
TIFF (tagged image file format)	The default files format for standard print production workflows. The TIFF format supports millions of colors, layers, transparency, alpha channels, and clipping paths.

Web Production Formats

For web work the main consideration is to create files with decent visual quality and a small file size and download time.

FORMAT	DESCRIPTION
JPEG (joint photographic experts group)	The default image format for photos and other continuous tone images. The JPEG format supports millions of colors.
GIF (graphic interchange file)	The default image format for limited tone imagery such as logos and other graphics. The GIF format supports up to 256 colors and, unlike the JPEG format, supports transparency and animation.
PNG-8 (portable network graphic, 8-bit)	Intended to be a replacement for the GIF format PNG-8 supports transparency and can display up to 256 colors.
PNG-24 (portable network graphic, 24-bit)	Intended to be a replacement for the JPEG format PNG-24 supports multiple levels of transparency and and contain millions of colors.

Video Production Formats

For video, the most important consideration have always been a high image quality and the ability to save transparent files.

FORMAT	DESCRIPTION
Tiff (Tagged Image File Format)	The default files format for standard print and video production workflows. The TIFF format supports millions of colors, layers, transparency, alpha channels, and clipping paths.
Targa (Truevision Advanced Raster Graphics Adapter)	The traditional and long-lived file format for video production workflows. The TARGA format supports millions of colors and alpha channels.
PSD (Photoshop Document)	The native format of Photoshop Elements, the psd file format, has become a staple of the Adobe Video production workflow. The format supports the use of millions of colors, alpha channels, layers and clipping paths. It allows the user to maintain all the original image data of the file in a lossless state for easy editing or modification.

It is important to note that if you are using another Adobe application for your video editing, motion graphics, or compositing, such as Adobe Premiere Elements or Adobe After Effects, it is usually better to keep your files in the native Adobe Photoshop Elements format .psd.

Index

A

About This Gallery text box, Adobe Bridge Output panel, 371
action safe area, 350
active layer, 235
Actual Pixels, 297
Add a Page button, photo book, 171
Add button
   Print Photos dialog box, 177, 180
   Watch Folders dialog box, 10
Add Media button, slide shows, 268
Add Noise dialog box, 320
Add Photos dialog box, 177, 180
Add Selected Items button, Online Album Wizard, 157
Add Text button, Editor workspace, 260
Add to Cart button, Adobe Photoshop Services web site, 277
Add to Selection option, Load Selection dialog box, 146
Add To Selection setting, Options bar, 140, 142
Add to Selection tool, Magic Extractor, 245
additive color model, 341
additive primaries, 127–128
Adjust Color Curves command, 111, 135
Adjust Color for Skin Tone command, 73–75
Adjust Color Intensity slider, Color Variations dialog box, 133
Adjust Hue/Saturation command, 136–137, 148
Adjust Sliders, Adjust Color Curves dialog box, 135
Adjustment Intensity sliders, Convert to Black and White dialog box, 147
adjustment layers, 82, 112–117, 217, 219–221, 231
Adobe Bridge
   Adobe Bridge Home, 376
   Collections, 367–368
   Favorites, making, 360–361
   file, opening from, 365
   Filter panel, 367
   folders, using in, 358–360
   metadata, 361–364
   navigating, 356–357
   overview, 355–356
   PDF contact sheet, 373–374
   Photoshop Elements, integration with, 376
   searching for files, 365–367
   Stacks, 368–369
   view, changing, 374–375
   Web Photo Gallery, 369–372
Adobe Bridge Home, 376
Adobe Color Picker, 309–310, 319
Adobe Creative Suite, 356
Adobe E-mail Service, 164, 166–168

Adobe ID, 155, 158
Adobe Photoshop Services web site, 172–173, 273–277
Advanced button, Page Setup dialog box, 182
After Only button, Guided Edit panel, 69
album categories, 19
Album Category drop-down menu, Online Album Wizard, 156
Album Category Name text field, Create Album Category dialog box, 40
Album Details panel, Organizer, 17–18, 38, 40
Album Groups, 16
Album icon, 39
Album Name text field
   Album Details panel, 18
   Online Album Wizard, 157
Album option, Add Photos dialog box, 177
albums, 37–42, 155–160
Albums panel, Organizer, 17–18, 24, 27, 38, 41
alert icon, Histogram panel, 215–217
Align command, 326
Allow Viewers to options, Online Album Wizard, 160
alpha channel, 351, 353
Also delete selected item(s) from the hard disk checkbox, Confirm Deletion from Catalog dialog box, 32
Also Show Hidden Media option, Add Photos dialog box, 177
Alt key, 118
Amount field
   Add Noise dialog box, 320
   Quick Fix panel, 61
   Unsharp Mask dialog box, 87–88, 298
Angle option, Brush tool More Options menu, 311
Animate checkbox, Save for Web dialog box, 210
animating text, 210–211
Animation section, Save for Web dialog box, 210
animation with text, creating, 206–208
anti-aliasing, 142
Apply Borders button, Stationery & Layouts Wizard, 165
Apply checkbox, Adobe Bridge Metadata panel, 363
Apply Metadata section, Photo Downloader, 8
Apply Pan & Zoom to All Slides check box, Slide Show Preferences dialog box, 259
Apply to Selected Text Item option, text style, 262
Arch option, Warp Text dialog box, 204
Arrange command, 65, 112, 114, 202–203, 238
arrow keys, 193
art. see also scrapbooking
   brushes, 307–314
   documents, creating, 306–307

overview, 305
patterns, 316–318
shapes, 314–315
As a Copy checkbox, Save As dialog box, 149
audio, 267–270
audio captions, 259
Auto button, Guided Edit panel, 68, 70
Auto Color, 63–64
Auto Contrast, 62–63, 216
Auto controls, 58
Auto Levels, 61–62, 216
Auto Select Layer option, Options bar, 237
Auto setting, Photomerge dialog box, 254
Auto Smart Fix, 60–61, 216
autofill feature, photo calendar, 274
Auto-Fill With Project Bin Photos, photo book option, 171
Automatically Download checkbox, Photo Downloader, 8
Automatically Fix Red Eyes option, Photo Downloader, 7, 9
Automatically Suggest Photo Stacks option, Photo Downloader, 8
automation tools, Adobe Bridge, 369–374
AutoPlay dialog box, 4
Auto-select, Options bar, 227

B

background, 171, 220
Background Brush tool, 242–243
background color, 295
Background Color option, Slide Show Preferences dialog box, 259
Background Contents drop-down menu, New dialog box, 232
Background copy layer, 101, 103
Background Eraser tool, 379
Background layer, 82, 85, 119–120, 221, 236–237, 238
backing up files, 183–186
Backup/Sync Now option, System Tray, 186
Backup/Sync only when Idle option, System Tray, 186
Backup/Synchronization Preferences dialog box, 184–185
Backup/Synchronize checkmark, Album Details panel, 38
Balance section, Quick Fix panel, 64
banding, 217
base layer, clipping group, 247
Basic panel, Camera Raw dialog box, 285
Before and After - Horizontal option, 60, 69
Bend field, Warp Text dialog box, 233
Bevels option, Effects panel, 249
Bicubic sharper, 92

bitmap images, 388
bitmap mode, 129
Blacks slider, Camera Raw dialog box, 282
blending modes, 84, 101, 119, 239–241, 310, 332–333
Bloat tool, 322–324
Blue channel option, 110, 122
Blue Skies brush style, 83
blue skies, enhancing, 82–85
Blur filter, using to create depth of field, 300–303
Blur tool, 316, 381
blurring, correcting, 86–88
BMP format, 150
border, scrapbook, 334–337
Border option, Print Photos dialog box, 175
Bridge. *see* Adobe Bridge
Bridge Home, Adobe, 376
brightness, 61–62, 105–112, 127
Brightness slider, Camera Raw dialog box, 282, 286–287
Brightness slider/text field, Brightness/Contrast dialog box, 105
Brightness/Contrast command, 105–106
Browse for Folder dialog box, 34–35
Browse with Adobe Bridge icon, 357
Brush drop-down menu, Options bar, 83
Brush Picker arrow, 223
brush presets menu, 307
brush size, 81, 243
Brush tool, 307, 380
brushes, 307–314. *see also specific brushes by name*
Burn tool, 316, 381
burning audio to disk, 270
Butterfly brush, 307–308

C

Camera Calibration panel, Camera Raw dialog box, 285
Camera Raw dialog box, 281–290
Camera Raw files, 280–290
Cancel button, Photo Downloader, 6
Caps Lock key, 222
Caption field, Print Photos dialog box, 179
captions, photo, 259
capture devices, profiling, 176
cartoon bubbles, 195–199
Change Settings button, Print Photos dialog box, 178, 180
Channel drop-down menu
    Histogram panel, 215
    Levels Adjustment panel, 122
    Levels dialog box, 110
Channel pop-up menu, Levels dialog box, 134

choppy images, 217

chroma, 127

Clarity slider, Camera Raw dialog box, 282

Clear Layer Style option, Layer Style menu, 251

Click Here to Add Audio to your Slide Show button, storyboard, 268

Click to add formatted text to your slide show button, Extras palette, 262

Click to Lock to Thumbnail Grid button, Adobe Bridge, 374

clipped shadows, 285

clipping groups, 247

Clone Stamp tool, 224–227, 379

Close button, Editor, 15

CLUT (color lookup table), 129

CMYK (Cyan, Magenta, Yellow, and Black) color mode, 341

Collections, Adobe Bridge, 367–368

color. see also selections
    adding to areas of image, 148
    adjusting in Edit Guided workspace, 130
    adjusting in Edit Quick workspace, 130
    cartoon bubble, 197
    Convert to Black and White command, 147
    correcting automatically, 63–64
    correcting in Full Edit, 132–137
    exporting images, 148–150
    file formats, 148–150
    HSB, 127–128
    image modes, 129–130
    management, 176
    overview, 125–126
    in PNG images, 348
    saving images, 148–150
    text, 194
    tonal range, adjusting in Full Edit, 131–132
    for video, 340–341
    for Web, 340–341

Color Auto button, Quick Fix panel, 63

color balance, 63–64

Color blending mode, 310

color cast, removing, 72–73, 132–134

color curves, 111–112, 135

color gamut, 176

color lookup table (CLUT), 129

Color Management section, Print Photos dialog box, 175

Color Mode drop-down menu, New dialog box, 232

Color Picker, 309–310, 319

color reduction algorithm, 348

Color Replacement tool, 380

Color Section, Quick Fix panel, 63–64

Color swatch, Gradient Editor, 309–310

color temperature, 281

Color Variations command, 133–134

color wheel, 126, 128

Colorize option, Hue/Saturation dialog box, 148, 328

Columns option, Print Photos dialog box, 178

combining images, 234

Command key, 359

Commit button, Quick Fix panel, 63

Commit Current Quick Fix Operation button, Quick Fix panel, 62

Common Base Name text field
    Export New Files dialog box, 187
    Rename dialog box, 33

comparing photos side by side, 35–36

composites. see photo composites

compression, 342, 344

Confirm Deletion from Catalog dialog box, 32

Consolidate All command, 114, 203, 234

Constrain Proportions option
    Image Size dialog box, 207
    Options bar, 334

contact book, e-mail, 161

Contact Sheet option, Print Photos dialog box, 178

Contents section, Fill Layer dialog box, 317

contrast, 62–63, 105–112

Contrast Auto button, Quick Fix panel, 62

Contrast slider, Camera Raw dialog box, 282, 288

Contrast slider/text field, Brightness/Contrast dialog box, 105

Convert to Black and White command, 147

Cookie Cutter tool, 316, 378

Copy command, 119, 246, 331

Copy Layer Style option, Layer Style menu, 251

Copyright option, Photo Downloader, 8

correcting photos. see photographic problems, fixing

crafts. see art; scrapbooking

Create a Calendar button, web-based calendar creator, 271

Create a new folder icon, Adobe Bridge, 359

Create a New Layer button, Layers panel, 226, 307–308, 335

Create adjustment layer button, Layers panel, 218

Create Album Category dialog box, 40

Create Brush from Selection option, Edit menu, 311

Create Category dialog box, 45

Create Keyword Tag dialog box, 46

Create New Adobe ID button, Online Album Wizard, 158

Create new album or album category button, Albums panel, 38, 40

Create new album or album group button, Albums panel, 17, 19

Create New Album radio button, Online Album Wizard, 156

Create new fill or adjustment layer icon, Layers panel, 121

Create new keyword tag, sub-category, or category button, Keyword Tags panel, 45

Create panel, 169

Create Subfolder(s) drop-down menu, Photo Downloader, 5, 7

Create tab, Organizer, 257, 271

Create warped text button, Options bar, 204, 233

Create your Calendar page, 275–276

creations, Photoshop Elements
    audio, 267–270
    overview, 253
    panoramas, 254–255
    photo calendars, 270–277
    slide shows, 255–267

Creative Suite, Adobe, 356

Creator: City field, Adobe Bridge Metadata panel, 363

Creator option, Photo Downloader, 8

Crop To Fit option, Print Photos dialog box, 174, 180

Crop to Fit Slide options, Slide Show Preferences dialog box, 259

Crop tool, 89–91, 93–94, 255, 283, 289, 330, 378

cropping images, 89

Ctrl key, selecting photos with, 18

custom brushes, 311

custom option, Duration drop-down menu, 265

Custom Overlay Color button, Refine Edge dialog box, 144, 219

Custom Pattern menu, Fill Layer dialog box, 317

Custom Shape tool, 195, 197, 315

Cyan, Magenta, Yellow, and Black (CMYK) color mode, 341

D

dark image, fixing, 68–69

Darken Highlights settings, Guided Edit panel, 68, 70

    Darken Highlights slider
    Quick Fix panel, 63
    Shadow/Highlights dialog box, 132

Darken section, Guided Edit panel, 68

date, sorting images by, 16, 47

Date field
    New Smart Album dialog box, 42
    Print Photos dialog box, 179

Default Brushes drop-down menu, Options bar, 140

Default Photoshop Elements Size option, New dialog box, 232

Define Pattern from Selection option, Edit menu, 317

Defringe option, Magic Extractor dialog box, 245

Delete a Page button, photo book, 171

Delete button, Narration tool, 269

Delete key, 32

Delete Options section, Photo Downloader, 6–7

Delete Selected Items from Catalog option, Edit menu, 32

deleting layers, 239

depth of field, creating with Blur filter, 300–303

Description Writer field, Adobe Bridge Metadata panel, 363

Deselect command, 14, 336

Destination field
    Process Multiple Files dialog box, 291
    Save Options dialog box, 290

destroying images, 216–217

Detail panel, Camera Raw dialog box, 285

Detail Smart Brush tool, 380

details, viewing in Adobe Bridge, 375

Details checkbox, Options bar, 25

Diffuse Glow filter, 293

digital files, 388–390

digital negative file, 290

digital photography, 2

Direction drop-down menu, Properties palette, 264

disk, burning audio to, 270

Display icon, Organizer, 36

Display in My Gallery checkbox, Online Album Wizard, 159, 160

distribution methods, slide show, 269

Distribution section, Add Noise dialog box, 320

dithering, 348

Document section, Adobe Bridge Output panel, 373

Document Size area, Image Size dialog box, 91

Document Size Width text field, Image Size dialog box, 92

Document Sizes option, status bar drop-down menu, 246

documents, creating from scratch, 306–307

Dodge tool, 316, 381

Done button, Frame From Video dialog box, 15

double arrow, Toolbox, 57

down arrow, navigating photos with, 30

Download Photos option, Online Album Wizard, 160

download time, 347

dragging and dropping slides on storyboard, 267

drawing tools, 316

Drop Shadows option, Effects panel drop-down menu, 205

Duplicate Layer dialog box, 100, 102, 209, 321

duplicating files, 131

Duration drop-down menu, Properties palette, 264–265

DVDs, 270

E

edges, smoothing, 142–144

Edit button, welcome screen, 3, 56

Edit drop-down menu, Hue/Saturation dialog box, 116, 136

Edit Full workspace. *see* Full Edit mode

Edit Guided workspace. *see* Guided Edit mode

Edit Photos button, Organizer, 15, 56

Edit Quick option, Editor workspace, 60

Edit Quick workspace, adjusting color in, 130

Edit Recipients In Contact Book option
    Online Album Wizard, 159
    Photo Mail dialog box, 165

Edit tab, Editor workspace, 57–58

Edit Text dialog box, 261

Edit with Photoshop Elements option, 56, 283

editing. *see also* Editor workspace; photographic problems, fixing; retouching photos
    layers, 236–239
    Magic Extractor selections, 245
    text layers, 193–194

editing modes, 58. *see also* Full Edit mode; Guided Edit mode

Editor workspace. *see also* color; photographic problems, fixing; retouching photos
    artists, 305–306
    creations, 253
    digital photography, 279
    entering, 56
    exposure, adjusting, 97–98
    fixing problems, 55
    organizing photos, 23
    overview, 57
    Panel Bin, 58
    panels, resetting, 1
    photo composites, 229–230
    Project Bin, 58
    sharing photos, 153
    type, working with, 189–190
    video clips, working with, 14–15
    Web and video graphics, 339

effects, adding to text, 200–202

effects icon, 248

Effects panel, 200–201, 206, 248–250

8-bit images, 129

Elliptical Marquee tool, 139, 219, 377

E-mail Attachments dialog box, 161–164

E-mail Client drop-down menu, Preferences dialog box, 167

E-mail Service, Adobe, 164, 166–168

e-mailing photos, 161–168

Emboss effect, 201–202

Enable Pan & Zoom checkbox, Properties palette, 265

Encapsulated PostScript (EPS), 150

End point thumbnail, Properties palette, 266

Entire Catalog option, Add Photos dialog box, 177

EPS (Encapsulated PostScript), 150

Eraser tool, 316, 379

Expand Selection dialog box, 335

Export New Files dialog box, 186–187

Export to CD/DVD option, Online Album Wizard, 156

Export to FTP option, Online Album Wizard, 156

exporting images, 148–150, 186–187

exposure
    adjustment layers, 112–114
    blending modes, 101
    brightness and contrast, adjusting manually, 105–112
    faded images, improving, 102–105
    Hue/Saturation adjustments, 115–117
    layers, 100
    overexposed images, improving, 102–105
    overview, 97–98
    Photomerge Exposure, 75–76
    selections, correcting, 115–123
    underexposed images, improving, 99

Exposure slider, Camera Raw dialog box, 281, 287

Extras palette, 262–263

eyedropper, 72, 74

Eyedropper tool, 116, 377

F

F1 key, 19

facial recognition. *see* People Recognition

Fade option, Brush tool More Options menu, 311

faded images, improving, 102–105

Favorites, Adobe Bridge, 360–361

feathering, 84, 142–144, 220, 245

File Info dialog box, 363–364

File name field, Save As dialog box, 149

File Naming section, Save Options dialog box, 290

File Type option, Export New Files dialog box, 186

Filename field, Print Photos dialog box, 179

Filename search criteria drop-down menu, New Smart Album dialog box, 42

filenames, 13, 32–33

Filenames area, Export New Files dialog box, 187

files
    backing up, 183–186
    digital, 388–390
    formats, 148–150, 342–343, 389–390
    locked, 362
    opening, from Adobe Bridge, 365
    saving audio as, 269
    saving for video, 351–353
    searching for in Adobe Bridge, 365–367

Fill Holes option, Magic Extractor dialog box, 245

Fill Layer dialog box, 221, 317, 325, 335
fill layers, 231
Fill Light slider, Camera Raw dialog box, 282
Fill Page With First Photo checkbox, Print Photos dialog box, 180
Filter button, Effects panel, 201
Filter Gallery, 295
Filter panel, Adobe Bridge, 367
filters, 295. *see also specific filters by name*
Find box, Keyword Tags panel, 50, 52
finding photos, 51–53
Fit Screen button, Quick Fix panel, 60
Fit Slides To Audio button, storyboard, 268
Fix tab, Organizer, 14, 15, 56
fixing photos. *see* photographic problems, fixing
Flash Player, 275
flattening images, 245–246
flow percentages, brush, 137
focus problems, fixing, 86–88
Folder option, Process Files From drop-down menu, 291
folders, using in Adobe Bridge, 358–360
Folders panel, Adobe Bridge, 357–358
font, text, 192
Font drop-down menu, Options bar, 233
Font Family drop-down menu, Options bar, 326
Font Name text field, Options bar, 200
Font Size text field, Options bar, 326
Foreground Brush tool, 241–243
foreground colors, adjustment layer mask, 220
Format field, Save As dialog box, 149
formats, file, 148–150, 342–343, 389–390
formatting text layers, 192–193
Frame From Video dialog box, 14–15
Free Transform command, 227, 315
fringe colors, removing from selection, 245
Full Edit mode
    color, correcting in, 131–137
    color cast, removing, 72–73
    comparing images in, 112
    overview, 71
    Photomerge Exposure feature, 75–76
    skin tone, correcting, 73–75
    tonal range, adjusting in, 131–132
Full Photo Edit, 79–80
Full Screen View button, Options bar, 36

G

Gaussian Blur, 295, 302–303, 320, 327
gears icon, Levels dialog box, 113
General Preferences dialog box, 183
Get Media button, Get Photos and Videos from Files and Folders dialog box, 12

Get Photos and Videos by Searching for Folders dialog box, 9–10
Get Photos and Videos from Files and Folders dialog box, 11–12
Get Photos button, Photo Downloader, 6
Get Photos from Scanner dialog box, 8–9
GIF (Graphics Interchange Format), 150, 342, 389
GIF 128 Dithered option, Save for Web dialog box, 210
Go back button, Adobe Bridge, 357
Go forward button, Adobe Bridge, 357
Grab Frame button, Frame From Video dialog box, 15
Gradient Editor, 308–310
Gradient Stroke Black & Gray effect, 208
Gradient tool, 308, 380
gradients, creating textures with, 307–311
graphics
    adding to slide shows, 263
    color, 340–341
    overview, 339
    resolution, 340–341
    safe margins, 350–351
    saving files for video, 351–353
    vector, 381
    video, preparing images for, 349
    Web, preparing images for, 341–348
Graphics Interchange Format (GIF), 150, 342, 389
grayscale images, 388
grayscale mode, 129
Green channel option, Levels Adjustment panel, 122
Greens option, Hue/Saturation dialog box, 116
Group as Stack command, 369
Group With Previous option, Layers panel, 247
Guided Edit mode
    adjusting color in, 130
    dark image, fixing, 68–69
    light image, fixing, 69–70
    overexposed image, fixing, 69–70
    overview, 67
    underexposed image, fixing, 68–69

H

hand icon, Navigator panel, 66
Hand tool, 66, 242, 283, 297, 377
hardness, brush tip, 141, 311
Healing Brush tool, 222–223, 379
Height field, New dialog box, 232
help, 19–20
hex colors, 319
Hidden icon, Organizer, 31
Hide All Effects option, Layer Style menu, 250
Hide Hidden Files option, Organizer, 32

hiding layers, 237

high resolution, 388

Highlight Clipping Warning, Camera Raw dialog box, 285

Highlight Details slider, Photomerge Exposure, 76

highlights, 106–107, 132

Histogram, Camera Raw dialog box, 285

Histogram panel, 108–111, 215–217

Horizontal Type Mask, 378

Horizontal Type tool, 191–193, 198–200, 204, 207, 233, 378

hue, 127, 136–137

hue, saturation, and brightness (HSB) color, 126–128

Hue Jitter option, Brush tool More Options menu, 311

Hue slider
    Hue/Saturation dialog box, 117, 136, 148
    Quick Fix panel, 63

Hue text field, Hue/Saturation dialog box, 328

Hue/Saturation command, 115–117, 136, 328

I

ICC Profile, 149, 345

image modes, 129–130

Image Size area
    Process Multiple Files dialog box, 291
    Save for Web dialog box, 346

Image Size dialog box, 91–92, 207, 341

Import Attached Keyword Tags dialog box, 12

Import Folders button, Get Photos and Videos by Searching for Folders dialog box, 10

Import into Album option, Photo Downloader, 8

Import option, Process Files From drop-down menu, 291

Import Settings section, Photo Downloader, 5, 7

Imported Keyword Tags category, Keyword Tags panel, 51

importing photos
    files and folders, adding to Organizer, 11–13
    overview, 1
    Photo Downloader, 4–8
    from scanner, 8–9
    searching for photos and videos, 9–10
    from video frames, 13–15
    Watch Folder, setting, 10
    welcome screen, 3
    workspaces, 16

Impressionist brush, 312–314, 380

Include Audio Captions as Narration check box, Slide Show Preferences dialog box, 259

Include Caption checkbox, Photo Mail dialog box, 165

Include Captions, photo book option, 171

Include in the Elements Organizer checkbox, Save As dialog box, 149

Include in the Organizer checkbox, 15

Include Photo Captions as Text check box, Slide Show Preferences dialog box, 259

Include Sound Effects checkbox, Slideshow Settings window, 157

Increase Contrast style, Adjust Color Curves dialog box, 111

Increase Red button, Color Variations dialog box, 133

indexed color mode, 129

Individual Prints option, Print Photos dialog box, 174

inkjet printers, 176

Input Levels section
    Levels Adjustment panel, 121
    Levels dialog box, 293

Inspiration Browser, 20

Interlacing option, Save for Web dialog box, 348

Inverse command, 146, 312, 352

Invert command, 120, 333

IPTC Core, 362

Iron-on Transfer option, Print Photos dialog box, 175

Is drop-down menu, New Smart Album dialog box, 42

Items area, Online Album Wizard, 157

J

Join Now button, Organizer, 155

JPCX format, 150

JPEG (Joint Photographic Experts Group) format, 149–150, 342, 343–345, 389

JPEG medium option, Save for Web dialog box, 344

JPEG Options dialog box, 59

K

keyboard shortcuts, 377–387

keyword Tag Cloud, 52–53

Keyword Tag option, Add Photos dialog box, 177

Keyword Tags panel, 24, 27, 45, 47–48, 52–53

keywords, 12, 44–47, 51–52, 363–364, 366

Keywords tab, Adobe Bridge, 363

Kodak, 169–173, 270, 273–277

L

Labels menu, Process Multiple Files dialog box, 291

Lasso tools, 138–139, 377

Layer blending mode drop-down menu, Layers panel, 310
layer style, adding to text, 205–206
layer style icon, 235, 251
layer styles
    applying, 249–250
    changing scale, 250–251
    copying between layers, 251
    hiding all, 250
    overview, 248–249
    removing, 251
    showing all, 250
layers. *see also* layer styles
    adjustment, 82, 112–117, 217, 219–221, 231
    animating, 209–211
    Background, converting into regular layer, 236–237
    blending modes, 239–241
    combining images, 234
    copying style settings between, 251
    editing, 236–239
    file, creating, 232
    in image modes, 130
    Layers panel, 235–236
    opacity, 239–240
    overview, 100, 231–232
    text, 191–194, 209
    type, 233
Layers checkbox, Save As dialog box, 149
Layers panel. *see also* layers
    blending mode, specifying, 240–241
    clipping group, creating, 247
    Clone Stamp tool, 226
    completing composite, 246
    flattening images, 245
    improving images, 218
    layer styles, 249–251
    Magic Extractor, 241–242
    opacity of layer, specifying, 240
    overview, 100, 231, 235–236
    shortcuts for working with, 386–387
layout options, Kodak photo book, 171
Layout section, Photomerge dialog box, 254
Lessons folder, 1, 11–12
Letter option, New dialog box, 306, 318
Levels adjustment layer, 112–114, 219
Levels Adjustment panel, 121–122
Levels Auto button, Panel Bin, 61
Levels command, 108, 109–111, 134
Levels dialog box, 113–114, 218–219, 293
light image, fixing, 69–70
Lighten section, Guided Edit panel, 68
Lighten Shadows slider
    Guided Edit panel, 68, 70
    Shadow/Highlights dialog box, 132

Lighting and Exposure section, Guided Edit panel, 68, 69
Lighting section, Quick Fix panel, 61–62
Lightness option, Hue/Saturation dialog box, 117, 137, 328
Link Layers button, Layers panel, 235, 315
Liquify dialog box, 322–324
lists, Adobe Bridge, 375
Load Selection dialog box, 120, 145–146, 301
loading opacity mask, 335
Location: field, Photo Downloader, 7
Location option, Export New Files dialog box, 187
locked files, 362
locked layer icon, Layers panel, 235
locking layers, 239
lossy compression, 344
low resolution, 388
Luminosity option, Blending Mode drop-down menu, 240
LZW compression, 342

M

Mac OS. *see* Adobe Bridge
Mac OS keyboard shortcuts, 382–387
Magic Eraser tool, 379
Magic Extractor, 241–245
Magic Wand tool, 138–139, 312, 352, 377
Magnetic Lasso tool, 139, 377
Make 'Group Custom Name' a Tag option, Photo Downloader, 8
Make New Folder button, Browse for Folder dialog box, 35
Map panel, 46
margins, safe, 350–351
Mark as Hidden option, Organizer, 29–30
Mark as Visible option, Organizer, 31
mask icon, Levels layer, 122
Mask mode, Selection Brush tool, 140–141
Match Zoom and Location option, Full Edit View, 65
Matte Color option, Save for Web dialog box, 348
Matte option, Save for Web dialog box, 345
Max Print Resolution option, Print Photos dialog box, 175
Maximum number of colors option, Save for Web dialog box, 348
Maximum Photo Size drop-down menu, E-mail Attachments dialog box, 162
Media Browser Arrangement drop-down menu, 16, 25, 47
Media Currently in Browser option, Add Photos dialog box, 177
media types, hiding and showing, 13, 15

medium resolution, 388
Merge Layers command, 327, 336
Merge Visible option, Layers panel, 209
Message text field
    E-mail Attachments dialog box, 162
    Online Album Wizard, 159
    Photo Mail dialog box, 165
metadata, 8, 361–364
Metadata panel, Adobe Bridge, 362
Midtone Brightness slider, Adjust Color Curves
  dialog box, 111
Midtone Contrast slider
    Adjust Color Curves dialog box, 111
    Guided Edit panel, 68, 70
    Quick Fix panel, 61
    Shadow/Highlights dialog box, 107, 132
midtone slider, Levels dialog box, 218
Midtones option, Color Variations dialog box, 133
Mode drop-down menu, Options bar, 141
monitors, color management, 176
Monochromatic checkbox, Add Noise dialog box,
  320
More Options button, Print Photos dialog box, 175,
  181
More Options menu, Brush tool, 311
Motion Blur filter, 321
Move Selected Items dialog box, 34–35
Move tool
    adding text to multiple images, 203
    cartoon bubble, 198–199
    Clone Stamp tool, 227
    effects, applying to text, 200
    Impressionist brush, 312
    Magic Extractor, 244
    overview, 377
    shapes, 315
    text layer, editing, 193–194
    type layer, creating, 233
Multiply blending mode, 84, 101, 103, 119, 333

N

name, searching for files by, 366
Name drop-down menu, Page Setup dialog box, 182
Name text field, New dialog box, 232
Narration tool, 268–269
National Television Standards Committee (NTSC),
  349
Navigation buttons, Print Photos dialog box, 173,
  178, 180
Navigator panel, 65–66
New Album Category option, Albums panel, 19, 40
New Album option, Albums panel, 19
New Category option, Keyword Tags panel, 45
New Collection button, Adobe Bridge, 367

New dialog box, 232, 306, 318–319, 325
New Keyword button, Adobe Bridge, 363–364
New Keyword Tag option, Keyword Tags panel, 45
New Layer button, Layers panel, 247
New Layer dialog box, 112, 226, 236–237
New Smart Album dialog box, 41–42
New Sub Keyword button, Adobe Bridge, 364
Next button, Photo Calendar dialog box, 272–273
NTSC (National Television Standards Committee),
  349
Number of Pages, photo book option, 171

O

One Photo Per Page option, Print Photos dialog
  box, 174
1-bit images, 129
Online Album option, Share tab, 156
Online Album Wizard, 155–160
online albums, 155–160
online help, 19
online photo services, 168–173
Only Show Media with Ratings option, Add Photos
  dialog box, 177
opacity, of layers, 239–240
Opacity drop-down menu, Layers panel, 103
opacity mask, loading, 335
Open File button, Camera Raw dialog box, 289
Open Image button, Camera Raw dialog box, 290
Open Organizer when Finished option, Photo
  Downloader, 7
Open preferences dialog box option, Camera Raw
  dialog box, 283
Open Recently Edited File option, File menu, 317
Opened Files option, Process Files From drop-down
  menu, 291
optimizing images, 341–348
Options bar, 24–25, 57, 140–141. *see also specific*
  options and tools by name
Order Photo Prints option, Online Album Wizard,
  160
ordering
    printed photo book, 170–173
    prints, 168–170
Organize button, welcome screen, 3, 5
Organizer
    albums, 37–42
    Albums panel, 27
    artists, 305
    color, adjusting, 125
    comparing photos side by side, 35–36
    creating album, 16–19
    creations, 253–254
    digital photography, 279

exposure, adjusting, 97
finding photos, 51–53
fixing problems, 55
hiding photos, 29–31
importing photos to, 4–13
Keyword Tags panel, 27
moving photos, 33–35
online album, creating, 155–158
Options bar, 25
organizing photos, 23
overview, 23
People Recognition, 47–50
Photo Browser, 25
Photo Browser Timeline, 26
photo composites, 229
photo retouching, 213
Properties panel, 26
removing hidden photos, 31–32
renaming photos, 32–33
reviewing hidden photos, 31–32
rotating photos, 28
sharing photos, 153–154
slide shows, 256–257
Stacks, 37
tagging photos, 43–47
type, working with, 189
Web and video graphics, 339
workspace overview, 24
Organizer button, Editor workspace, 15–16
Original Name option, Export New Files dialog
  box, 187
Output button, Options bar, 269
Output drop-down menu, Adobe Bridge, 370
Output panel, Adobe Bridge, 370–374
overexposed images, improving, 69–70, 102–105

P

Page Numbers field, Print Photos dialog box, 179
page options, 182–183
Page Setup dialog box, 182
Paint Bucket tool, 319, 380
PAL (Phase Alternating Line) video standard, 349
palettes, shortcuts for working with, 387
Pan & Zoom effect, 265–266
Panel Bin, 57, 58
panels, resetting, 1, 55
panning, in slide shows, 259
panoramas, 254–255
Paper Size drop-down menu, Print Photos dialog
  box, 178, 180
Paste command, 119, 246, 331
Paste Layer Style option, Layer Style menu, 251
Pattern Stamp tool, 379
patterns, 316–318

Pause Backup/Synchronization option, System Tray,
  186
PDF (Portable Document Format), 150, 269
PDF contact sheet, 373–374
Pencil tool, 316, 380
People Recognition, 43
Performance section, Preferences, 300
Phase Alternating Line (PAL) video standard, 349
Photo Book option, Create tab, 170
Photo Browser, 24, 25, 161
Photo Browser Timeline, 26
Photo Calendar dialog box, 272–273
photo calendars, 270–277
photo composites. *see also* layers
    clipping groups, 247
    completing, 246
    flattening images, 245–246
    layer styles, 248–251
    Magic Extractor, 241–245
    overview, 229–230
    welcome screen, 230
Photo Downloader, 4–8
Photo Mail, 164–166
Photo Prints button, Create panel, 169, 173
Photo Project (PSE) format, 148, 150
photographic problems, fixing
    cropping images, 89
    editing modes, 58
    Editor workspace, 57–58
    Full Edit mode, 71–76
    Guided Edit mode, 67–70
    overview, 55
    Quick Fix, 58–66
    Red Eye Removal tool, 78–79
    resizing images, 91–94
    rotating images, 90–91
    sharpening images, 86–88
    skies, enhancing blue, 82–85
    teeth, whitening, 80–82
    Toolbox, 77
    welcome screen, 56
photography, digital, 2
Photomerge dialog box, 254
Photomerge Exposure feature, 75–76
Photomerge Panorama option, File menu, 254
Photos to Share folder, 155
Photoshop (PSD) format, 114, 123, 148–149, 150,
  351, 389–390
Photoshop EPS (Encapsulated PostScript), 150
Photoshop help, 19
Photoshop PDF (Portable Document Format), 150
Photoshop Raw format, 150
Photoshop.com, 20, 168, 183–186
Photoshop.com Backup/Synchronization Agent
  icon, 186

Photoshop.com option, Online Album Wizard, 156
PICT format, 150
picture packages, 173
Pixar format, 150
Pixel Dimensions area, Image Size dialog box, 91
pixels, 340–341, 388
Place command, 334
Place on Map button, Create Keyword Tag dialog box, 46
Place Order option, Adobe Photoshop Services browser, 173
Play button, slide show, 259, 266
Playback Options section, Adobe Bridge Output panel, 373–374
plus icon, New Smart Album dialog box, 42
PNG (Portable Network Graphics) format, 150, 342, 345–348
PNG-24 (portable network graphic, 24-bit), 345–348, 389
PNG-8 (portable network graphic, 8-bit), 345, 348, 389
Point Eraser tool, 245
Polar Coordinates filter, 328–330
Polygonal Lasso tool, 139, 377
Portable Document Format (PDF), 150, 269
portable network graphic, 24-bit (PNG-24), 345–348, 389
portable network graphic, 8-bit (PNG-8), 345, 348, 389
Portable Network Graphics (PNG) format, 150, 342, 345–348
Portraits style option, Convert to Black and White dialog box, 147
Position photo in Frame, photo book option, 172
Poster Edges dialog box, 322
preferences, e-mail, 161
Preferences dialog box, 183
Preset drop-down menu
    New dialog box, 232, 306, 318
    Save for Web dialog box, 344, 346
Preset section, Save for Web dialog box, 210
Preview checkbox
    Brightness/Contrast dialog box, 105
    Shadow/Highlights dialog box, 132
Preview in Browser button, Adobe Bridge Output panel, 371
Preview In icon, Save for Web dialog box, 210
Preview option
    layer styles, 250
    Magic Extractor, 243
Preview Quality option, Slide Show Preferences dialog box, 259
preview window, Unsharp Mask dialog box, 87
primary colors, 127–128
Print option, File menu, 173

Print Photos dialog box, 173–175, 178, 180–181
print production formats, 389
Print Sizes drop-down menu, General Preferences dialog box, 183
Print Space drop-down menu, Print Photos dialog box, 175, 181
Print with Local Printer button, 173
Print x copies of each image section, Print Photos dialog box, 174
printed photo book, ordering, 170–173
Printer button, Page Setup dialog box, 182
printers, 176, 182–183
printing photos
    contact sheets, 178–179
    in Organizer, 173–175
    overview, 173
    picture packages, 180–181
    Print Photos dialog box, 177–178
prints, ordering, 168–170
problems. see photographic problems, fixing
Process Files From drop-down menu, Process Multiple Files dialog box, 291
Process Multiple Files command, 291
profiles, managing color with, 176
progress bar, Backup/Synchronization Preferences dialog box, 185
Progressive check box, Save for Web dialog box, 345
Project Bin, 57–58
Properties button, Page Setup dialog box, 182
Properties dialog box, 35
Properties panel, 24, 26, 263–266
protect brush, Recompose tool, 94
PSD (Photoshop) format, 114, 123, 148–149, 150, 351, 389–390
PSE (Photo Project) format, 148, 150

Q

Quality slider, E-mail Attachments dialog box, 162
Quick Fix
    Auto Contrast, 62–63
    Auto Levels, 61–62
    Auto Smart Fix, 60–61
    color, correcting automatically, 63–64
    Full Edit view, comparing images in, 65
    Navigator panel, 65–66
    overview, 58–59
Quick Photo Edit option, Fix tab, 14
Quick Reorder menu, 267
Quick Selection tool, 118, 139, 378
Quick Share panel, 168
QuickEdit panel, 36

R

Radius text field, Unsharp Mask dialog box, 87–88, 298–299

random setting, slide transition, 264

ranking menu, Photo Browser, 51

ratings, 36, 43–44

Raw format, 150

Recompose tool, 93–94, 378

Record button, Narration tool, 268

Recovery slider, Camera Raw dialog box, 281, 286–287

Rectangle Shape tool, 195

Rectangle tool, 315

Rectangular Marquee tool, 138–139, 219, 294, 317, 377

Red, Green, and Blue (RGB) color model, 126–128, 341, 388

red eye, fixing automatically, 9

Red Eye Removal tool, 78–79, 283, 378

Redo button, Unsharp Mask, 88

Reduce Noise filter, 300

Refine Edge command, 84, 143–144, 219–220, 302

refreshing Organizer, 15

remove brush, Recompose tool, 94

Remove button, Print Photos dialog box, 178

Remove Color Cast command, 72–73

Remove Color option, Enhance menu, 292, 321

Remove From Selection tool, 245

Remove JPEG Artifacts option, Reduce Noise dialog box, 300

Remove Selected Items button, Online Album Wizard, 157

Rename dialog box, 33

Rename Files section, Photo Downloader, 6–7

Repeat Soundtrack Until Last Slide check box, Slide Show Preferences dialog box, 259

Resample Image option, Image Size dialog box, 91–92, 207

Reset button
  Camera Raw dialog box, 286
  Editor workspace, 58
  Guided Edit panel, 68, 70
  Magic Extractor dialog box, 243

Reset Panels command, 55

Reset Standard Workspaces command, 362, 374

Resize Images option, Process Multiple Files dialog box, 291

resizing images, 91–94

resolution, 207, 340–341, 388

Resolution field, New dialog box, 232, 306, 319

Resolution text field, Image Size dialog box, 92

Resume Backup/Synchronization option, System Tray, 186

Retouch tool, 283

retouching photos. *see also* photographic problems, fixing
  adjustment layer, making selective changes with mask, 219–221
  brushing on corrections, 221–222
  Clone Stamp tool, 224–227
  destroying images, 216–217
  Healing Brush tool, 222–223
  histogram, 215–216
  overview, 213–214, 218–219

Reveal in Finder command, 362

Reveal recent file or go to Recent folder drop-down menu, Adobe Bridge, 357

reversing text effect, 330

reviewing photos, 31–32, 35–37

RGB (Red, Green, and Blue) color model, 126–128, 341, 388

RGB Color in the Editor command, 148

RGB option, Histogram panel, 215

Rotate buttons, Print Photos dialog box, 174, 180

Rotate command, 329–330

rotate icons, Options bar, 25

Rotate image icons, Camera Raw dialog box, 283

Rotate Left button, Options bar, 28, 44

rotating images, 90–91

Rotation buttons, Print Photos dialog box, 178

Roundness option, Brush tool More Options menu, 311

S

safe margins, 350–351

Sample All Layers checkbox, Options bar, 225, 352

saturation, 127, 136–137

Saturation slider
  Camera Raw dialog box, 282
  Hue/Saturation dialog box, 117, 136–137, 148, 328
  Quick Fix panel, 63–64

Save As a File option, Slide Show Output dialog box, 269

Save As dialog box, 59, 61–63, 66, 131, 149

Save As drop-down menu, Get Photos from Scanner dialog box, 9

Save As Type option, Save for Web dialog box, 210

Save for Web dialog box, 210–211, 341, 343–348

Save Image button, Camera Raw dialog box, 290

Save in Version Set with Original checkbox, Save As dialog box, 59, 149

Save Optimized As dialog box, 345

Save Options dialog box, 290

Save Selection dialog box, 119, 145

Save Slide Show dialog box, 269

Save to Disk button, Adobe Bridge Output panel, 372

saved selection, 351, 353

saving
  audio files, 269
  images, 148–150

Scale Effect option, Layer Style menu, 250

Scale slider, Print Photos dialog box, 174, 178, 180

scanners, importing photos from, 8–9

Scatter option, Brush tool More Options menu, 311

Scitex CT format, 150

scrapbooking
  borders, creating, 334–337
  images, adding, 334–337
  overview, 318
  text, adding to background, 331–333
  text, effects, 324–330
  textures, creating, 318–324

Screen blending mode, 101, 332

Search box, Options bar, 25

Search button, Get Photos and Videos by Searching for Folders dialog box, 9

Search Criteria section, New Smart Album dialog box, 42

Search Options section, Get Photos and Videos by Searching for Folders dialog box, 9

Search text box, Adobe Bridge, 366–367

searching for files, in Adobe Bridge, 365–367

Select a Frame drop-down menu, Print Photos dialog box, 180

Select a Layout drop-down menu, Print Photos dialog box, 180

Select a Style box, Adjust Color Curves dialog box, 135

Select All command, 331

Select All option
  Add Photos dialog box, 177
  Import Attached Keyword Tags dialog box, 12

Select Print Size drop-down menu, Print Photos dialog box, 174

Select Printer drop-down menu, Print Photos dialog box, 174, 178, 180

Select Recipients list, Photo Mail dialog box, 165

Select Recipients section, E-mail Attachments dialog box, 163

Select Type of Print drop-down menu, Print Photos dialog box, 174, 178, 180

Selected Brush Preset, 307

Selection Brush tool, 139, 140–141, 145, 378

Selection drop-down menu, Load Selection dialog box, 145

Selection mode, Selection Brush tool, 140–141

selections
  adding to, 142
  creating brushes from, 311

Hue/Saturation adjustments, 115–117

importance of, 138

inverting, 146

keyboard shortcuts for, 383–384

layer, 237

with Magic Extractor, 241–245

modifying new with saved, 145–146

moving to new layer, 119–123

overview, 115, 138

Quick Selection tool, 118

saving, 118–119, 145

Selection Brush tool, 140–141

shortcuts for working with, 384–385

subtracting from, 142

tools, 139–140

working with, 117

Send E-mail To box, Online Album Wizard, 159

Sender Verification code, 167

Set Background & Foreground colors to default tool, 381

set icon, Layers panel, 235

Shadow Clipping Warning, Camera Raw dialog box, 285

Shadow/Highlights command, 106–107, 132

shadows, 106–107, 132

Shadows slider, Photomerge Exposure, 76

Shape drop-down menu, Options bar, 196, 315

shape layers, 231

shapes, 314–315

Share tab, 155–156, 161

Share to Photoshop.com checkbox, Online Album Wizard, 158

Share To section, Online Album Wizard, 156

sharing photos
  albums, 155–160
  e-mail, 161–168
  online services, 168–173
  overview, 153, 154
  Quick Share panel, 168
  welcome screen, 154

Sharing tab, Online Album Wizard, 157

Sharpen tool, 316, 381

sharpening images, 86–88, 295–299

Shift key, selecting photos with, 17

shopping cart, Adobe Photoshop Services web site, 277

Show All button, Photo Browser, 28, 33, 38–40, 51

Show All Effects option, Layer Style menu, 250

Show Bounding Box, Options bar, 198

Show File Names feature, Organizer, 13, 16

Show Guides command, 352

Show Only Hidden Files option, Organizer, 31

Show Print Guides, photo book option, 171

Show Print Options checkbox, Print Photos dialog box, 179

Show Printer Preferences button, Print Photos dialog box, 174
Show selected brush presets drop-down menu, Options bar, 224
Show/Hide Slideshow settings button, Slideshow Settings window, 158
showing layers, 237
Shutterfly, 169–170, 270
Sign In link, Adobe Photoshop Services browser, 172–173
Sign In option, Organizer, 155
Simple Blending mode, Photomerge Exposure, 76
Site Info section, Adobe Bridge Output panel, 371
Size And Quality option, Export New Files dialog box, 186
Size drop-down menu, New dialog box, 306, 318
Size field, Options bar, 140, 200, 233
skin tone, correcting, 73–75
Slide Order drop-down menu, 267
Slide Show Editor, 259
Slide Show Output dialog box, 269–270
Slide Show Preferences dialog box, 258–259
slide shows
    audio, adding, 268
    graphics, adding, 263
    narration, adding, 268–269
    overview, 255–259
    panning, 265–266
    reordering slides, 267
    slide order, setting, 267
    text, adding, 260–263
    transitions, applying, 264–265
    zooming, 265–266
Slideshow Settings window, 157–158
Small Thumbnail Size button, Options bar, 31–32
Smart Album, 41–42
Smart Blending mode, Photomerge Exposure, 76
Smart Brush tool, 80–85, 140, 380
Smoothing Brush tool, 245
Smudge tool, 316, 381
snap shot, Undo History panel, 300
Soft Edge Drop Shadow effect, 205
Soft Light, 318, 322
softening selections, 220
Solarize filter, 327
sound effects, slideshow, 157
soundtrack, slide show, 269
Source area, Photo Downloader, 5–6
Spacebar, selecting video frame with, 15
Spacing option, Brush tool More Options menu, 311
Special Effect Brushes, 307
Sponge tool, 137, 316, 381
Spot Healing Brush tool, 222–223, 379
Stack Selected Photos option, Organizer, 37

stacking order, layers, 238
Stacks, 37, 368–369
star ratings, 36, 43–44, 51
Start bounding box, Pan & Zoom effect, 266
Start people recognition button, Keyword Tags panel, 47
State text field, Adobe Bridge Metadata panel, 363
Static Duration drop-down menu, Slide Show Preferences dialog box, 259
stationery, 164
Stationery & Layouts Wizard, 165
Stop Backup/Synchronization option, System Tray, 186
Stop button, Narration tool, 269
Stop Share Album dialog box, 160
storyboard, dragging and dropping slides on, 267
Straighten tool, 283, 378
Style drop-down menu, Warp Text dialog box, 233
Style Info section, Adobe Bridge Output panel, 371
Style Settings dialog box, 249
Styles drop-down menu, Adobe Bridge Output panel, 371
subkeywords, 364
Subtract from selection brush, 81, 83
Subtract From Selection setting, Options bar, 140, 142
subtractive color model, 341
subtractive primaries, 127–128
Support Center, 20
Swap Background & Foreground colors tool, 381
switching image modes, 130
synchronizing files, 183–186
System Tray, 186

T

Tag Cloud, 43, 52–53
Tagged-Image File Format (TIFF), 150, 351–353, 389–390
tagging photos, 43–47
Talk1 shape, 196–197
Targa (TGA) format, 150, 390
Temperature area, Camera Raw dialog box, 281
Temperature slider
    Adjust Color for Skin Tone dialog box, 74
    Quick Fix panel, 64
Template drop-down menu, Adobe Bridge Output panel, 371, 373
Template to Use option, Photo Downloader, 8
text
    animating, 210–211
    animation with, creating, 206–208
    background, adding to, 331–333
    cartoon bubbles, 195–199

effects, 200–202, 324–330
layer style, adding to, 205–206
layers, 191–194, 209
multiple images, adding to, 202–203
overview, 189
shortcuts for working with, 385–386
slide shows, adding to, 260–263
stroke, adding effect to, 208
warping, 204–205
welcome screen, 190
text alignment drop-down menu, cartoon bubble, 199
Text Properties palette, 263
Text tool, 260, 326
textures, 307–311, 318–324
TGA (Targa) format, 150, 390
Threshold text field, Unsharp Mask dialog box, 87–88, 298–299
Thumbnail checkbox, Save As dialog box, 149
thumbnail slider, Options bar, 25
thumbnails, 31–32, 157, 375
TIFF (Tagged-Image File Format), 150, 351–353, 389–390
Tile All in Grid option, 65, 112, 202
Timeline, Organizer, 24
Tint area, Camera Raw dialog box, 281
Tint slider, Quick Fix panel, 64
Tips and Tricks link, welcome screen, 20
title safe area, 350
Toggle layer visibility button, Levels dialog box, 218
tonal adjustments, 108–112, 215–216
Toolbox, 57, 77. see also specific tools by name
tools, 78, 377–381. see also specific tools by name
Transition drop-down menu, Slide Show Preferences dialog box, 259
Transition Duration drop-down menu, Slide Show Preferences dialog box, 259
transitions, applying to slide shows, 264–265
transparency, 342, 351
Transparency option, Save for Web dialog box, 348
Trim Guidelines option, Print Photos dialog box, 175
TV, sending audio to, 270
Twirl Clockwise tool, 322–324
2 Digit Serial Number option, Save Options dialog box, 290
type layers, 231, 233
Type tool, 191, 326

U

Unconfirmed tab, People Recognition window, 49
underexposed images, improving, 68–69, 99
Undo button, Unsharp Mask, 88
Undo History, 299–300
Undo option, Edit menu, 251
undoing retouching, 223, 225
unlocking
  files, 362
  layers, 239
Unsharp Mask, 86–88, 295–299
Unstack photos option, Organizer, 37
Upgrade Membership option, Backup/Synchronization Preferences dialog box, 185
U.S. Paper option, Preset drop-down menu, 306, 318
USB cable, 4
Use drop-down menu, Fill Layer dialog box, 317, 335
Use Lower Case Extensions checkbox, Save As dialog box, 149
Use Original Format option, Export New Files dialog box, 186

V

VCD (video CD), 270
vector graphics, 381
Vector Shape tools, 381
vector-based shapes, 314
verification e-mail, Adobe E-mail service, 167
Version Set, 76
Vertical Type Mask, 378
Vertical Type tool, 378
Very Pearly Whites option, Smart Brush tool, 80
Vibrance slider, Camera Raw dialog box, 282, 288
video
  color, 340–341
  importing photos from frames, 13–15
  preparing images for, 349
  production formats, 390
  resolution, 340–341
  saving files for, 351–353
video CD (VCD), 270
view, Adobe Bridge, 374–375
View, Edit, Organize in Full Screen button, Options bar, 25
View as List button, Adobe Bridge, 375
View Content as Details button, Adobe Bridge, 375
View Content as Thumbnails button, Adobe Bridge, 375
View drop-down menu, Quick Fix panel, 60
View Keyword Tag Cloud button, Keyword Tags panel, 52
View Keyword Tag Hierarchy button, Keyword Tags panel, 53
viewing images, shortcuts for, 382
vignetting, 220, 292–295

visibility icon, 82, 85, 235, 237
volume, slide show audio, 268

W

Warp Text dialog box, 233
warping text, 204–205
WBMP file format, 343
Web graphics
    color, 340–341
    image formats, 342–343, 389
    JPEG, creating, 343–345
    PNG, creating, 345–348
    resolution, 340–341
Web Photo Gallery, 369–372
web-based calendar creator, 271
welcome screen
    Adobe Bridge, accessing, 356–357
    color, adjusting, 126
    exposure, adjusting, 98
    fixing photographic problems, 56
    importing photos, 3
    photo composites, 230
    Photoshop.com link, 20
    sharing photos, 154
    text, 190
White Balance tool, Camera Raw dialog box, 281,
 283, 286
white slider
    Levels Adjustment panel, 121
    Levels dialog box, 109
whitening teeth, 80–82
"Who is this?" field, 47–48, 50
Wind filter, 329–330
Windows keyboard shortcuts, 382–387
Windows Media Video (.wmv) format, 269
Wipe option, Properties palette, 264
Workspace drop-down menu, Adobe Bridge, 362
workspaces, 3, 16

Z

Zoom tool
    Camera Raw dialog box, 283
    Magic Extractor, 242
    overview, 377
    Red Eye Removal tool, 79
    retouching, 222
    Smart Brush tool, 80
    Unsharp Mask, 88
    using on all open images, 65
zooming, slide show, 259

Wiley Publishing, Inc.
End-User License Agreement

(b) WPI AND THE AUTHOR(S) OF THE BOOK DISCLAIM ALL OTHER WARRANTIES, EXPRESS OR IMPLIED, INCLUDING WITHOUT LIMITATION IMPLIED WARRANTIES OF MERCHANTABILITY AND FITNESS FOR A PARTICULAR PURPOSE, WITH RESPECT TO THE SOFTWARE, THE PROGRAMS, THE SOURCE CODE CONTAINED THEREIN, AND/OR THE TECHNIQUES DESCRIBED IN THIS BOOK. WPI DOES NOT WARRANT THAT THE FUNCTIONS CONTAINED IN THE SOFTWARE WILL MEET YOUR REQUIREMENTS OR THAT THE OPERATION OF THE SOFTWARE WILL BE ERROR FREE.

(c) This limited warranty gives you specific legal rights, and you may have other rights that vary from jurisdiction to jurisdiction.

6. Remedies.

(a) WPI's entire liability and your exclusive remedy for defects in materials and workmanship shall be limited to replacement of the Software Media, which may be returned to WPI with a copy of your receipt at the following address: Software Media Fulfillment Department, Attn.: *Adobe Photoshop Elements 8 Digital Classroom*, Wiley Publishing, Inc., 10475 Crosspoint Blvd., Indianapolis, IN 46256, or call 1-800-762-2974. Please allow four to six weeks for delivery. This Limited Warranty is void if failure of the Software Media has resulted from accident, abuse, or misapplication. Any replacement Software Media will be warranted for the remainder of the original warranty period or thirty (30) days, whichever is longer.

(b) In no event shall WPI or the author be liable for any damages whatsoever (including without limitation damages for loss of business profits, business interruption, loss of business information, or any other pecuniary loss) arising from the use of or inability to use the Book or the Software, even if WPI has been advised of the possibility of such damages.

(c) Because some jurisdictions do not allow the exclusion or limitation of liability for consequential or incidental damages, the above limitation or exclusion may not apply to you.

7. U.S. Government Restricted Rights. Use, duplication, or disclosure of the Software for or on behalf of the United States of America, its agencies and/or instrumentalities "U.S. Government" is subject to restrictions as stated in paragraph (c)(1)(ii) of the Rights in Technical Data and Computer Software clause of DFARS 252.227-7013, or subparagraphs (c) (1) and (2) of the Commercial Computer Software - Restricted Rights clause at FAR 52.227-19, and in similar clauses in the NASA FAR supplement, as applicable.

8. General. This Agreement constitutes the entire understanding of the parties and revokes and supersedes all prior agreements, oral or written, between them and may not be modified or amended except in a writing signed by both parties hereto that specifically refers to this Agreement. This Agreement shall take precedence over any other documents that may be in conflict herewith. If any one or more provisions contained in this Agreement are held by any court or tribunal to be invalid, illegal, or otherwise unenforceable, each and every other provision shall remain in full force and effect.